PELICAN BOOK
A722

THE TREASURY UNDER THE TORIES
1951–1964

SAMUEL BRITTAN

Samuel Brittan, who was born in 1933, read economics at Jesus College, Cambridge, and took first-class honours. For some years he worked on the *Financial Times* as feature writer, leader writer, economic correspondent, and American editor. Since 1961 he has been economics editor of the *Observer*.

D0611040

THE TREASURY
UNDER THE TORIES
1951–1964

SAMUEL BRITTAN

Penguin Books

Penguin Books Ltd, Harmondsworth, Middlesex, England
Penguin Books Inc., 3300 Clipper Mill Road, Baltimore 11, Md, U.S.A.
Penguin Books Pty Ltd, Ringwood, Victoria, Australia

—

First published simultaneously by Secker & Warburg and by Penguin 1964
Copyright © Samuel Brittan, 1964

—

Made and printed in Great Britain
by C. Nicholls & Company Ltd
Set in Monotype Baskerville

TO THE MEMORY OF MY MOTHER

Contents

Acknowledgements

I wish to thank the following for permission to reprint extracts:

Professor Ely Devons, for an article in the *Listener*, 27 March 1958.

The Bodley Head, publishers of Viscount Chandos's *Memoirs*.

John Wiley & Sons Ltd, publishers of *Presidential Power: The Politics of Leadership*, by Professor R. E. Neustadt.

Thames and Hudson Ltd, publishers of *Prosperity Through Competition*, by Professor Ludwig Erhard.

'The authorities' has always been an anonymous description and 'the authorities' have been able to get away with anything. But if the 'authorities' divided themselves into bits, and issued their own apologia, it would break up confidence in the whole system.

> Mr. R. A. Butler, 19 December 1958 (giving oral evidence to the Radcliffe Committee on the Monetary System).

Introduction

THE Treasury is one of the oldest of Government Departments and also one of the most distinguished in intellectual calibre. Since Sir Stafford Cripps became Chancellor of the Exchequer in 1947, this venerable and high-powered body has been responsible for guiding the economic destinies of the country. Yet the nation seems to have stumbled from crisis to crisis, and Britain's record has often compared unfavourably with many other advanced industrial nations.

To what extent has the Treasury really been responsible for the disappointing record? Was the failure of the Conservative Governments of the 1950s and early 1960s to put up a better economic performance due to the politicians, Civil Servants, or the hard facts of Britain's position in the world? The more discerning Conservatives are fully aware that the movement of public opinion against them in the early 1960s had its roots in the economic troubles of the 1961 Pay Pause crisis; and the issues raised are thus political as well as economic.

These are perhaps the more obvious questions that this book attempts to answer in its account of the Treasury's guidance of our economy. There is also a second more elusive, but equally important theme; and that is Treasury policy as a case study of where power lies in a complex society like Britain where myth and reality so largely diverge.

There have been times in the last year or two when it has looked as if we were entering a new and improved economic phase. At other times yet another drearily familiar crisis seems to have been staring us in the face. It is anyone's guess just how the situation will seem by the time this work appears on the book stalls. It may all depend on the chance movement of a few erratic trade figures or other fortuitous developments.

Recently, too, there have been modest, but encouraging, signs of a new outlook in Whitehall, and particularly in the Treasury itself, which may lead to a more successful policy whichever Party is in power. Events will show how deep or otherwise these changes go.

In the long run my instincts are on the side of the optimists, both about Britain's economic position, and about the way in which policies and institutions are likely to develop. But this certainly does not mean that all our troubles are over, or that the conundrums with which successive Governments have wrestled will not recur. Still less does it mean that changes can be left to take place by themselves without further pressure from public opinion.

Readers will see from the following pages why some students of economic policy have come to the conclusion that if greater success is to be achieved in future a new ministry is necessary to take over the Treasury's function of economic overlord. This proposal formed an important part of the Labour Party's platform for the 1964 election. Whoever wins the election the idea is likely to remain very much in the air.

In one sense, indeed, the period of the Treasury's greatest supremacy was coming to an end even before the 1964 election.* The establishment of the National Economic Development Council in 1962 and the appointment of a major Conservative figure, Mr Edward Heath, as Secretary of State at the Board of Trade with a wide reforming brief

---

* The expression 'the Treasury' is ambiguous. Strictly speaking this is a composite whole, including the Chancellor of the moment. But very often it is used in a more restricted sense to describe the body of officials that advises the Chancellor rather than the Chancellor himself. This second meaning has normally been used in this book, except where it is obvious from the context that the other meaning is intended.

The expression 'Treasury policy' is on the other hand a much looser one; and its use in this book does not imply that the policy in question originated with officials rather than ministers.

in 1963, showed that rival centres of economic power were coming into existence. In the last analysis, however, the Treasury's control of the financial taps, its responsibility for sterling, and its links with the Bank of England, will still give it an essential economic role whatever new ministries are formed.

Part I of the present work is designed mainly to set the scene and starts off with a description of the Treasury in its Civil Service context. The following chapters go on to analyse the Treasury's own special functions in the period up to the middle of 1964 and a little of that Department's special ethos and background. (Most of the activities described are likely to remain in the Treasury whatever new ministries are started, and the others will certainly continue to be performed.) Part I ends with some practical examples, including an account of how the budget is prepared.

Part II is by far the longest of the book. It discusses the interaction of politicians and their advisers in the light of the events of the past few years. In the main it deals with recent Conservative Governments, but is prefaced by a few general observations on the post-war Labour Governments. It attempts to shed new light on such topics as the genesis of the Pay Pause and seven per cent Bank Rates, the selection of Chancellors, the role of Mr Macmillan and other Prime Ministers, the Conservative conversion to 'Planning' and Whitehall's flirtation with the Common Market.

In Part III an attempt is made to draw together a few of the conclusions and recommendations which have emerged from the first two parts. My own views on the proposal to establish a brand new Economics, Production or Planning Ministry additional to existing Government Departments are given in the last chapter. Economic policy is not a field where final solutions are likely; and it seemed more useful here to express a personal view rather than to try to guess the finer details of what Mr Wilson might, in the first instance, do if he formed a Government.

Both the workings of the Civil Service and the conduct of

economic policy have come in for a good deal of critical discussion during the time this book was in the press. A good many of the suggestions in it inevitably reflect the general climate of opinion and are common property among the critics; a few are a conscious reaction from that climate, and one or two may even be new. But if the following pages have any originality, it is mainly in the attempt to link the discussion of institutions to some of the actual policy questions with which Governments have had to grapple, and to get away from discussing 'the machinery of government' in a vacuum.

These subjects are large enough in all conscience and it is necessary to limit the field. The book is principally concerned with the Treasury in its role of economic helmsman and it does not attempt to provide more than an outline guide to all the other varied functions of that Department in the years covered. There is far more to be said, for example, about the Treasury's watchdog functions over Government spending. I have said a little about the determination of the broad totals of expenditure, but hardly anything about the elimination of detailed waste and inefficiency in administration. This is not because the latter subject is unimportant, but because – as recent cases make all too clear – it requires a separate book to itself.

The reader with no previous knowledge of the topics discussed ought readily to be able to catch the drift of the argument even if he misses out the Appendixes and more complex footnotes. He might like to take a bird's eye view of the book and first read Chapter 2 on Civil Service habits, jump to *the first half* of Chapter 5, go on to read those parts of the historical Chapters 6–8 which happen to catch his fancy, and then skim the two concluding chapters, before tackling the book in more detail. On the other hand, those familiar with the ways of Whitehall may well want to turn over the pages of Chapter 2 fairly quickly – although I hope that even they will find some things of interest in it, especially towards the end.

There is more published material on the way in which the Treasury and other Government Departments take their decisions than is generally realized, if only one is prepared to hunt around for it. I have placed at the end of the book some of the sources I have found most useful.

All the same, any work of this kind must be heavily dependent on conversations with men and women at the centre of public affairs. In the course of preparing it, I have had lengthy interviews with about sixty or seventy different people, a few of whom I have bothered more than once. Since most of them must remain anonymous, it would be better not to single out any of them. But I would like to take this opportunity of thanking these extremely busy people for their very generous help, without which the book could not have been written.

In a different category, I should like to thank the Information Division of the Treasury, which went out of its way to assist me in my efforts by arranging interviews and giving me all the information which it properly could, even though my requests often came at very short notice. Officials with whom I have spoken have been helpful on factual matters within the limits imposed by the bar against their discussing their advice to, or relations with, ministers. In absolving them and the Information Division from any responsibility for what appears here, I should make it clear that the help they gave me was confined to Part I of the book. Even here it represented only a small part of my material, the greater part of which was derived from other sources.

I should like to thank the many friends and colleagues who have helped me at various stages. A special debt is due to Mr Nigel Lawson and my brother Mr Leon Brittan who both read every word of my original draft and discussed it with me in great detail. I am extremely grateful to them for the patience and speed with which they read my manuscripts and for their useful and pertinent comments. Professor Alan Day made some very helpful comments on

Chapter 5, and on the first two Appendixes to Chapter 3, and Mr David Henderson did the same with Appendix III of that chapter. My brother also gave me some most valuable editorial assistance with the structure and organization of the book.

I should also like to express my gratitude to the *Financial Times* and the *Observer* for the valuable insight I gained into the evolution of economic policy, with the first as Economic Correspondent, and with the second, in my current post of Economic Editor. The Editor of the *Observer*, the Hon. David Astor, has also been very generous in the time and facilities he has placed at my disposal to enable me to write this book.

Messrs Allen & Unwin were kind enough to allow me to read in proof Lord Bridges's book *The Treasury* in the New Whitehall Series. This was very helpful to me both as a source of reference and as a stimulus. The National Institute of Economic and Social Research went out of its way to provide any figures that I requested, again often at unpardonably short notice. The Librarian of the Royal Institute of Public Administration was another great source of aid and comfort in my efforts to gather information. In this connexion too I must thank Miss Gritta Weil of the *Observer* for important assistance.

I must gratefully acknowledge the permission of the Editor of the *Banker* to incorporate in modified form passages from two articles I contributed to his journal. An earlier version of the chart on page 290 originally appeared in the *Banker* of September 1962.

Finally I must express my deep gratitude to Miss Anne Melson, Mrs Anne Shotts and Miss Janet Pearson who bore the brunt of the typing and correcting with great forbearance and efficiency.

The usual disclaimer that none of the people or organizations mentioned above is responsible for any part of the book needs special emphasis and applies both to statements of fact and questions of interpretation.

August, 1964

Part I

THE TREASURY AT WORK

CHAPTER 1

An *Élite* Within an *Élite*

ALTHOUGH the Treasury itself has large responsibilities, it is very small in numbers. Its total staff, according to the 1963 Civil Estimates, amounts to only 1,453. Of these, 807 are messengers, typists, telephonists, and others who come under the general heading of Office Services. The Treasury staff proper is little more than 600, including members of the clerical grades of the Civil Service. The Inland Revenue, by comparison, employs 57,000; the Ministry of Pensions 37,000; the Ministry of Aviation 22,000, and the Ministry of Labour 20,000. The Treasury is very small, too, compared with some of the other central Economic Departments. The Board of Trade has a staff of about 7,000 and the Ministry of Transport is of a similar size.

But 'the Treasury', in the popular sense, is even smaller than these total figures suggest. For one must remember that the British Civil Service is divided into three general grades: Administrative, Executive, and Clerical. There are also important specialist and scientific grades and a mass of 'non-established' general workers. These distinctions are not, as some might think, a unique product of the British class system, but exist in astonishingly similar forms in most continental countries.

The title of the three main grades is misleading, for much of the real administration is in fact done by the Executive grades. Executive officials will, for instance, grant licences, listen to public complaints, see that clerical work is organized properly, and make sure that discussions on policy are not hampered by bad filing or inadequate tabulation.

The 'Administrative' Civil Servants have a very different job. An American author once described them as 'permanent politicians'.* It is to these Civil Servants that 'the minister, who may be changed more than once in the lifetime of a Government, looks for advice and help in the development of the policies of his Department, in his contributions to general Cabinet policy, and in his direction of existing policies'. These frank words are used by the Civil Service Commission in its recruiting pamphlet. For faced with the serious job of bidding for high-quality graduates in a very competitive market, the Commission cannot afford to undersell its goods. But its doctrine will have to be modified quite a lot when we come to consider the Plowden Report.

The Administrative class is a tiny proportion of the Civil Service – 2,500 out of 630,000, or less than half of one per cent. Of these hardly more than 150 are in the Treasury. When people curse or praise 'the Treasury', it is this tiny handful of men and women they have in mind.

Oxbridge and the Reform

It is a complete myth to suppose that Administrative Civil Servants in the Treasury or elsewhere are mostly public-school products. An analysis of thirty top Civil Servants in 1960 showed that only eleven came from public schools and the remainder came mostly from grammar or other State-aided schools. The Foreign Office alone remains to some extent a public-school preserve.

The figures for club membership shown in a recent survey are in some ways even more revealing. Almost half the Civil Servants for whom data were collected belonged, in equal proportions, either to the Reform Club or one of the university clubs. Hardly any of the ministers or top City figures were members of either. A good many blue-blooded clubs, such as White's, the Turf, and Pratt's, which were well represented among the Tory ministers, had hardly any

* J. Donald Kingsley, *Representative Bureaucracy*, Yellow Springs, Ohio, 1944, p. 269.

Whitehall members at all. The only real point of contact seemed to be the Athenaeum to which a (no doubt distinguished) minority of about one eighth of those surveyed in all three groups belonged.

One characteristic that Whitehall does have in common with other *élite* groups is its overwhelmingly Oxbridge character. About eighty-five per cent of all graduate entrants to the Administrative class between 1957 and 1962 came from either Oxford or Cambridge. The percentage, moreover, has been steadily increasing over the last few years and is now higher than it was before the First World War. Of the non-Oxbridge entrants, nearly all come from London or the Scottish universities. Less then four per cent come from Redbrick proper.

Why the provincial universities should do so badly is something of a mystery. It is difficult to imagine that the older universities which cater for a very small proportion of the undergraduate population, turn out twenty-five times as many high-quality products as all the others combined. The Oxford and Cambridge colleges cannot be that good at skimming off the cream.

The Civil Service Commissioners are themselves worried by the trend, which can hardly be explained away by any social bias at the entrance interview. In fact the greatest slaughter of the Redbrick competitors takes place in the written competitive examination. The Commissioners themselves emphasize that 'the idea of a public service career is neither part of their family background nor a tradition in their universities'. This is borne out by the statistics. Not only is their success ratio dismal – about one in forty-two – but, far more significant, the number of Redbrick candidates is very, very small indeed in relation to their share in the university population.

In the late nineteenth century and early twentieth century, when the present traditions of the Home Civil Service finally took root, the majority of its members did indeed have an upper middle-class public-school background. They were not the capitalist *bourgeoisie*, whom Marx wrongly believed had captured the state machine, but the non-commercial middle classes – the sons of Army officers, clergymen, dons, doctors, or the lesser landed gentry. Their families would tend to have small private incomes invested in government stock or other fixed interest securities, and would be thus ultra-sensitive to any threat of inflation or currency debasement.

Although the social basis of recruitment is now very much broader, something of the old tradition lingers on and is gradually acquired by new recruits from a different background. As late as 1950 over a third of senior Civil Servants were themselves the sons of Civil Servants, clergymen, dons, or school teachers; and even today an official in the Executive or Clerical grades will regard a career as an Administrative Civil Servant as a natural ambition for any of his children with scholastic ability.

The qualities required in an Administrative class Civil Servant have been well summed up by the 1955 Royal Commission as the capacity 'in an unusual degree' to 'master and marshal detail in many different fields at different times, to interpret effectively the ideas and policies of others, and to operate a complex administrative machine. It is rare to find these qualities in balanced proportion in one individual.' I shall argue later that it is even a mistake to seek the combination.

How to Become a Treasury Knight

The normal first step for anyone whose ambition is to become a Treasury knight is to join the Administrative class of the Home Civil Service. About forty per cent of the places in this class are filled by promotion from the Executive grades (which are largely recruited from people who have left school at eighteen) and the remainder are filled by the competitive examination already mentioned, taken by young graduates in their early twenties. As a report by a group of Conservative M.P.s points out, 'the system makes it inevitable that young men and women who enter this branch of the Civil Service should be unacquainted with the problems of industry'.*

Candidates can either enter under Method I, in which they are examined in their own subject, but also have to face an interview which accounts for thirty per cent of their possible marks, or by Method II, which involves general papers, personality tests, and intensive interviews. (The nickname 'country house method' is abominated and is no longer accurate.)

In either case entry is as far as possible confined to those with First and Second class degrees. There are about forty or fifty vacancies every year in the Home Civil Service, and the chances of success for those who actually sit the competitions are about one in seven. Until about 1960 the Civil Service Commissioners used to complain that they were not getting enough candidates of the right quality. Today they find recruitment 'a little easier' but are still not getting as many as they would like.

Nearly all the Administrative class officials in the Treasury have come directly from university (wartime entrants apart). The proportion promoted from the Executive grades is far less than the forty per cent normal for the Civil Service as a whole. The Treasury is far and away the chief preference of graduates successful in the Civil Service exams; and candidates who came near the top of the competitions have a very good chance of going to the Department of their choice.

Whitehall works on the assumption that the Treasury requires a higher standard of intellectual sophistication than the other Departments. In pre-war days no one was appointed to the Treasury as his first post, but some came earlier to it than others.

Some of the most successful Treasury men are later sent

---

* *Change or Decay*, Conservative Political Centre, 1963, p. 20.

ANALYSIS OF ADMINISTRATIVE CLASS FIRST
PREFERENCES 1960–2 (SUCCESSFUL
CANDIDATES ONLY)

Department	No. Giving it as first preference	No. actually assigned
Treasury	46	8
Home Office	20	4
Ministry of Education	13	7
Board of Trade	9	16
Scottish Departments	6	7
Ministry of Labour	4	5
Ministry of Transport	4	8
Admiralty	3	5
Ministry of Housing and Local Government	3	3
Ministry of Aviation	2	7
Export Credit Guarantee Dept	1	1
Ministry of Health	1	7
Post Office	1	5
Dept of Technical Operation	1	—
Ministry of Public Buildings and Works	1	3
Ministry of Agriculture	0	10
Air Ministry	0	5
Customs and Excise	0	3
Inland Revenue	0	3
Ministry of Pensions	0	5
National Assistance Board	0	2
Ministry of Power	0	5
War Office	0	1
No Preference	4	—
TOTAL	119	120

N.B. The Commonwealth Relations and Colonial Offices, which
are in some ways more akin to the Foreign than to the Home Civil
Service, have been excluded. This is one reason why the totals do
not add up. Source: The Civil Service Commission.

out to colonize. Out of twenty or so Permanent Secretaries of big home Departments about six have come up through the Treasury.

The Making of a Mandarin

What kind of background training does the Treasury Administrator have before he is let loose on the economy or on other Departments? About three fifths of all graduate recruits to the Administrative Civil Service have degrees in classics or history, with classics winning by a short head. The two subjects together have actually been increasing their lead over the last few years. Classics students are incidentally distinguished by a very high ratio of successes to total competitors. Scientists and mathematicians together make up two to three per cent of all new entrants. Graduates in economics or in politics, philosophy and economics, make up only twelve to thirteen per cent, a considerably smaller proportion than in the early 1950s. But there is a suggestion that the Treasury has a larger minority of recruits who have done some academic economics.

This last point may not be entirely an accident. Until very recently the orthodox doctrine was that the Civil Service could not care less which subject a candidate had read. Any training required was given on the job. But the pendulum has started to swing towards professionalism. The Treasury is now on the look out for, instead of being averse to, the new recruit with an economic qualification. Mr Cairncross, who has been Economic Adviser since 1961, keeps a list of the detailed qualifications of all new recruits to Whitehall who have studied economics at university.

Until 1963, about the only economic instruction new recruits who had read other subjects received was a book list for use in their own free time. At the top was a note warning them that the list was 'daunting'. New Assistant Principals, it was stressed, were asked 'not to regard them as urgent compulsory reading; that way lies indigestion. The lists constitute a menu to be tasted with discretion and to return to if necessary over the years.'*

The opening of a Centre for Administrative Studies in October 1963 marks a fundamental change of heart, which it would be carping to play down. All Assistant Principals in the Home Civil Service will go there for a fourteen-week course, at the end of their probation, and a few young men from the Foreign Office are at present also attending as an experiment. About half the time is devoted to simple economics and statistics, and half to a mixed collection of topics, including Parliamentary procedure, drafting bills, local government, industrial structure, trade-union organization, business management, and international problems. Those who attended the first courses seemed to want more economics, much more statistics, and less of subjects like parliamentary drafting, which they correctly thought they could learn on the job.

Assistant Principals from the 'economic Departments', which are defined as the Treasury, Board of Trade, and Ministries of Labour and Housing, will do a further seven-week course on subjects such as the balance of payments, economic forecasting, and growth in the U.K. and in underdeveloped countries.

* The list is divided into two sections. One is of publications 'of general interest to everyone working in the Treasury'. This is almost entirely devoted to Treasury and Whitehall organization, and to the control of Government spending. Professor Brian Chapman's *The Profession of Government*, dealing with the European Civil Service, is included here. The second section is meant for someone who has not read economics and who wishes 'to acquire some basic knowledge of the subject. It concentrates on what is most likely to be of most immediate use to him in his work in the Treasury.' The main text recommended on economic theory is Samuelson's *Introductory Analysis*, where the chapter on the Keynesian theory of employment and business activity is picked out as 'essential reading'. Much less enlightened is the sparse selection of books (apart from official statements) on current problems and recent economic history. The unorthodoxies of other generations and other countries are represented by two volumes of Keynes's essays and by two of Galbraith's books. It seems rather petty to exclude from the list Andrew Shonfield's *British Economic Policy Since the War*.

The young dons who are assisting at the courses could not conceivably be called 'fuddy-duddy' even by the sourest critics. There are also visiting speakers from business and Whitehall; but formal lectures have been kept to a minimum and the emphasis is on discussion groups, exercises, visits, and reports. There is no examination or test of any kind at the end of the courses (although the Director of the Centre has occasionally been asked by Departments to report on their members attending it).

How does the training to be given at the new Centre compare with that received by French Civil Servants who are now trained at the famous École Nationale d'Administration? Only the middle year of the three-year course in the École is devoted to academic studies. At the end of that year the student specializing in Financial and Economic Affairs not only has to take a six-hour paper in his own field; he must also take two general papers with compulsory questions on constitutional matters, social and health administration, international affairs, and international law. He has to draft an administrative report on a specified subject and take an oral examination in a foreign language. It can plausibly be argued that the British Assistant Principal at Regents Park will not learn all that much less about economics during his training period than his French counterpart who has so much else to absorb.

There are, however, other differences between the French and British attitudes. Unlike the Civil Service Commission, the French authorities are extremely interested in the subjects studied at university. The qualifying examination for admission to the École Nationale contains one paper on political, social, and economic history since the mid eighteenth century. A second paper deals with the political institutions of the major states. A third paper has an economic slant – it may for example be an essay on European monetary policies since 1945. There is, too, an examination in a foreign language. Those who pass these preliminary hurdles have to take, if they want to enter the

Finance Ministry, more specialized tests in public finance. All candidates must also attain certain standards in running, jumping, climbing, swimming, and putting the shot.

A much more important difference between the French and British systems is in the training a French Civil Servant receives in his first and third year at the École. During his first year he is sent to assist one of the Prefects who represent the Central Government in a provincial centre. The psychological motive for sending him is not disguised. 'It is to give the student a complete break from all past associations and ideas, to force the metropolitan man to live in the provinces, and to bring him into contact with those parts of French society which, once started on his career, he will have no further chance to contact or explore.'* In his third and final year, a student is sent for two or three months to a large industrial, commercial, or agricultural undertaking: he then returns to the École for specific instruction on the work of the Department to which he has been assigned.

In Britain on the other hand, while there is some interchange of junior staff between the Foreign Office and a very restricted number of commercial concerns such as Shell and B.P., the Treasury and other home Departments do not have a similar scheme.

Amateurs on the Retreat

Apart from the Administrative officials who have made the Civil Service their career, there were, in the summer of 1964, twenty-five or so professional economists inside the Treasury, of whom six were very junior. About nineteen were actually working in the building. The remainder were scattered in different places; one, for example, was on loan to the Foreign Office, one was on sabbatical leave at the National Institute of Economic and Social Research, one

* Brian Chapman, op. cit. pp. 115–16. This book contains a full account of the École Nationale.

with an international organization in Paris; and another had been seconded to the Ministry of Transport.

Mr Cairncross has in fact been successful in building up the staff of the Economic Section which contained only twelve or thirteen members when he arrived in 1961. The normal term of service for a professional economist is five years, which can be renewed. One of Cairncross's achievements has been to borrow some economists for shorter periods of a couple of years from academic life. There were five such academics in the Treasury in mid-1964 compared with two in 1961. Apart from the full-time staff, he has persuaded quite a number of academics to undertake on commission part-time studies of specific problems.

There are still many criticisms to be made, as we shall see, of the status, role, and numerical strength of Treasury economists. But much bigger criticisms can be made on this score of other economic Departments which deal more directly with the real world. The Inland Revenue, and the Ministries of Labour, Transport, Housing, and Aviation may have had professionals who once studied or even taught economics; but for most of the last decade they have not had a single economist professionally employed as such. Many of the mistakes in Transport policy in the pre-Beeching days of the 1950s can be attributed to the absence of an economist for so long. The Board of Trade did without an economist for well over ten years, and has only just made one not particularly senior appointment. The absurd concentration of analytical power on the problems of economic steering at the expense of industrial and social issues in the 1950s and early 60s has now provoked a reaction which may well go too far.

Whitehall in general and the Treasury in particular are in rather a mixed-up mood about specialists. On the one hand it is still maintained that for the bulk of its work the Treasury needs *professional administrators* rather than experts in any particular subject. On the other hand official calculations were made in 1963 to show that eight out of the twelve top

Treasury officials then had outside economic qualifications of some kind (and fifty-three out of 152 Board of Trade senior officials). These 'outside economic qualifications' should be taken with a pinch of salt. In one case an official held a minor post in a bank branch office before the war. And people who once took a subsidiary paper in economics in the first year of a long-forgotten university course are included in the tabulation.

But there is more to Whitehall rethinking than these debating points. Confidence in the 'intelligent layman' as the best possible critic of Government spending plans is waning a little, and there are ideas in the air for bringing in appropriate specialists to help appraise complicated projects in defence, education, and the social sciences. In the reorganization of 1962, the Treasury accepted the case for a substantial degree of specialization in its different sections. The more technical Finance divisions already contain officials who have worked there for many years and would not be lightly transferred elsewhere. Unfortunately the dividing line between specialized knowledge and the unreflective observance of time-honoured thought-skipping rituals is very difficult to draw.

There is now a great deal of talk in Great George Street of a Treasury whose officials will have varying degrees of economic expertise, but where everyone will be 'economically literate'. The tide is flowing in the right direction and on this issue the outside critic is already speaking to the half-converted. But it is still a distant aim with many human obstacles in the way. Meanwhile, too much of the serious analysis still comes from junior people; and the success of economic policies depends very much on the particular official to whom they happen to be reporting.

The Promotional Tree

An Assistant Secretary is the highest rank which an Administrative Civil Servant can expect to reach as of right.

General	Treasury only	Salary[1]	Approximate age range
	Permanent Secretary to the Treasury[2]	£8,800	45–60
Permanent Secretary[3]	Second Secretary	£8,265	45–60
Deputy Secretary	Third Secretary	£5,850	45–60
	Under Secretary	£4,766	40–60
	Assistant Secretary	£3,115–£3,965	36–60
	Principal	£1,959–£2,711[4]	26–43
	Assistant Principal	£846–£1,474[5]	21–28

1. Scale for Inner London Area.
2. Secretary to the Cabinet is equivalent in rank.
3. Large Department. The Permanent Secretary of a small Department is equivalent to the Deputy Secretary of a large one.
4. Receives an extra £270–£395 if Private Secretary to Minister or Senior official.
5. Receives an extra £165–£240 if Private Secretary to Minister or Senior official

From this point onwards, age is less important, and promotion depends on the normal combination of merit, luck, and ability to please. About one in three Assistant Secretaries rises to Under Secretary. From this position he has an almost fifty-fifty chance of going higher still.

Although promotion between ranks is very slow, there is a great deal of sideways shifting. For the Treasury as a whole (excepting a few of the Finance Divisions) the normal length of stay in one post has up to now been very short. The average over the past few years (which have of course included the upheaval of the 1962 reorganization) is as follows:

Under Secretary	3 years
Assistant Secretary	3 years
Principal	$2\frac{1}{2}$ years
Assistant Principal	1 year

With periods as short as this, the Treasury is still open to the gibe that no sooner has a man learnt his job than he is transferred somewhere else. There is no contradiction in urging more movement between Departments, and between Whitehall and the outside world, and also advocating longer periods of service in each individual post.

The head or deputy head of a Department has to cover far too many subjects to be a real expert on any one of them. A large part of his time is inevitably devoted to directing and criticizing the work of those below him. Only the Under and Assistant Secretaries in the middle ranks are junior enough to have a detailed knowledge of their own particular subjects – if they have been allowed to stay long enough to acquire it – but sufficiently senior to be in contact with the Permanent Secretary. They are thus in a key position for certain kinds of policy making – regional development would be a good example.

The key position of the Treasury among Whitehall Departments emerges in yet another way from the table. Not only is the rank of Permanent Secretary to the Treasury superior to the Permanent Secretary of other Home Departments, but a Treasury Second Secretary is equal in rank to the Permanent Secretary of other large Departments. Indeed a Treasury Second Secretary will often take the chair at a meeting where other Departments are represented by their Permanent Secretaries. When in the late 1940s Sir Henry Wilson-Smith, who had been head of the Ministry of Defence, returned to the Treasury as Second Secretary in charge of Overseas Finance, this was certainly no demotion.

The Treasury now has two Permanent Secretaries – Sir Laurence Helsby, who looks after the Civil Service, and Sir

William Armstrong, who is in charge of the financial and economic side – and three Second Secretaries. This gives the Treasury five men of Head of Department rank, compared with one for normal Ministries.

The unhappiest aspect of the hierarchy just described is the fifteen or twenty years which the ablest young men have to endure as Assistant Principals and Principals before they are given a real voice in policy discussions. No wonder many of the more adventurous and enterprising young graduates prefer to take a gamble on getting ahead more quickly in the outside world rather than enter the Civil Service. During the war the usual formalities were waived, and many officials were promoted while still very young, but the Civil Service afterwards lapsed back into 'normal' routines. Indeed the wartime promotions represent an entrenched group of senior officials blocking promotion today. This promotion blockage is, as much as anything else, the clue to the politely suppressed frustration that one senses among some of the younger Whitehall Administrators.

Men with ideas are also put off by the general atmosphere of civilized scepticism. Despite all the reforms which have already taken place they still feel that it is not done to show enthusiasm for any idea, or to take too seriously the national objectives discussed in the newspapers. The worst thing that can be said about a proposal is that it is 'political', and the next worst that it is journalistic. The words 'there is nothing new under the sun' seem to be written on the walls in invisible ink; and the place is full of kind, intelligent people (and just a few less kind ones) whose real interests are private ones far removed from the political and economic arena.

'Scepticism' of the Whitehall variety is a very different animal from the Cartesian doubt of the philosophers, which questions old-established assumptions as a prelude to a new synthesis. British official scepticism is more often directed towards new, reforming ideas than towards accepted beliefs and is not necessarily a prelude to anything at all.

Pay and the Exodus

The salary structure itself is probably rather less important as a source of discontent. The Assistant Secretary level marks the parting of the ways on salaries as in other matters. Up to this level Civil Servants' pay and conditions, taken together, are meant to be broadly comparable to equivalent jobs outside. Actual salaries seem to be somewhere between university and business scales.

Above the level of Assistant Secretary the principle of 'comparability' in salaries no longer applies with full rigour. The 1955 Royal Commission on the Civil Service emphasized the traditional doctrine that the financial rewards of the Higher Civil Service could not match 'the highest rewards' in commercial employment.* An independent Standing Advisory Committee, now under the chairmanship of Lord Franks, has advised the Prime Minister on Higher Civil Service salaries since 1957. So far its recommendations have invariably been followed.

Judged by any overseas comparison, the knights of Whitehall should have little complaint. According to no less an authority than Professor Brian Chapman, 'the British Civil Servant has a far higher salary than his opposite number in any European country and he enjoys a considerably higher standard of living. This is true for all grades.'† In America too, Government servants come very much lower down in the U.S. salary scale than do British officials.

It is tempting to leave the matter here. After the 1963 pay revision neither an Assistant Secretary nor an Under Secretary can feel grossly underpaid, although he may be left behind in the salary race in the four or five years before the next review falls due. The 1963 review deliberately makes no allowance for future inflation, and not all Civil Servants may enjoy the process of setting an example. All the same

---

* *Royal Commission on the Civil Service 1955* Cmd 96113 H.M.S.O., Chapter IX.

† *op. cit.*, pp. 43-4.

it is extremely unlikely that promising men in the middle reaches of Whitehall are consciously aiming at chairmen's jobs. Most ambitious officials of forty or so are much too preoccupied with their own immediate prospects to plan for ten years ahead.

But it is at the bottom and at the top that good people of unascetic tastes may be deterred by the pay and conditions. During the long years of work as Assistant Principal and Principal, when promotion still depends on age and seniority, some of the brightest young men are likely to feel that they would have more money as well as better positions in the outside world.

At the very top too, the money gap between the business world and Whitehall is immense, despite the recent widening of differentials. Civil Service salaries give a false impression as they take no account of the various tax avoidance measures or benefits in kind obtainable in business which are completely absent in Whitehall.

Financial considerations therefore to some extent explain the exodus into industry since the mid 1950s of so many slightly older Whitehall men. (But the exodus, which has only been at the very top, has not been enough to remove the promotion blockage discussed above.) In the U.S., key officials arrive at their posts with a change of President, stay a few years, and then go back to the business or academic worlds. Their financial sacrifice is therefore a much more temporary one than that of the Treasury knight who remains in Whitehall.

There is still a slight danger, therefore, that the patient mandarin and the monastic will tend to be attracted to the Civil Service while the more full-blooded hedonist will try to make his living elsewhere. This tendency is reinforced by the fact that the Civil Service offers honours instead of a money reward at the top. A brilliant career in Whitehall will never be the way to a fortune. Yet we might get a slightly different type of Civil Servant if pay at the top were made just that little bit more attractive to people 'responsive', in Professor Samuelson's words, 'to good, clean money' rather than 'bad, dirty power'.*

But when all this is said and done, it is doubtful if money is the complete explanation of why top Whitehall men, who could have had the Permanent Secretaryship of almost any ministry they wanted, should have suddenly left the scene. Surely, if these men had known what to do about national policy, and had felt able to do it, more of them would have stayed?

A Set but not a Clique

Treasury officials do not see a great deal of each other socially in their own homes. A few senior officials, especially on the overseas side, have to attend an endless proliferation of official lunches and cocktail parties, mostly to meet foreign visitors and Embassy representatives. But these officials are very much in a minority; and contacts with industry are almost non-existent until Civil Servants come very near the summit of the Treasury.

A handful of the most important Treasury men also come together for more informal and private dinner discussions at one or two dining groups, chiefly the Political Economy Club and the Tuesday Club, where they are joined by a few selected dons and one or two very senior financial journalists.

More important today than these contacts with economic orthodoxy are the links with the economic Left through the National Institute of Economic and Social Research. The links here are of a different kind and perhaps not quite so near summit level. Instead of a convivial dinner party, there may be a phone call about a statistical discrepancy or a lunch to argue *tête-à-tête* about the trend of productivity.

To the innocent reader of the City columns, no two bodies could be further apart in outlook than the Treasury

* Professor Paul Samuelson, *Problems of the American Economy*, University of London, Athlone Press, 1962, p. 15.

and the National Institute. When the Treasury is cautious the National Institute wants to put on the accelerator, and *vice versa*. While the Treasury puts 'the pound' first, the Institute in its quarterly reviews documents Britain's lagging growth rate and puts the case for devaluation. Outsiders do not realize that the whole argument is conducted like an eighteenth-century battle, with the commanders on each side on the friendliest of terms. Both sides use forecasting techniques first developed in the Economic Section of the Treasury, and interchange of staff is frequent.

Indeed the National Institute's widely quoted quarterly *Review* emerged as a direct result of the desire of Sir Robert Hall, the Government's Economic Adviser from 1947 to 1961, to have an independent check on the Treasury's forecasts.

So far from wanting to do battle with the Institute, the Great George Street pundits are often inclined to minimize differences between the two sets of forecasts, by pointing out for example that the periods of time covered are not the same or that the figures are expressed in different ways. The Treasury has even given the Institute money for long-term research. Of course this dove-like toleration does not extend to all issues, nor is it always reciprocated by the fiercer spirits in the Institute. Yet when all such qualifications are recorded, the Treasury economists and the National Institute have more in common with each other than with any other group of laymen or economists in the whole of the country.

Another organization, which is neither on the Right nor on the Left, with which many Treasury men have connexions is Nuffield College, Oxford. This college specializes in politics, economics, and social studies. The Warden, D. N. Chester, is the editor of a journal, *Public Administration*, to which many Civil Service knights contribute, and its Fellows include people like Sir Donald MacDougall, the Economic Director of NEDC. Ministers and officials frequently come to dine at Nuffield, and Mr Maudling, Mr Heath, and Mr Callaghan have all been Visiting Fellows.

Whitehall at Work

There are certain distinctive characteristics of nearly all Whitehall work. These are best explained in the words of the Civil Service knights themselves who appear in print (in suitably recondite journals) far more than the outsider would suppose.

The first of these characteristics has been called by Lord Bridges, who was Permanent Head of the Treasury and the Civil Service from 1945 to 1956, the *departmental point of view*.* Out of each Department's 'store of knowledge and experience', Lord Bridges writes, a 'practical philosophy' takes shape. Every Civil Servant going to a new job 'finds himself entrusted with this sort of inheritance'. The good official will 'improve' and 'mould' his inheritance, but 'it is something he will ignore at his peril'.

The Treasury's own Departmental philosophy is more general and less rigid than that of, say, the Board of Trade or Ministry of Housing. It is largely a well-justified suspicion that the projects of other Departments will cost much more than appears at first sight, and that total Government spending has an inherent tendency to get out of control. This philosophy has been carried over into the Treasury's newer responsibilities, where it has become a perennial fear that the whole economy is likely to become overstrained, that as a nation 'we are trying to do too much'.

The second Whitehall characteristic concerns *the way in which advice is given to ministers*. The view that senior Civil Servants are pliant mind readers, executing policies which they have had no say in making, is absurd. The opposite view, that senior officials blatantly urge one single course of action on minister after minister is equally false, if stated in this crude form. The truth is between the two extremes, although some Permanent Secretaries are nearer one than the other.

The usual procedure, in the words of Sir Burke Trend,

* *Portrait of a Profession*, Cambridge University Press, 1953.

now the Cabinet Secretary, is to indicate 'both the range of possible decisions open to ministers and the probable consequences of adopting any one of these rather than any other'.* Lord Plowden has written of the 'procedures by which matters are prepared for ministers'.† And from America Professor Samuelson has noticed 'it is all done in oh-so-subtle and pleasant a way as to make the Minister feel that he is enjoying Hegelian freedom – that delicious freedom which represents the cheerful recognition of necessity'.‡

The Labour statesman Arthur Henderson once said: 'The first forty-eight hours decide whether a minister is going to run his office, or whether his office is going to run him.'§ This is true of most ministries, but I suspect that in the Treasury first impressions may be very deceptive. A Chancellor may start off with every appearance of intending to be master in his house, but eventually become swallowed up by the sheer complexities of the issues. On the other hand a Chancellor who begins by dutifully reading his briefs may astonish his officials by acquiring later on some rebellious ideas of his own.

The Treasury deals in issues, which are much more technical and more abstract than those of any other Department. (The homely analogies sometimes used by Chancellors in their television chats – 'the nation is like a family and can't spend more than it earns' – simply confuse the issue, and are invented after the real decisions have been taken.) In this situation the dice are hopelessly loaded against the conventional type of politician; and it is almost inevitable, as Lord Woolton has remarked, that 'the Civil Servants in the Treasury should have a very large, if not dominant, say'.||

* *International Bulletin of Social Sciences*, Vol. VIII No. 2, Unesco 1955, p. 242.
 † *Control of Public Expenditure*: Cmd 1432, H.M.S.O., 1961, p. 5.
 ‡ *Op. cit.*
 § Quoted in *High Tide and After*, by Hugh Dalton, p. 15.
 || Lord Woolton: *Memoirs*, Cassell, 1959,

THE TREASURY UNDER THE TORIES

A third keynote of Whitehall life is *the duty to 'protect' one's minister*, an activity which is supposed to have nothing to do with Party politics. Lord Bridges has once again put the matter very frankly. Some minister, he explains, will get the praise and blame for all that Civil Servants do. This 'absence of direct responsibility' is perhaps 'responsible for the Civil Servant's highly developed sense of caution'. Lord Bridges also mentions the official's 'vigilance in defence of his minister. For this reason he is at times too unwilling to admit anything which looks like a defect, and he wishes to be certain that a decision made in a particular case will not be used as a lever for other concessions which might embarrass his minister.' Lord Bridges regards these faults as occupational maladies, like housemaid's knee.

A recent Fabian study has put the point more sharply. 'Most of the time advice is concerned with *ad hoc* problems rather than with wider questions of general policy. Political pressures, the sovereignty of Parliament, the need for apparent consistency between policies which have to be described in public, tend to cause officials to be cautious and to take account of many different things before making a decision or giving advice'.* These pressures are aggravated by a tendency to emphasize procedures rather than policies and to develop a crisis mentality, grappling with an issue only when it becomes urgent.

When officials negotiate with a foreign power or business groups at home, they are affected by similar influences. 'The important thing,' the Fabian authors suggest, 'is to avoid concluding an agreement which will lead to extensive criticism rather than to register an outstanding success.' Such negotiations are characterized by a relative lack of personal involvement on the part of the Civil Servants participating. There are no direct bonuses for success or penalties for failure. (Ministers are at another, and equally absurd, extreme. Negotiations, to which their name is attached, become vastly over-personalized, and their

* The Administrators, Fabian Tract 355, June 1964.

prestige is disproportionately affected by successes or failures which may often be quite outside their power to avert – as both Mr Maudling and Mr Heath discovered in their successive attempts to come to terms with the Common Market.)

The closeness of Civil Servants to ministers also leads to a degree of political consciousness very far removed from the popular picture of a super-bureaucrat above the battle. Most of the leaders of the two main Parties are very empirical in their outlook, and innocent of the deep-seated beliefs which political philosophers and economists ascribe to their Parties. Many of them would be quite happy to adopt policies their officials assume are unacceptable on political grounds.

Nevertheless, so long as an individual minister is in charge he can, despite all that has been said, in the last resort assert his own authority over his officials – even, if he insists hard enough, over the way they 'prepare' their material. The place where Civil Servants have the greatest independence relative to ministers is in what Lord Bridges has called the 'extremely elaborate system of interdepartmental Committees, many of them with interlocking membership'. As these interdepartmental committees themselves report to *committees* of ministers their instructions are unlikely to be clear-cut, for no one minister is in a position to give the committee orders or interfere with it in the course of its work.

It is in these committees that the fourth key Whitehall characteristic I want to mention is most apparent. This is what Sir Burke Trend has called the *disposition to seek agreement*. There is a working rule that every Department affected, however remotely, by any change of policy should be consulted and an attempt made to 'carry it' before ideas are put to ministers. Even friendly critics of the Whitehall machine have suggested that the proliferation of these committees has gone too far.

These strictures apply more to the formulation than to the execution of policy. A Government which knows its own mind can make inter-departmental committees perform in a way that is truly wondrous to behold. Before the final decision to apply for Common Market membership was taken in 1961, the Whitehall machinery was chewing, regurgitating, and evading the point. But the moment Mr Macmillan announced his decision, all the officials concerned harnessed their energies to a single end, as if all their lives they had been waiting to do nothing else but take Britain into Europe.

The fifth Whitehall habit which must be mentioned here is its *obsession with secrecy*. This is partly due to the Official Secrets Act which makes it a criminal offence for a Civil Servant to communicate any note, document, or information to any unauthorized person. But it is also rooted in the doctrine that ministers alone are responsible for policy and that how they reach their decisions is no one's business but their own. Lord Normanbrook, who was Head of the Civil Service from 1956 to 1962, was a great believer in the anonymity of officials, who were strongly discouraged from any personal contacts with the Press. He is said to have ruled that any information not officially made public counts as an Official Secret.

At the beginning of an academic article on the economic techniques employed in the British and Dutch Governments, the author, Robin Marris, has to warn his readers that 'whereas the Dutch officials willingly discuss their methods and problems with outside research workers, the Treasury pursues a policy of deliberate secretiveness – which its members are bound to follow – often extending to the finer points of social accounting'.*

The sixth characteristic to be mentioned here is peculiar to the Treasury alone. This is that *the Treasury normally deals with the outside world through other Departments*, which act as its eyes, ears, and arms. If Treasury economists want to find out how industry is feeling, they must act through the Board of Trade's regional officers; if they want to make a sugges-

* The *Economic Journal*, December 1954, p. 762.

tion to the coal industry, they must go through the Minister of Power; if they want to change the tax system they must work through the Inland Revenue. Indeed they are more likely (although the chances are not great) to visit Paris, Washington, or Brussels in the course of their official duties than Newcastle, Liverpool, or Glasgow.

The strict doctrine of always operating through other Departments is, it is true, getting just a tiny bit frayed at the edges. At least one chairman of a nationalized industry never hesitates to telephone his Treasury contacts directly. And at summit level, someone like the Director-General of the Federation of British Industries can always call on the Permanent Head of the Treasury – he would not invariably feel obliged to go through the Board of Trade side-door. The Permanent Secretary, the Economic Adviser, and perhaps the odd Second Secretary might be seen at board-room lunches. But all these contacts are at a very high level indeed. Most Treasury officials mix very little in industry or the City.

There is also a seventh characteristic peculiar to the Treasury. As the Department is responsible for economy in government spending *it feels bound to set a parsimonious example in its own activities*. Most of its divisions do not have enough staff. So much has to be done in a normal day's work that very little time is left for reflection or for planning future strategy. If anyone wanted to remedy these defects the 150 or so officials of Administrative rank might have to be doubled in number.

The normal office amenities enjoyed by executives in any medium-sized commercial firm are often lacking. Principals writing papers on high State policy have no proper secretarial assistance, apart from the use of a common typing pool, and even have to correct their own carbons.

This pinch-penny atmosphere puts the Treasury at a great disadvantage, compared with the Bank of England which enjoys an independent income of its own. The Bank has for instance far more permanent representatives abroad than the Treasury, which used to have a large number, but now has only two – an important mission in Washington and a single man in Delhi. In the very early stages of the recent discussions on 'world liquidity', the Bank prepared, as a routine job, a very big dossier, which summarized all the plans for improving world payments, and analysed their strengths and weaknesses. Treasury officials would not have had time for such a project, unless it were expressly ordered from No. 10 or 11 Downing Street.

From Kent to 'The New Public Offices'

Until the war the Treasury was housed in a distinguished building more appropriate to its importance than to its traditions of frugality. This was William Kent's 'Treasury' built in 1737. It faces on to Whitehall, just on the left-hand side as one comes out of Downing Street. The rooms are lofty and elegant; the state rooms for ministers were once the best in Whitehall, and even the garrets used to be spacious by Whitehall standards. The Board Room where the early Georges used to meet the Treasury Lords and where later Chancellors have presided in lonely majesty, has been described as 'a model for all board rooms in proportions and furniture'.*

The older members of the Treasury look back nostalgically on Kent's building which they had to leave after a wartime air-raid. Although its reconstruction has now been completed as part of the Downing Street scheme, it is no longer big enough for the present Treasury staff (which, small though it is, has multiplied threefold since the war). The old 'Treasury' now houses the Cabinet Secretary, who can walk through a passage to No. 10 Downing Street without once venturing out into the open air.

The Treasury itself now occupies a singularly charmless

* A. J. D. Winnifrith, *Country Life*, 14 November 1957. This is a fascinating article, attractively illustrated.

1908 building known as the 'New Public Offices'; one irreverent inmate now retired nicknamed it 'the mausoleum', but its most common title is simply the 'Great George Street Front'. The exterior of the Great George Street Front has been described as a gentlemanly copy of the Italian style, which looks as though it had been designed by Inigo Jones when suffering from indigestion. The interior resembles a municipal hospital. One end of the building, containing the Ministry of Housing, faces Whitehall. The other end, overlooking St James's Park, used to be the home of the Ministry of Defence and is now used as extra office accommodation by several Government Departments.

The Treasury is between the two in the long stretch looking out on to Great George Street and Parliament Square. But many other ministries and offices, including that of the Ministers without Portfolio, are buried inside its labyrinths.

Papers and Meetings

Members of the Treasury, like members of any other organization, conduct a certain amount of the really important business by word of mouth – during lunch at the Reform, or in the course of a chat in a colleague's room. A five-minute telephone call to the Bank of England or a half-hour's telephone conversation with one or two overseas Finance Ministries can sometimes be the basis of quick and important decisions.

Although a large amount of paper is sent up to the Chancellor, most Chancellors are far too busy to read it all and prefer to be advised at informal meetings around their long thin table. But the officials will have met among themselves beforehand and tried to hammer out a common line. All such discussions are preceded and followed by a vast amount of documentation, and every proposal and decision has to be recorded in meticulous detail together with all the arguments used in the discussion. Papers presented to

45

ministers try to harmonize conflicting views as much as possible; and where different opinions are mentioned, no names are given (except in the case of Mr Cairncross, who is in a special position).

Nearly all the Chancellor's important meetings are with the Department's top brass – in other words Second and Third Secretaries. By and large, the Chancellor does not often talk to the real experts on many of the detailed subjects in question.

In the Foreign Office, by contrast, the man in charge of a particular area or region is as a matter of course summoned to top secret meetings, and personally interrogated by the Foreign Secretary. An ultra-conscientious Chancellor could always ask to see the original papers put in by Principals and Assistant Secretaries with the comments of their superiors in the margin – but this does not often happen.

Policy papers are usually of a fairly simple, pragmatic kind. There are theoretical appendixes, but they can be all too easily skipped. I wonder, for example, if the Treasury house doctrines on unemployment, growth, and inflation (sometimes miscalled the 'Paish' Theory to the fury of Treasury intellectuals), discussed in the Appendix to Chapter 9, have ever been adequately presented to ministers.

Economic forecasts and assessments are nearly always circulated in written reports. A paper on any subject that is long and technical will usually be divided up. There may be a summary at the beginning, or, alternatively, the main paper will be kept short and the technicalities relegated to an appendix.

The differing 'schools of thought' which were such an exciting feature of the Treasury in the 1950s are now strongly discouraged. These sharp contrasts of opinion, top Treasury men now say, reflected mainly a lack of hard information. In 1951, for example, the Bank Rate weapon was reintroduced after twenty years and no one had any idea what the effects would be. Yet I personally doubt whether the multiplication of data can compensate for the blurring of intellectual distinctions.

In the middle and lower reaches of the Treasury the only way to push an idea is to circulate a carefully drawn-up paper – which will have to devote most of its space to a discussion of objections, snags, and loopholes. New recruits soon find that an attempt to write anything that remotely resembles either an academic paper or an article in one of the intellectual weeklies will be greeted with a pitying smile. The shrewdest authors of Treasury papers will take careful verbal soundings before putting pen to paper to make sure the climate is right. Anything that cuts across the work of several parts of the Department – still more if it affects other ministries – is sure to be a hot potato.

CHAPTER 2

What the Treasury Does

THE first job of all Finance ministries all over the world is to raise money to finance Government spending.

Though the present British Treasury is far too sophisticated ever to admit to believing anything so old-fashioned, consciously or not, it is like all other Finance ministries, primarily concerned to restrain Government spending and combat tax proposals that threaten the revenue. This crude rule of thumb must now be qualified by many exceptions; but it is still a better practical guide for anyone trying to predict the Treasury's behaviour than the more sophisticated doctrines which that Department nowadays proclaims and even believes.

The Treasury is, because of its great age, one of the few Whitehall Departments whose functions are not defined by statute. As a result, its powers and responsibilities have always been the subject of confusion and argument.

It was only in 1919 that the Permanent Secretary to the Treasury was first officially made Permanent Head of the Civil Service, and it was first laid down as recently as 1920 that the Prime Minister's consent was required for the appointment or removal of the chief officers of all Departments. The object of the last reform was not of course to strengthen the Prime Minister, who could only know a very few of the individuals involved, but to strengthen the Treasury which advised him.

The title 'Permanent Head of the Civil Service' touched off a great deal of acrimonious discussion in the 1920s and 1930s; and the last parliamentary debate on the subject was held in 1942. These controversies centred around Sir Warren Fisher, an unusual and to my mind distasteful figure who was Permanent Secretary to the Treasury from 1919 to

1939. His main object in life was a unified, and in practice self-regulating Civil Service; and he would sometimes send out circulars about the four Crown Services, the Army, Navy, Air Force, and the Civil Service.

In Sir Horace Hamilton's authoritative biographical article* on Fisher there is not one reference to the Great Depression, the Gold Standard, the General Strike, Reparations, or any of the other big financial problems of the inter-war years.

Fisher was followed by Sir Horace Wilson, the Government's Chief Industrial Adviser who became Chamberlain's *éminence grise* on foreign policy. He reigned from 1939 to 1942 when the Treasury was at its wartime ebb and was succeeded by Sir Richard Hopkins, who, incredible as it may seem, was actually an authority on finance.

The Spell of Keynes

Hopkins had the usual Civil Service reserve towards all great projects, but it was a deeper and more personal scepticism than the professional mask worn by most of his colleagues. Between the wars Hopkins had been the fountainhead of the Treasury view that nothing could be done through Government spending to relieve unemployment. Yet this hardened empiricist, as Sir Roy Harrod calls him,† was also a highly individual and unpredictable character. During the war he came under the spell of Keynes and threw all his influence behind that great economist's ideas. Nor was his respect born of fear, for Hopkins was perhaps the only man in public life who was ever able to stalemate Keynes in an argument on a subject of Keynes's own choosing.‡

Hopkins was followed in 1945 by Sir Edward (now Lord)

* 'Sir Warren Fisher and Public Service', *Institute of Public Administration*, 1951.
  † Sir Roy Harrod, *The Life of Keynes*, p. 529.
  ‡ *Ibid*, pp. 420–2.

Bridges who held office until 1956. Bridges was the last Permanent Secretary to preside over both financial and economic policy and the management of the Civil Service. In every other way too he was the last great man of the old school. He was the son of Robert Bridges, the poet, and deeply interested in all the arts. He carried his broad humanist principles into his official work and his lectures, extolling 'the principle of the intelligent layman', have through their frankness and clarity, provided an inexhaustible quarry of quotations for radical critics.

By his time the Treasury work had expanded so much that the man at the top could not hope to be equally at home in all its aspects. Bridges never pretended to be an authority on economics. He had spent the seven years before his appointment as Secretary to the Cabinet and his heart probably lay in the more personal work of looking after the Civil Service.

More Than an Accident

Bridges's period in office, which spanned the first post-war decade, was, in fact, an extraordinarily eventful one. The most important changes, from the point of view of the Treasury's own responsibilities, occurred in 1947. For it was as recently as this that the Treasury was made the chief economic ministry.

The Treasury had long had responsibility for money and credit. These functions arose naturally from its relations with the Bank of England, and its responsibility for government borrowing. But responsibility for questions such as production, exports, wages, and manpower and the co-ordination of economic policy between Departments was the job of a separate minister outside the Treasury. During the war years and until 1947 the job was done by the Lord President of the Council, Herbert (now Lord) Morrison. In that year his planning responsibilities were taken over by the late Sir Stafford Cripps who was appointed Minister of

Economic Affairs. Sir Stafford had hardly been in his job for six weeks when the Chancellor of the Exchequer, Dr Dalton, resigned over a minor and innocuous Budget leak. When Cripps succeeded him as Chancellor he took with him his economic responsibilities and his personal staff.

There was of course more to the move than the personality of Cripps. The Labour Government after some disastrous experience in its first two years of office was moving rapidly away from the idea of detailed regulation of particular industries. Critics sneered that the Economic Survey of 1950 marked the end of all attempts to plan the economy. Whether this was so or not depends entirely on the meaning attached to the word 'plan' – an old verbal dispute now topical once more.

The Labour Government's latter-day doctrine was in fact stated quite explicitly by Sir Stafford Cripps in 1950. In his Budget speech of that year he pointed out that it was not always sensible to decide from the centre all the details of production. Such day-to-day decisions must obviously be made by individual undertakings within the broad framework of national policy. 'Indeed the Budget itself can be described as the most important control and the most important instrument for influencing economic policy that is available to the Government.' The idea, which is based on the doctrines of Keynes, is that when there is too much unemployment, or unused industrial capacity, the Chancellor reduces taxes or allows government spending to rise. In this way, more goods are bought and jobs created. If, on the other hand, the Chancellor wants to restrict business activity – because a boom is getting out of hand or the gold reserves are running out – he raises taxes and tries to take a tough line on government spending. In other words, the government controls businessmen and consumers by acting on their pockets, but leaves them to spend their money in their own way. Thus was born what later came to be called the Butskellite doctrine, now rather out of fashion. With the end of rationing in the early 1950s, and the abolition of most of the remaining physical controls by the Conservative Government, the Treasury became still more important as the only remaining Department with effective economic sanctions.

The next big change came after the retirement of Bridges in 1956, when it was at last recognized that no single man could carry the whole responsibility of the Head of the Treasury. The Permanent Secretaryship was accordingly split into two parts, roughly as shown in the chart on page 55. One Joint Permanent Secretary, Sir Roger Makins, was put in charge of economic and financial policy, and another, Sir Norman Brook (now Lord Normanbrook), became Head of the Home Civil Service. For the following six years Brook combined his Treasury post with his old job of Cabinet Secretary which he had held since 1947. It was not until the 1962 reorganization that the three separate jobs of Cabinet Secretary, Head of the Civil Service, and Head of the economic and financial sides of the Treasury, were finally disentangled and given to three different people.

The choice of Sir Roger Makins (now Lord Sherfield), until then Ambassador in Washington, as the Treasury's economic chief was a bold gamble that did not quite come off. The country's economic problems were too complex for anyone, however intelligent, with a mainly Foreign Office background, to pick up overnight.

Sir Frank Lee, who succeeded Makins at the beginning of 1960 and who had previously been Permanent Secretary to the Board of Trade, was the first post-war Head of the Treasury to be fully at home in current economic controversies. Basically he was a man of affairs who got on well with industrial tycoons. He was himself succeeded in 1962 by Sir William Armstrong, who was dramatically promoted at the age of forty-seven from the ranks of Third Secretary. Armstrong has probably a better grasp of the conceptual framework of modern economic policy than any previous Permanent Secretary. The practical influence of both these men will be discussed in the next few chapters.

Trouble Shooting

The Treasury has of course never been the only ministry with economic functions – although it is the only one with effective power over the level of employment and business activity. Whatever happens to the proposal for a Production or Economic Ministry, we already have the Board of Trade, and the Ministries of Labour, Housing, Works, Power, Transport, and Pensions which are all concerned with production, trade, or movements of money in one form or another.

The Cabinet's *Economic Policy Committee* (known as the E.P.C.), over which the Chancellor presides, is mainly a trouble-shooting body. Its meetings deal with many subjects, from tariffs to local unemployment; its main aim is to spot political trouble or iron out conflicts between ministers. Although most subjects of importance – with the huge exception of budgetary and monetary policy – come up before it sooner or later, it would be bizarre fantasy to suppose that discussion in the E.P.C. in the early 1960s centred around the nation's four per cent growth programme and the obstacles in its way. If we ever have an Economics Minister, one of his first acts will presumably be to take over from the Chancellor as chairman of the E.P.C. (as well as the better known NEDC).

Top officials meet at irregular intervals at the *Economic Steering Committee*, which is presided over by the Permanent Secretary to the Treasury. The Permanent Heads of all ministries, including Departments like the Foreign and Colonial Office, are encouraged to come along or send deputies; and a good average turn-out would be a dozen. The Committee usually discusses the Treasury's Monthly Economic Report and two or three other papers on topical subjects. The main object of this Committee is to keep everyone in touch and (in the gentlest possible way), to stop deviationists from rocking the boat. It would be an abuse of words to call it a planning committee. There are, of course, a great many other committees on specific subjects, many of them with Treasury chairmen.

In view of the Treasury's wide ramifications it is hardly surprising that it should possess a large number of lesser ministers apart from the Chancellor – although not nearly as many as the Foreign Office.

The Chancellor has been assisted since the eighteenth century by a junior minister known as the Financial Secretary. This post, which is normally a stepping stone to full ministerial office, has certain traditional duties connected with the Budget and the Government's spending Estimates. At most times since the war, the Chancellor has also been assisted by a second junior minister, the Economic Secretary. The Financial Secretary has usually taken a special interest in the Inland Revenue, and the Economic Secretary in the Customs and Excise. Either could without too much difficulty be upgraded into a special minister in charge of these tax Departments.

In 1961 a second Cabinet minister with the title of Chief Secretary was appointed to the Treasury by Mr Macmillan. He was given special responsibility for controlling Government spending; and this was supposed to leave the Chancellor with more time to think about economic strategy. (This followed the appointment in 1960 of a second Cabinet minister to the Foreign Office to relieve the Foreign Secretary.)

The whole question of whether there should be a second Cabinet minister at the Treasury, and what his responsibilities should be, is still very uncertain, and all kinds of experiments are likely.

The Two Sides

So much for the ministers and their relations with their colleagues. The rest of this chapter and the next will be an attempt to probe the role and responsibilities of the mysterious officials who advise them on Britain's perplexities. The reorganization of 1962 makes this much easier, as the administrative set-up for the first time reflects the real division of functions.

The usual wall charts tell one next to nothing about how a Department actually works. The diagram below is included simply as a map to which the reader can refer if he gets lost in the following pages.

How the Treasury is Organized

Chancellor and other ministers

Pay and Management Side	Finance and Economic Side
Joint Permanent Secretary	Joint Permanent Secretary
Sir Laurence Helsby	Sir William Armstrong
P. Allen	Economic
(Second Secretary)	Adviser
	Prof. A. K. Cairncross

Pay Group Mrs E. M. Abbot (Third Secretary)	Management Group W. W. Morton (Third Secretary)	Finance Group Sir Denis Rickett (Second Secretary)	National Economy Group D. A. V. Allen (Third Secretary)	Public Sector Group Sir Richard Clarke (Second Secretary)

* Summer 1964.

The Treasury is now divided into five main 'groups'. Reading from left to right in the order shown in the chart they are as follows:

1. *Pay.* This is concerned with wages and salaries in the public services.
2. *Management.* This is concerned with Civil Service

staffing methods study, recruitment, and promotion, and the organization of Whitehall.

These two groups together form what is now called the *Pay and Management Side*. This side of the Treasury, as we have already mentioned, has a separate Permanent Secretary, Sir Laurence Helsby, who is also Head of the Home Civil Service.*

Sir Laurence reports directly to the Prime Minister, rather than the Chancellor, on major questions of Civil Service policy and promotion.

3. *Finance.* This group is concerned not with taxation, but with borrowing and lending, and foreign exchange. It is also in charge of international financial negotiations.

4. *National Economy.* This is a new group bringing together most of the officials concerned with inflation, deflation, unemployment, long-term growth, incomes policy, forecasting and similar topics on which Chancellors are prone to sermonize. The Economic Adviser has some responsibilities for this group, but is also an influence in his own right.

5. *Public Sector.* Although, by an accident of layout, it comes last on the list, this all-important group discharges the Treasury's central role of controlling spending.

These last three groups form what is called the *Finance and Economics Side* and come under the other Permanent Secretary, Sir William Armstrong, who reports, of course, to the Chancellor. If an Economics or Production Ministry is formed, the nucleus will consist of *part* of the Treasury's National Economy Group and staff transferred from NEDC.

The work in the Pay group which regulates wages and conditions in the public services is very different from the

* Even now the distinction is not free from all ambiguities. Sir Laurence Helsby has one economic responsibility, incomes policy, on which he reports to the Chancellor. This partly arises from Sir Laurence's responsibility for Civil Service Pay.

rest of the Treasury. The qualities required include strong tactical skill, a feeling for trade-union psychology, and the ability to present a case to an arbitration tribunal in front of a hostile and articulate public gallery. It is decidedly not a place for a young man who wants to let off intellectual sparks. The government's incomes policy is worked out in the National Economy division, and the Pay group's own powers are strictly limited by compulsory arbitration. Most of the work consists of detailed comparison to make sure that pay and conditions keep in step in all Departments and in all grades. An independent Pay Research Unit has been established to compare Civil Service earnings with the outside world.*

The Great and the Good

The Management group deals, on the whole, with rather more interesting subjects than the Pay group, although here too there is a mass of humdrum administration which would make no appeal to men with opinions on policy.

One of its principal jobs, for example, is to control the number of staff in different grades employed throughout Whitehall – a process known as 'complementing'. It is in charge of recruitment policy and gives the Civil Service Commission an idea of likely vacancies. In addition, it coordinates superannuation for the three million employees in the public services as a whole. The group also runs a sort of management consulting service for Whitehall.

* The public services, excluding the nationalized industries, employ three million people, with a pay and pension bill of over £2,500m. – about a seventh of the national total. But the Treasury's say varies enormously from one public service to another. It is in full charge of the employers' side on Civil Service and Forces pay. It can influence the Health Service and the Police through the Health Ministry and the Home Office. On the other hand its responsibilities for teachers' pay are notoriously muddled and controversial. In the case of local authority staff the government has no power at all; but as it foots so much of the bill it does quietly insist on its right to whisper a word of advice.

Officials in this section are concerned too with the burning question of Civil Service promotion. Although the bulk of junior and middle level promotions are made within Departments, the Treasury is consulted about all the key positions. One of its main jobs is to move people from one Department to another, on the argument that 'disturbance and discomfort can induce extra growth in the right kind of human plant'.* Promotions to Permanent and Deputy Secretary are discussed at a very high level by an informal club of the most powerful existing Permanent Secretaries, before a recommendation is made to the Prime Minister.

The Management group is entrusted with one very solemn responsibility: it keeps the book of the 'Great and the Good'. This is the list of worthy, public-spirited citizens from whom members of Royal Commissions and other government Committees are chosen and a Treasury Third Secretary is responsible for looking after the list. Suggestions for the list come in from all over Whitehall; and every few years there is a drive to find new names. To call the result unadventurous would be a gross understatement. A meticulous balance is maintained between all powerful interest groups, and active members of political parties. The main qualification is that one must be safe, respectable, and, above all, over fifty.

Another of the group's responsibilities is Civil Service training. Most of this work is as unexciting as the arrangement of courses for typists. But the group is also responsible for studying the whole range of controversial questions about recruitment and training of Civil Servants raised in Professor Chapman's *British Government Observed*.

But perhaps the most interesting responsibility of the

---

* W. W. Morton, *Public Administration*, Spring 1963, p. 32. One of the least attractive aspects of the British establishment is the language it has developed for discussing subordinates. There is a lot of talk about jobs which will 'stretch' a person, and there are many head-shaking discussions on whether some unfortunate person has a low-capacity engine, or does not use enough petrol.

Management group concerns the 'machinery of government'. The hot potatoes of current political discussion, such as regional planning and the government's relation with science, come on to the plates of officials in this part of the Treasury.

The work of the Pay and Management groups may seem to the reader to be a world of its own having little in common with the rest of the Treasury, and the groups do now report, as we have seen, to a separate Joint Permanent Secretary, who has hardly anything to do with economic policy.* But the two sides cannot yet be regarded as two separate ministries for the following reason.

There are more transfers from one 'side' of the Treasury to the other than from either to the rest of Whitehall. Officials on one 'side' usually have more day-to-day contacts with officials on the other 'side' than they do with Civil Servants in other ministries. They are situated in the same building, and, above all, somehow feel themselves to be members of the same organization; and the Management side is after all responsible to the Chancellor for controlling the size and pay of the Civil Service. Indeed, the rather strange presence of two Permanent Secretaries symbolizes the compromise reached between those who wanted to hive off the management of the Civil Service on to a separate Department, and the traditionalists who wanted to keep it all inside the Treasury.

Defenders of the £

The Finance group is an appropriate place to start a tour of the other side of the Treasury, as far and away that group's most important responsibility is the defence of the pound sterling. For this reason it is the most conservative influence in the whole of Great George Street. The seven

* The November 1962 reorganization abolished the last of the 'mixed divisions' which were concerned both with Civil Service management and the general control of expenditure.

per cent Bank Rates and the other restrictive measures of the
past decade have nearly always been the result of pressure
from Finance officials for prompt action to stop a drain on
the reserves. No Economics Minister who does not have
direct and personal control over the Treasury's Overseas
Finance divisions* can really live up to his title.

The Finance group had unfortunately to fight for a long
time with one hand tied behind its back. For almost the
only way it was able to influence the balance of payments
in the decade up to mid 1964 was by depressing home
demand. (One can always reduce imports by reducing
business activity at home. The effects on exports are more
controversial.) This was to some extent its own fault, as it
showed very little sign of wanting the politicians to give it
alternative weapons.

The Treasury's main links with the Bank of England are
through the Finance group, which is another professional
reason for the group's conservatism. Most of the key
decisions on subjects such as whether to change the Bank
Rate, relax or tighten credit, or borrow from foreign
Central Banks are made at highly confidential meetings
between a small number of top Bank of England and
Treasury officials. More of the real business is done in
conversation and less is put down on paper than anywhere
else in Whitehall.

The Treasury has no practical contacts with the financial
markets. Its operations are conducted for it by the Bank
of England in both the foreign exchange and the domestic
money market. The Bank itself still claims to have the
initiative on Bank Rate changes, which are announced in
the Governor's name 'with the approval of the Chancellor'.
Fantastic though it may seem, no other member of the
Cabinet, apart from the Chancellor (and in exceptional

* Until 1962 there was a separate section of the Treasury entitled
Overseas Finance. For this reason the expression 'Overseas Finance' is
used occasionally in this book, especially in reference to past events. In
1962 Overseas and Home Finance were merged into one group.

cases the Prime Minister), has any say at all on Bank Rate changes.

Spokesmen of the City

What then, can one say of the role of the *Bank of England*, which seems to have a greater part in many important matters than Her Majesty's ministers? The Bank likes to think of itself as at one and the same time the Chancellor's instrument in the City, and the spokesman of the City in government circles. This latter role is, of course, enormously important in its own eyes. The theoretical contradictions between the two functions are no worse than those faced by the Ministry of Agriculture, which is both a Government ministry and an unashamed advocate of farmers' interests. They are less than those of the National Economic Development Council, which is sandwiched midway between the Government and industry. The contradictions are only harmful when Bank apologists pretend that they do not exist. Some of the spurious arguments they advance – e.g. that what is good for any part of the City is necessarily good for Britain – only discredit the Bank in more thoughtful circles.

The present Governor, the Earl of Cromer, accepts in practice as well as in theory that the Bank must conform to the overall financial policy laid down by the Chancellor. Lord Cromer, who was appointed in 1961 at the age of forty-three, is, despite his title, thoroughly at home in the twentieth century. Although he is forthright in pressing his own views on the Chancellor, he would not dream of indulging in the narrow-minded obstructionism of some of his predecessors.

The Bank is, nevertheless, obsessively concerned to show that it is not a Government Department and that it reports to the Chancellor as an independent entity. In the days of Montagu Norman (who reigned from 1920 to 1944) the Governor of the Bank of England would normally go alone to see the Chancellor and no Treasury officials would be present. As late as the mid 1950s only the top Treasury knights were allowed to talk to their opposite numbers in the Bank. There is no exchange of staff between the two institutions: Mr Butler, in evidence to the Radcliffe Committee, wondered whether a man trained in one stable would be welcome in the other.

There are people in the Bank as intellectually high-powered as almost anyone in the Treasury. Some very good economists have been taken on as 'Advisers to the Governor' and one has recently been made an executive director. The executive directors too are now – they were not until the early 1960s – all men who can easily hold their own in any forum on practical monetary policy.

But the typical Treasury Civil Servant and Bank of England official could hardly be more different in approach, temperament, and training. This shows itself at every level below the top. The Bank has no graduate training scheme, and any graduate entrant has to spend years in little more than clerical work. It is not surprising that the Bank tends to recruit straight from public school rather than university.

Since the publication in 1959 of the highly critical Radcliffe Report on the monetary system there have been more detailed discussions of policy between Bank and Treasury officials, including sometimes Treasury econo-mists. A team from the Treasury, Central Statistical Office, and Bank is at present trying to put the mass of ill-assorted published financial statistics into some logical form, from which trends can be established and judgements drawn. But it would be idle to pretend that it has yet had any influence on policy, and in the infinitely more important sphere of overseas Finance there is no such technical committee.

Advice to the Chancellor on monetary issues is usually thrashed out at *ad hoc* meetings between a very few Bank and Treasury officials. Tactics to adopt at a meeting of the International Monetary Fund will often be discussed be-tween Sir Denis Rickett, the head of the Treasury's Finance

Group, Mr Cairncross, the Government's Economic Adviser, and Mr Maurice Parsons of the Bank of England. Parsons, as a good Central Banker, will tend to be the most cautious of the three in the initial discussions; but once a policy has been accepted he will work the hardest to get it accepted by other countries.

At every international monetary conference Parsons's tall figure can be seen above the throng of bankers, being polite to all of them and arranging to talk privately to the one or two who really matter, or enduring indescribably boring parties for the sake of advancing monetary co-operation one tiny step further.

There is no one who can beat Parsons at talking round a hardened Swiss or German Central Banker who is not very interested in economic argument, but is convinced in his innermost being that Britain is engaged in a rake's progress at someone else's expense.

Parsons can also be very impressive indeed in warning British ministers against schemes which he regards as dangerous. Most Chancellors would think many, many times before overruling him on an issue where he has chosen to bring out all his guns. When he warns in a deeply serious but unpompous voice of the profound risks one might be running in some suggested scheme, he really does know his subject matter, and sounds as if the candles of monetary civilization may go out any moment. It is not his fault that there is no one on the radical side a fraction as impressive.

The Bank of England has two main jobs that are important for policy-making. It is responsible for managing the foreign exchange market and for running the market in government securities. Just as its responsibility for restraining government spending is a better clue to how the Treasury will behave ninety per cent of the time than any more highfalutin theory, so these two functions of the Bank enable an outsider to predict many of its attitudes.

The Bank is more interested in whether foreigners are buying or selling pounds, and less in theoretical calculations about the balance of payments than the Treasury. And its judgements of the business situation at home depend on the mood its executive directors pick up from individual businessmen, rather than on any elaborate calculation of National income trends.

As the Bank is interested in foreigners holding pounds, it abhors any suggestion that devaluation might ever in any foreseeable circumstances be a legitimate action. It dislikes exchange controls nearly as much, partly because it believes that they weaken the attraction of London as a financial centre.

If the reserves start running out the Bank will favour swifter and severer action than the Treasury. But once the scare is over and confidence has returned, the Bank is less cautious than the Treasury in taking off the brakes. On the home front the Bank may start worrying about recession more readily than Treasury officials – who are very cynical about businessmen's tales of woe – even though it places domestic expansion lower down its list of priorities.

When gilt-edged securities were unpopular with investors, the Bank of England was a fanatical advocate of economy in Government spending. For the smaller the gap between expenditure and revenue the less the Bank has to borrow for the government on the gilt-edged market.*

* There were, of course, several ways round this difficulty. Long-term interest rates could have been forced up to a point where investors were happy to hold gilt-edged. But by the laws of simple arithmetic, when long-term interest rates move up, gilt-edged securities fall in value; and the idea of deliberately depressing government stock was regarded by the Bank of England in Lord Cobbold's day as analogous to spitting on the Union Jack. Alternatively, the government's borrowing requirements could have been met through the issue of Treasury Bills; and the expansionary effects of these bills on the banking system could have been offset by a call for Special Deposits. This expedient would have been regarded by the Bank as a form of legalized fraud. The third alternative, appropriate to certain economic circumstances, of raising taxes, was almost as great an anathema to the Bank. Yet anathema or not, a combination of all three methods was introduced quietly and without fuss in 1960–1.

The doctrine of an 'overall Budget balance' which we shall come across in the following chapters, and which makes such nonsense in economic terms, falls into place as the rule of thumb of an unhappy bond salesman operating in a depressed market.

Because of certain changes in the personalities at the top, the Bank is today slightly less likely to expound such over-simplified doctrines.

Aid and Payments

After this digression on the Bank of England, it becomes easier to see the unenviable position of the Treasury's own Finance group which falls professionally between two stools. As one of its jobs is to convey the Bank of England's views to Whitehall, it is inevitably infected with the Bank's approach, and as it is professionally concerned with maintaining the value of the pound, it cannot adopt the detached attitude to gold reserve movements advocated by some economists. On the other hand, it has no direct contact with the speculators and traders who actually sell sterling; and its own special contribution lies in the presentation of (often excessively pessimistic) balance of payments statistics.

The Treasury was not always so detached from the Foreign Exchange market as it is today. Before the war this market was largely managed from the Treasury end by two expert officials, Sir David Waley and Sir Frederick Phillips. In the post-war period the Treasury has on the whole had less influence on overseas financial questions, where the Bank is supposed to be acting as a mere agent, than in domestic credit where the Bank officially takes the initiative.

On many financial questions the Treasury has succeeded in delaying the Bank but not stopping it. The Treasury's Finance divisions are too often simply a negative force saying 'not yet' to initiative which comes from the Bank. This was true, for instance, of sterling convertibility which was postponed from 1955 to 1958.

The Treasury Finance group is also concerned with aid to underdeveloped countries. This is a fairly new function: up to 1957 grants and government loans were mostly confined to the Colonies, which ceased to qualify on reaching independence. The total annual aid programme has been almost trebled in three years, and it is now running at around £200m. Although advice is given by other government Departments directly concerned, the Treasury is for practical purposes the Aid Ministry. The arrangement works better than one might expect, as Rickett and his subordinate officials are genuinely keen on aid, and are, for example, particularly sympathetic to the Indian Five Year Plans.

Another section of the Finance group, which is entitled 'Overseas and Coordination' has been mainly concerned with Europe and was responsible for coordinating the British position in the Common Market negotiations so abruptly terminated by General de Gaulle in January 1963.

Two Advisers

Officials in both the Finance and Public Sector groups are, of course, handling economics all the time, whether they know it or not (like Molière's M. Jourdain who discovered that he had been speaking prose all his life). The difference between these officials and the Treasury's 'professional economists' is that the latter are not career civil servants, but have usually worked in universities or research institutes and are normally hired on a five-year engagement, which can be renewed.

The holder of the imposing title *Economic Adviser to Her Majesty's Government* has an independent role in his own right at top-level conferences. In theory he can by-pass the Chancellor and go straight to the Prime Minister. But neither Sir Robert Hall, who was Economic Adviser from 1947 to 1961, nor his successor, Mr Alexander Cairncross, has made much if any use of this privilege.

Any Economic Adviser is under constant suspicion of being a head-in-the-clouds theorist; and as a result the occupant of the post leans over backwards to avoid giving this impression. This has been true of both Sir Robert Hall and Mr Cairncross.

The similarities do not end here. Both have been described by politicians who have watched them at work as 'pretty middle-of-the-road Establishment economists' (although since he retired Hall has not tried to hide his Labour sympathies). One minister told me that it was quite impossible to tell the difference between a report by Hall and one by Cairncross, until he came to the signature at the end. Indeed Hall was said to have suggested Cairncross as his successor.

For all the similarities, there are still interesting differences between the two men. Hall was unflappable and stable in his views; Cairncross occasionally surprises ministers by his volatility. Many Civil Servants, including some who wanted to learn about economics, found Hall somewhat inarticulate; Cairncross is just the opposite; he explains everything very fully and is ready with a quick reply to any point raised.

Cairncross's advice is less personal. He is, as was mentioned at the end of the last chapter, much better at organizing other economists and he has done a great deal to improve morale in the Economic Section.

And yet there are some very hard-headed witnesses who insist that Hall may have had more influence on policy than Cairncross has had in his much shorter period at the Treasury. Hall had, in fact, a remarkable feeling for the way the economy was going, which worked almost like a feminine intuition.

In his first few years Hall had something of a reputation as a radical, which had worn off completely by the time he retired. He gave the impression during the last few years in office that it was useless to expect politicians, buffeted in all directions by electoral pressures, to see economic sense. An important factor in his change of front was the departure in 1953 of Plowden, who was an incisive practical operator, with great sympathy for Hall's ideas. Together they formed an almost unbeatable team, the loss of which may help to account for some of the Treasury's later shortcomings.

Mr Ian Little, a former Deputy Head of the Economic Section, has emphasized, in an article written in early 1957, that the short-run balance of supply and demand overshadows all other problems as far as the Treasury's professional economists are concerned.* Questions such as 'Are we moving into a boom or a slump?' are therefore their special province. It is fashionable to belittle these questions today as insufficiently specific; but they still formed the one area where professional economists rather than career Civil Servants had the main responsibility for advising ministers from Cripps to Maudling.

It was these broad 'macro-economic' questions that mainly interested Sir Robert Hall, who was a disciple of Lord Keynes, and did more than anyone else to make the Treasury think in terms of output and employment, instead of in purely money terms. Hall was also interested in certain other broad problems: he put up a long fight for an incomes policy which succeeded only after he left, and he was keen to encourage labour-saving investment and get rid of the restrictive, protectionist mentality of the 1930s.

In the same article Little regretfully pointed out: 'Professional economic advice still plays a rather small part in influencing the many rather disjointed decisions which together determine the long-run influence of the government on the structure and functioning of the economy.' He was referring to issues like fuel and transport policy, the social services, the distribution of industry, and the composition of government expenditure. Things began to change after 1961, thanks partly to Cairncross's success in bringing in more economists to study such problems.

* 'The Economist in Whitehall', *Lloyds Bank Review*, April 1957.

Cairncross, as one Whitehall man has put it, is 'more encyclopaedic' in his interests than Hall. He once said that the main job of an official economic adviser was to check silly actions rather than to select the right course, and this remark has, perhaps unfairly, been quoted against him ever since. But he is known in Whitehall for his keen scrutiny of even minor detail and his unwillingness to take any figures for granted. Although he has plenty of interesting things to say about growth models showing the behaviour of the economy as a whole, he is probably at heart a 'micro-economist'; in other words someone whose main interest is the forces affecting individual firms and industries. He sometimes gives other economists the impression that economic growth is a matter of getting shipwrights to knock nails into ships faster – and there is a fundamental level at which this view is right.

But irrespective of personal temperament, the Economic· Adviser to the central financial Department like the Treasury inevitably still spends the greater part of his time on the central problems of growth, inflation, and the balance of payments.

The Economic Adviser, whoever he is, usually becomes in time the most expansionist influence inside the Department. This is not because he wears a halo, but because he is the one top official who is paid to think specifically about production and employment. In the pre-Budget meetings the Finance group is concerned with the pound sterling; the Public Sector group with restraining Government spending. In these discussions, the Economic Adviser, on the other hand, looks at the real forces: he asks whether home and export demand will grow fast enough to keep the economy reasonably fully employed; and he will often want a more generous Budget than the Chancellor's other advisers. (This argument does not, of course, apply in quite the same way to periods when demand is excessive and the economy is under strain, and there have been occasions when the whole influence of the Economic

Adviser and his staff has been on the side of restraint.)
Moreover, the Economic Adviser also tends to be more
sympathetic to physical controls than the permanent Civil
Servants who are obsessed by the administrative difficulties.* But on all the key questions affecting the balance of
payments and the pound sterling the Economic Adviser is
only one voice among several, and not usually the
loudest.

Although the Economic Section has reported to the
Chancellor since the days of Cripps, it was nominally
attached to the Cabinet Office until 1953. Even after 1953
it kept for several years what the official announcement
called its 'special identity'. Until well on into the 1950s its
members could be regarded as licensed rebels within Great
George Street; and what they were saying often bore little
relation to what was being said in the rest of the Treasury.
Before a good many Budgets there would be great battles,
with Hall fighting for domestic expansion against the
cautious instincts of the other Treasury knights.

But although these differences of emphasis remain, there
has been a great closing of the ranks; and the Treasury now
presents a united front to all comers. Behind this front
the Economic Section is much more influential than
ten years ago; but the price it has paid is greater
orthodoxy, and absorption into the Great George Street
machine.

The seal was set on this process in the November 1962
reorganization already mentioned, when most of the
economists were put together with Administrators in the
National Economy group which is now a part of the ordinary Treasury. The role of the licensed rebels was taken over
first by the National Institute, and then by the National
Economic Development Office. Could it eventually pass to
yet another body – a new ginger group Ministry acting

* Sir Robert Hall wrote in the *Economist* of 23 September 1961 that
he was very doubtful 'about attempts at price control', but added
'though we have set our faces against it even more than we need'.

within the Government machine? Politics apart, the experiment will sooner or later be tried.

Crystal Gazers in Chief

A handful of economists work with the Public Sector or Finance groups. But the majority work in the National Economy group which itself contains two divisions with the revealing titles of 'N.E.1' and 'N.E.2'. A few economists work in both N.E.1 and N.E.2. The members of N.E.1 are concerned with trends and forecasts for the economy as a whole. Nearly all are professional economists, and the total staff works out at a little over ten, including the chief, Mr Bryan Hopkin. As the indicators of production, employment, exports, and all the rest come in, they are rushed through the division and up to Cairncross who may write a minute to the Chancellor or the Permanent Secretary, if he sees anything that calls for possible action. These various indicators are collected together for the Treasury's monthly report on the economic situation.

Three times a year, in February, June, and October, the Treasury economists together with officials of the Board of Trade, Bank of England, and Central Statistical Office make a much more ambitious and systematic 'National Income Forecast'. The February forecast, which forms the basis of the Budget, is of course the most important. All the forecasts try to give a picture of how the economy will move ahead quarter by quarter; the one that is made in February 1965 will try to predict in detail the behaviour of the economy for an eighteen-month period covering the whole of 1965 and the first half of 1966. It will also try and add a few more general remarks on the months up to spring, 1967, thus making two and a quarter years in all. Each National Income forecast is accompanied by a World Trade and by a U.K. balance of payments forecast. These are both made by a combination of Treasury economists, officials from the Treasury's Finance group, and the Board of Trade.

An interesting innovation in the summer of 1964 was to put Bryan Hopkin in charge of the balance of payments as well as the National Income forecasts. The idea was to look at all the forces affecting the economy, domestic and foreign, in a single operation. Previously payments forecasts had come under one of the Finance divisions. The new set-up might in the end prove a first step towards the unified Forecasting Office mentioned below; but its future obviously depended on the result of the election and on the exact organization of any new Economics Ministry if Labour were to win.

There is often a conflict between the different parts of the forecast. The National Income estimate may suggest the need for quite big tax reliefs to stimulate production, while the balance of payments outlook may give rise to an opposite recommendation; and if such disagreements did not exist the whole exercise would be rather dull.

Export forecasting has a particularly bad record – even worse than forecasting in general. In the last few years shaking dice might actually have led to better results.

The June forecasts are mainly a check to see if the Budget calculations are working out correctly. They may give the Treasury its first warning that something extra may have to be done in the autumn. A few adjustments can also, as a last resort, be made to the April Budget, as the Finance Bill does not receive its Third Reading until July.

The October forecast gives Budget planners a useful first guess on which to work, and the Expenditure officials some idea just how tough to be in bargaining with the Departments on the coming year's estimates. Nowadays it is also used to see if the Chancellor may need to do anything in the autumn without waiting for the Budget. There is in fact no longer anything abnormal or crisis-like about measures which amount to an autumn Budget in all but name. We more or less had one in 1962.

Members of N.E.1 have to observe a strict rule: 'Forecasting should not be mixed up with policy.' They are supposed to predict what will happen, on the basis of existing policies, not what should happen.* The task of drawing up policy recommendatons on the basis of these forecasts rests mainly with a triumvirate of Cairncross, Allen, and Hopkin.

As well as the short-term forecasts N.E.1 is responsible for a long-term five-year crystal-gazing exercise made each spring. On its long-term estimate hangs both the government's own spending plans and the line the Treasury takes in discussions with NEDC.

The Treasury's long-term forecast is quite different in method and approach from its short-term one. No attempt is made to work out business cycle trends or to ask whether the balance of payments will allow us to work the economy near capacity. On the contrary it assumes that the fifth year from now will be a 'normal' one with neither slump nor boom and that somehow or other the balance of payments will work out all right.† The forecast thus becomes almost entirely a matter of guessing long-term productivity trends (correcting for any foreseeable trends in the proportion of the population wanting to work or in the average hours actually worked).‡

The second economic division, N.E.2, contains more

* This is a very dubious procedure. No prediction can be made without some assumptions about the Government's policy. There is no unique way of translating 'No change' into specific assumptions about what the Government will do in response to hypothetical situations. See the discussion in Chapter 4 on the difficulty of defining a neutral Budget.

† Technically, as in the NEDC exercise, balance of payments equilibrium is treated as a 'precondition' of any forecast.

‡ In theory the model is a very radical one, which assumes that, having established an initial margin of unusual capacity, output will not be held down for balance of payments or any other reasons. The National Economy divisions play the game perfectly straight; but I suspect there is a lot of double-think higher up in the Treasury and that officials argue for a cautious view of productivity trends, when they subconsciously want to hold output back for the sake of the balance of payments.

administrators than economists. It is concerned in a more down-to-earth way with the practical problems of the British economy – labour mobility, regional policy, technical training, pricing policy, incomes policy, competition, and monopoly. N.E.2 is the Treasury's main link with outside bodies such as NEDC or the T.U.C., and is more likely than N.E.1 to move to any new economic planning ministry.

Both the Economic Divisions come under Mr Douglas Allen, the head of the National Economy Group, a career Civil Servant who studied economics at university and has many interesting ideas on the workings of the U.K. economy.

Problems of a Planning Ministry

Sufficient has been said to dispose of the crude theory that there are no economists in the Treasury or that the ones that are there are not taken seriously. Enough is wrong with the organization of economic advice in the Treasury without resorting to exaggeration.

One major fault is that the handful of professional economists have to waste too much time on minor tasks such as answering recherché Parliamentary questions or letters to the Chancellor. Like their administrative colleagues they spend too much time in what the Fabian study has called 'the delicate manipulation of sentences', most of which is just laborious stonewalling.

This links up with another point of criticism: their status and salaries are too low. A further deterrent is that they have very little opportunity of rising up the normal Departmental tree. It is very difficult to persuade an economist of standing to give up his university career for five years, forego the right to publish freely, and miss many opportunities of academic preferment. Government posts would be much more attractive to certain types of people if they were given the option of becoming established Civil Servants at a reasonably senior level, if they made the grade and chose to stay on. At the moment the last thing to advise any young economics graduate who wants to rise to the top of the Treasury, rather than become a don, is to enter in his professional capacity, or even to take too many periods off for special studies. This type of activity may even, in the Whitehall euphemism, 'narrow' a person's career prospects.

An additional weakness concerns the place of the National Economy Group within the Treasury structure. The work of the Treasury still revolves around the Public Expenditure and Finance groups. Things are a little different in practice, largely because Sir William Armstrong tries to give a push to the National Economy divisions whenever he can, and bases his own advice to the Chancellor to a large extent on their work. But anyone who believes that Finance and the control of Government Expenditure should be subordinate to a long-term economic strategy will get a rude shock after a few days inside Great George Street.

At the moment the long-term forecasts are only forecasts. No systematic attempt is made to isolate the obstacles to growth that emerge and put them right. There is, however, just a chance that if the function of the Board of Trade expands in accordance with Mr Heath's plans, or if a Labour Government sets up a planning or production Ministry, that the forecasts might be used, some time or other, as a prelude to detailed action in individual industries.

But before this can happen the forecasts themselves will have to be worked out in more detail; and they should not be made by the same people who work on year-to-year problems in preparation for the Budget. On the contrary, the long-term strategists should work out the basic goals and targets, to which short-term policy should be as far as possible geared. Of course, any long-term strategy is likely to be full of mistakes and should be very flexible, but it is still better than a hand-to-mouth existence.

Forecasting would present quite a problem if a new

ministry were set up to concentrate on long-term growth. One solution would be to transfer long-range forecasting to the new Department and retain short-term forecasting inside the Treasury, leaving the two to work out some sort of relationship.

Whitehall would probably regard this expedient like King Solomon's judgement of cutting the disputed baby into two. Left to itself it might prefer to move the whole of economic forecasting into an enlarged Cabinet Office – which could be regarded as a suitably neutral place! The ideal would then be a unified Forecasting Office to serve all Government Departments and perhaps NEDC as well. One hardly needs to emphasize the potential power of a Forecasting Office independent of two fiercely rival ministries and reporting directly to the Prime Minister. But the real argument against this idea is that working out long-term assessments of productivity is intrinsically a different exercise from plotting the course of the trade cycle, however much the two inter-relate; and that there would be loss as well as gain in mixing the two together.

Administration or Ideas?

Finally, before the plunge in the next chapter into the mire of Government spending, a word should be said about the reorganization the Treasury had in November 1962. This was the first really big shake-up since 1938, or even, in some reckonings, 1919, although in many ways it simply brought to a head developments which had been going on for a number of years.

The Treasury, has, for the first time, been organized according to the logical functions it performs. In Norman Macrae's words it has become 'even tidier, even more hierarchical, and therefore potentially even more immobile than it was before'.* Every proposal goes into a vast machine; and while this may lead to a more thorough and

* *Sunshade in October*, p. 30.

professional examination, it multiplies second thoughts, reservations, compromise, and delay.

Like Mr Macrae I have a lingering affection for the pre-1956 system when the Chancellor drew his advice 'from a gaggle of co-equal advisers' below Permanent Secretary level. But having made the decision to appoint a single Permanent Secretary as a financial overlord, it was better that he should be served by a good organization than by a bad one. Between 1956 and 1962 the Treasury had all the disadvantages of a great hierarchical machine with few of its compensating benefits.

My own worry is that an administrative reorganization has been used as a substitute for the reorganization of ideas which was really required. All the emphasis in the middle and lower ranks, where most of the detailed work is done, is on the collection of data and interpretation of trends. There is not enough analysis of alternative policies and their implications. If the latter were to be done seriously it would require as much time as the more factual studies – and therefore a larger Treasury. Policy ought not to be left to a few overworked men at the top.

CHAPTER 3

Plowden Versus Gladstone

OFFICIALS in other ministries still think of the Treasury as the Department which stops them spending too much money. The wider economic responsibilities discussed in the last chapter are something they read about in the Press. And if one takes a deep breath and asks 'Doesn't the Treasury actually push forward spending projects which will help economic growth?' a look comes into their eyes which makes one drop the subject at once. It is indeed a fact that far more Treasury Civil Servants are concerned with controlling government spending than with any kind of broader economic policy. This is brought out by the following table showing the distribution of Administrative grade officials between the main Treasury groups. (Permanent and Second Secretaries are omitted, as are people working in Private Offices.)

Public Sector group	48
Pay group	22
Management	23
	—
Total of above	93
Finance group	45
National Economy group	7
	—
Grand Total	145
	—

The Pay and Management groups (whose functions were reviewed in the last chapter), have been put with Public Expenditure because, in the eyes of most Civil Servants, their main job is to stop ministries spending too much money on staff and salaries. Most of the officials in the National Economy group spend nearly all their time in their own offices interpreting figures and working out trends, and are relatively unknown outside the Treasury. Even if we include the professional economists in the National Economy group it still does not amount to many more than twenty. The numerous officials of the Finance group also tend to spend a lot of time making calculations in their own offices. Their activities are regarded with admiring incomprehension by the typical official in, say, the Ministry of Labour or Transport. As far as they have dealings with the outside world these are mostly with the Bank of England, or with overseas Finance Ministries.

The Public Sector, Pay, and Management groups are assisted by a phalanx of over 260 Executive officers – four or five times as many as in the rest of the Treasury put together. These assistants give the 'stopping spending' groups of the Treasury an appearance of massiveness completely lacking in the economic divisions, which have virtually no Executive officers, and would probably have no use for them if any turned up.

The Centre of the Treasury

Despite the forbidding nature of its functions, the Public Sector group is the part of the Treasury that has changed most in recent years. Rightly or wrongly, it is this part which is still the centre of the Treasury, and places in it are regarded by many young Treasury men as among the most lively and exciting to work in the whole of Whitehall.

The control exerted by the Treasury over government spending has, as Sir Ivor Jennings has stressed, in the last resort 'no basis save in the authority in the Cabinet of the Chancellor of the Exchequer. If his authority is overborne, the Treasury must comply.'* But, subject to this proviso, the Treasury's authority rests on three time-hallowed rules.

The first is the famous Standing Order 78 of the House of Commons, which dates back to 1713. This prevents any

* *Cabinet Government*, 3rd edition, p. 163.

member of the House of Commons from putting forward any Bill, or amendment, which would cost the Treasury money without the Government's consent.

The second rule, which was formulated in 1924, but had existed in substance before, is that no memorandum proposing additional expenditure should be circulated to the Cabinet until it has been discussed in draft with the Treasury.

Thirdly, any proposal involving an increase in expenditure or any new service, whether or not involving an increase in the total expenditure of the Department concerned requires Treasury sanction. This principle was first made explicit in 1884. Even when the Treasury has agreed to a new service in the Estimates, its consent has still to be sought separately for each item of expenditure as it is incurred.

The Exchequer accounts are audited eight or nine months after the year is over, by the Comptroller and Auditor General, who is a House of Commons official with a staff of 500 or 600. The Comptroller himself is theoretically responsible for spotting illegal expenditure; but nowadays he is personally mainly concerned with waste and extravagance. His reports are made to the House of Commons' Public Account Committee (P.A.C.), which is chaired by an Opposition M.P.; for a long time Harold Wilson. It dates back to 1861, and was a truly formidable body when the House was very economy-minded. Even today it still has pretty fierce teeth. It is the P.A.C. which recommends whether a Permanent Secretary should have to make good irregular spending out of his own pocket, a penalty last imposed in 1919.

Another House of Commons body, the Select Committee on Estimates, picks out individual topics which seem worth exploring. A recent example is the investigation of Government policies on transport aircraft which led the Committee to some critical observations on the Anglo-French Concorde supersonic project. Its reports go more into policy

matters than the more Gladstonian P.A.C., but, unfortunately, it does not have the same prestige. It only started
in its present form in the 1920s and it has had a rather
chequered career. Yet it was the Select Committee and not
the P.A.C. which carried out the highly critical analysis of
Treasury control methods in 1957–8, which sparked off the
revolutionary Plowden Report. The Treasury is sometimes
accused of taking a rather superior attitude to its findings,
accepting a point here and there, but rejecting many others
as impracticable. It would not dare to do this with the
P.A.C.

Nothing has been said of the formidably complex rituals
by which Departmental spending plans are vetted inside
Whitehall before the House of Commons gets to work.*
They consist mostly of devices for strengthening the lock on
the stable door when the horses are already many miles
away!

The End of Candle-Ends?

The influence of these time-honoured rituals has been
eroded by a much more modern approach, which is known
to the initiated by the one word 'Plowden'. Lord Plowden,
who is now Chairman of Tube Investments, has served in
the Treasury as Chief Planning Officer (a post since
abolished) between 1947 and 1953.

Between 1959 and 1961 he was asked back into Whitehall
on a part-time basis, to bring up-to-date the whole theory
and practice of Treasury control of spending. The Committee over which he presided consisted partly of officials
and partly of other discreet businessmen with Whitehall
experience.

The published version of the Plowden Committee Report,
which came out in 1961, was incomprehensible except to

* For a full and up-to-date account of the processes see *The British
Budgetary System* by Sir Herbert Brittain, Macmillan 1959. Another good
source is Lord Bridges's book, *The Treasury*, Allen and Unwin, 1964.

connoisseurs of Whitehall sign language. It is difficult to believe that Lord Plowden wrote the final draft. While his speeches in the House of Lords are crisp, clear, and concise, the Plowden Report is vague, elusive, and smothered in cotton wool. As D. N. Chester suggests, it must have gone through 'that lengthy process of redrafting, during which the sharp edges, the pungent phrases, and any handle to outside critics were all removed'.*

Four main recommendations can be extracted from the Reports. (I should warn the reader that there are many translations of the Plowden Bible and not everyone would agree with my version.) One Plowden suggestion, which has never up to now been published, is that there should be a special Cabinet Expenditure Committee of a very few senior ministers. These would meet to work out an order of priorities for government expenditure in the light of the tax burden they think people are willing to bear. It would include ministers like the Lord Chancellor, the Home Secretary or the Leader of the House, as well as the Chancellor, and ought ideally to be chaired by the Prime Minister. The big spending ministers would have been excluded on the grounds that a man cannot be judge in his own case. The main idea behind it is that the choice of spending priorities is not an esoteric financial matter, but a highly political judgement – perhaps the most important a Government has to make; and that the Prime Minister cannot escape giving a lead.

This suggestion was unfortunately rejected in Selwyn Lloyd's day and the Chief Secretary experiment was introduced as a substitute. There was originally supposed to be no appeal to the Chancellor above the Chief Secretary's head, but it has not in practice worked out this way.

A second key point of the Report was muffled up in the cliché 'importance of management'. What does this mean? 'I think if Lord Plowden were asked, he would say that the head of a large-scale industrial concern spends the major

* *Public Administration*, Spring 1963, p. 5.

part of his time not on policy but on ... putting the right man in the right job, seeing that the right kind of people were being recruited – and so on.'* Although advising on policy is more fun, the public would be better served, in Plowden's opinion, if Permanent Secretaries spent more time on the humdrum duties of running their Departments and less on the more glamorous job of advising ministers.

The Administrative class has not taken kindly to this change of role. Its members do not, as one official remarked, 'typically think of themselves as managers. By training and inclination they are fitted to regard themselves as advisers to Ministers and to the small group of very senior officials who help to fashion ministerial policies. This is, they feel, the essence of their function. This is where the excitement lies. This is a field where brilliance may be displayed and advancement won.'†

More and more converts are nevertheless being made to Lord Plowden's view. If this trend goes very far, the qualities required in Civil Servants will be different from those proclaimed by the Civil Service Commission. Instead of the Permanent Politician who so much enjoys telling his minister what to say in the House, the call will be made for the business executive, who might be almost as much at home in the large private enterprise boardroom.

As a result of its stress on management, the Plowden Committee threw overboard completely the candle-ends approach to Treasury control. This is the third key point to emerge from its Report. The best way the Treasury can get value for money, according to Plowden, is to see that other Departments are properly run.

As part of the new approach the Treasury has delegated some of its powers over spending. Until 1939 not a single extra charwoman could be hired by a Department without Treasury approval. As late as 1957, individual building projects by the Ministry of Works had to be sanctioned by

* D. N. Chester, *op. cit.*, p. 11.
† The *Economist*, 8 August 1964, 'The Civil Service Examines Itself'.

the Treasury if they exceeded £1,000. But today the general expenditure limits are much higher. They vary from sector to sector, of course. For public building projects they now stand at around £200,000. For main road schemes it is even higher – not far removed, in fact, from the £1m. mark. For many kinds of military research and development projects the spending limits are around £100,000. All these delegated powers are, of course, exercised within total spending limits already agreed with the Treasury.

There has recently been a reaction against the Plowden Report, in favour of more detailed Treasury scrutiny of individual items of expenditure. This seems to be Mr Wilson's view and it comes out very forcefully in a recent report by the House of Commons' Estimates Committee.

Unfortunately, some Whitehall Departments do not seem to be in a fit state to be trusted with their own financial management; and the Management group of the Treasury, as the Select Committee makes all too clear, has a long way to go before it is in any position to put their houses in order. A number of recent cases, such as the muddle over the V.C.10 aircraft, and the excessive Ferranti profit on Bloodhound, have played into the hands of the Gladstonian counter-revolutionaries.

Financial administration seems to be especially weak when anything to do with weapons, missiles, aircraft, space or atomic energy is involved. Some Conservatives feel the trouble lies in the remoteness of the Civil Service both from practical business and from space-age technicalities. When Mr Aubrey Jones was Minister of Supply in 1957–9, he had a regular system for calling in professional business consultants to advise on important contracts for a new weapon, but the system was dropped when he left the Government.

Although it would be other-worldly to ignore the very powerful lobbies in the whole defence–space–aviation area, the commercial element is almost the least worrying of the forces involved. Many Tory Back-benchers feel passionately that Britain's national prestige depends on our staying in the Big League in all these fields; and woe betide any Conservative minister who tries to give up an independent missile system or abandon British aircraft. Nor would it be easy for a Labour minister to abandon this prestige hardware. Labour Members are particularly sensitive on the employment aspects and sometimes sound as if they believe that full employment means that no one should ever change his job.

Another Select Committee was recently struck by the contrast between the lack of detailed study of the financial implications of the Concorde and the intensive study of its technical aspects.* There really can be no justification for the Treasury having been absent from the Anglo-French Committee on the Concorde – until it was forced to change its attitude by House of Commons pressure. Expenditure of £160m. at the very least is involved; and the whole thing could easily turn out a bigger white elephant than any previous financial shock. The one-sided way in which the Treasury has delegated its powers has played into the hands of the anti-Plowden school. The laxity in the defence-prestige fields contrasts with the continued pinch-penny atmosphere which still prevails in some civilian fields.

Despite the freer rein given to Departments, there is still in some ways an enormous amount of fussy detail. At the monthly meetings of the NED Council, the Treasury pay for the food consumed at lunch, but not the drink. Members of the NED office have personally to foot the bill for Dr Beeching's wine.

Five-Year Plans

The fourth Plowden idea is to plan Government expenditure several years ahead. The conventional financial year,

* Second Report of the Estimates Committee, Transport Aircraft Session 1963–4, 1964 House of Commons Paper 42.
7th Special Report of the Estimates Committee, Transport Aircraft (Departmental Observations) House of Commons Paper 241, 1964.

which has grown out of the agricultural crop cycle, is a ludicrously short period for expenditure control. Every modern industrial firm works to a longer time horizon, and it is quite amazing that the idea of long-term Government programmes should be regarded as revolutionary. To take a simple example: the education bill depends to a large extent on the number of trained teachers in the country (assuming that no significant numbers are forced to leave the profession or remain unemployed). It takes about three years to build a teachers' training college and another three years to put a trainee through one. So the main effect on the current education bill of the decision to build such a college is not felt for six years.

Separate four- or five-year spending plans have been in existence for some years in separate sectors. Mr Selwyn Lloyd had an unpublished defence plan made when he was minister in 1955, and in 1956 Sir David Eccles, as he then was, launched a five-year plan for technical education.

The novelty of the Plowden approach is that it goes beyond the piecemeal scrutiny of individual sectors. All the different spending plans are now added up and considered together, against a forecast of the probable growth of the National Income. The first of these comprehensive surveys was made in 1961, and one has been made every year since.

The early surveys were amateurish affairs; and one reason why Treasury officials were for a long time reluctant to publish them was the fear that they might look silly in the light of events. They were also afraid that policy might be tied down too rigidly for too many years in advance if the Government committed itself too precisely in public. The decision to publish was taken in December 1963 in the heat of a pre-election campaign despite a good deal of official head-shaking.

The following table is taken from the White Paper then published (Cmd 2235).

TOTAL PUBLIC EXPENDITURE

	£ million at 1963 prices		
	1962/63	1967/68	% Increase
Defence	1,905	2,170	14
Benefits and assistance	1,745	2,105	21
Education	1,260	1,570	24
Investment by nationalized industries	1,135	1,330	17
Housing, etc.	1,135	1,315	16
Health and welfare	1,020	1,160	14
Administrative, etc.	705	725	●
Assistance to industry, transport, and agriculture	665	620	●
Roads	360	470	30
Aid and overseas spending	310	365	●
Children's services	290	315	●
Contingency allowance	—	250	●
Police and prisons	200	230	●
Adjustments	180	200	
Total public expenditure	10,910	12,825	17½

● In some cases percentages would give a misleading idea of the size of the actual increase in view of the smallness of the base year figure.

The published exercise is incomplete. The missing half is the long-term National Income forecast. Unless one tries to guess how large the national product is going to be, how fast private savings are likely to rise, and the claims of private investment and exports, it is quite impossible to say what the implications of the White Paper are for taxation. The White Paper was said by ministers to demonstrate that the Government programmes were 'within our resources' (presumably this means at roughly existing tax rates – otherwise the phrase has no sense). In the absence of the unpublished economic half, no such assertion could possibly be demonstrated. But reading between the lines of the cryptic concluding paragraph it looked as if the Treasury thought that personal savings would have to rise improbably fast if long-term tax increases were to be avoided.* This explains why the Treasury went out of its way in the 1964 Budget to show that the small increase in taxation then imposed was meant to be permanent, and that there might be further increases to come.

The preparation of these forward surveys has now begun to acquire a timetable of its own, just like the Budget and the Annual Estimates. Each spring, once the Budget is out of the way, the main spending Departments send in forward estimates for four or five years ahead. Some of these will be based on definite programmes already agreed with the Treasury, for example hospital building and roads. In other cases such as the nationalized industries or housing, they are simply forecasts or projections of trends related to statements that ministers have made on policy. The very large increase in benefits and assistance is based partly on the increase in the number of pensioners, and partly on a statement in a Macmillan speech that the old would fully share in growing national prosperity. Defence spending is regulated by an understanding that it should not exceed 7–8 per cent of the G.N.P.

The military chiefs have often been caught out by this formula. They have a chronic tendency to underestimate the cost of their programmes, partly because they are not very good at this sort of thing, and partly because they do not take the seven per cent limit seriously enough. Hence the long list of abandoned weapons and missiles.

These long-term surveys are not really on all fours with the Annual Estimates. Neither the Treasury nor the

* This need not cause great alarm, as the Treasury may be too pessimistic about the growth of output. But whether this is so or not, the White Paper did not prove what the politicians said it proved.

spending Departments are committed to the figures they contain. They are regarded as a 'costing' of existing Government policies. Long-term programmes or under-standings now exist in some sectors as already explained; where they do not, the Treasury does not have the power to cut Departmental forecasts by a single penny.

The officials responsible for the forward looks have already discovered that expenditure usually turns out greater than they thought; and this explains the contingency allowance shown in the table, which really ought to have been con-siderably larger than £250m. The secrecy of these surveys encouraged some Departments to underestimate and hope for the best. But a healthy knowledge that the forecasts are liable to be published may make for greater realism in the future.

In 1961 when the Treasury's national growth target was only three per cent per annum, it was hoped to limit the average annual real increase in the Government's own spending to two and a half per cent. There was, of course, a sterling crisis at the time and the Treasury was looking for a sop to the European Central Bankers, and to the late Dr Jacobsson of the International Monetary Fund who held strong prejudices about Government spending. These first forecasts soon proved wishful thinking, and were abandoned fairly quickly.

Near the end of 1963, the Chancellor simply pointed out to his colleagues that public spending plans for the next five years would fully absorb the resources available without extra tax, even if the economy did grow by four per cent, and warned them against taking on any more plans. This is not a very rational procedure, as there may be new ideas far more worth carrying out than existing plans already in-cluded in the forecasts.

The whole process of regulating and surveying public spending still falls short of the ideals set out by Plowden and endorsed by the Treasury chiefs. The surveys are made the wrong way round – from the bottom upwards. Estimates of

future spending are first made in all the Whitehall ministries by very junior officials acting in a vacuum. The
papers put forward by the spending ministries are full of
vague words like 'desirable' and 'necessary' and make little
attempt to establish more elaborate criteria of national
benefit or social priority.

The root of the trouble is that, for all its great powers, the
Treasury is basically a coordinating and regulating Department. This is a point on which all the traditional standard
reference books have always insisted. The initiative in
raising policy questions rests with the other Departments;
and so long as this is true the Treasury cannot make a real
plan for the public sector, but only arbitrate among the
spending ministers.

The Treasury is able to take a strong line on defence
because of the agreed Cabinet formula that defence spending should not go much above seven per cent of the G.N.P.
The present fashion in Great George Street is to advocate
similar formulae for most other categories of public spending
as a way out of the present confusion. There are one or two
other similar formulae already in operation – spending on
health, for example, is allowed to rise by 3.3 per cent a
year in real terms. If this solution were generally adopted
the spending Departments would be told that their total
expenditure could increase by x per cent a year; and how
the Department spent it would be its own business. Such
a solution would transform the old type of Treasury control
into a watching brief on Departmental efficiency along the
lines that Plowden recommended.

But the simple laying down of percentages based on a
'political decision' made by ministers on heaven knows what
basis is not a satisfactory way out of present dilemmas. Before
any sensible evaluation can be made of the relative merits
of, say, an increase in the share of defence spending, one
would need to know a great deal about the kind of risks that
a defence policy was supposed to insure us against, and
something about the way in which the money would be

spent. To arrive at a reasonable percentage share out it is desirable to work both from the top downwards and from the bottom upwards. There is no escape from the detailed comparative study which is necessary before one can pick the right pattern of spending. It does in the end all come down to a matter of judgement, but the judgement should be an informed one.

Appendix 1: Where will the Money come from?

In the last few years the Expenditure divisions of the Treasury have in theory been converted to the doctrine of 'real resources'. In other words they are supposed to ask, not 'How much extra money will be spent on a project?', but the Keynesian question: 'How much extra load is it going to put on the labour and other resources that might have been doing other work?'

This is not just a pedantic quibble. Money is simply a measuring rod, useful enough on most occasions, but sometimes a very imperfect measure. To take a practical example: a sum of £1m. spent on a public project in a high unemployment area such as the north-east does not cost the country anything like £1m. Perhaps £500,000 will be spent on local labour and other resources which would otherwise have remained unemployed. The other £500,000 will leak out into the full employment areas, and impose a burden on the economy. (The new incomes generated in the north-east will themselves be spent partly on goods and services produced in the north-east and partly on 'imports' from elsewhere.) Theoretically, if they followed their own doctrines, officials engaged on expenditure control should count £1m. spent in areas like the north-east as equivalent to £500,000 (or some other sum of money different from £1m.) for the country as a whole.

But although this point is accepted in principle, and has induced a laxer attitude to expenditure proposals for such areas, one can be pretty sure that Treasury officials do not carry the principle to its logical conclusion. If an extra £100m. of spending for the north-east were to take total Government spending above certain limits, they will not say 'Ah but these are north-eastern pounds which should be reckoned at only £50m. in any economic accounting', as they ought to do, once they have pierced the veil of money symbols.

A broader example is the electricity investment programme which runs to almost £2,800m. for the five years up to March 1967. The question 'Where will the money come from?' is an inappropriate one. (The Bank of England printing works at Debden.) The real question is whether, given all the other calls likely to be made on the economy, in school-buildings, new houses, roads, private investment, exports, and consumer spending, the power station programme, is it likely to overload the economy? If the answer to this question is: 'No', there is no separate problem of 'finding the money'.

The total amount of government expenditure which can safely be financed from borrowing, whether on electricity generators or anything else, depends entirely on the balance of supply and demand in the economy. If as a result of the pre-budget calculations, it looks as if a borrowing requirement of £1,000m. (or £2,000m.) will not (allowing for its effect on the banking system) cause an excessive demand for goods or for labour, it is a first-class logical howler to go on to ask: 'Can the money be raised?' It is indeed characteristic of non-economists to be obsessed by money.

Yet the habit of thinking about 'finding the money' dies hard, and even those Treasury officials who themselves preach the gospel of 'real resources' sometimes slip back into purely financial ways of thinking.

But however incomplete their conversion to real resources, they are infinitely more advanced than the general public, which still insists in thinking in terms of 'where will the money come from?'. So far from being generally accepted as obvious common sense, the doctrines of Keynes run contrary to the way in which people have been taught to think about good housekeeping from childhood onwards; and economists will have to become propagandists, if they are not to lose touch completely with the informed public on whose backing they ultimately depend.

Appendix II: Public Spending and the Tax Burden

Definitions are a matter of convenience, and a definition which may be good for one purpose may be bad for another. Unfortunately the Treasury has come to adopt as *the* definition of public spending one which is misleading for many purposes for which it is liable to be used. There are no prizes for guessing that the definition errs on the side of making it seem too high.

The definition, which has emerged from the Treasury's long-term surveys, covers all expenditure by the Central Government and local authorities, the total outgoings of the National Insurance funds and the investment outlays (but not the current spending) of the nationalized industries. It is the inclusion of this last item which gives rise to all the criticism.*

The new official definition gives a good answer to the

* Interest on the National Debt is not part of the forward surveys, but is added to the computation later.

question: 'How much of the nation's spending is, in the last analysis, under the control of the public authorities?' This is the respectable argument advanced on its behalf, and it is not one lightly to be dismissed. But the question which most people ask when they see a projection of expenditure several years ahead is: What will this mean for taxes? The official definition is badly designed for answering this question.

According to the current definition some forty-four per cent of the Gross National Product goes to the Public Sector. This percentage is in part an index of the degree of public ownership – politically interesting, but irrelevant to taxation. If electricity were denationalized the proportion would go down to less than forty-two per cent. If steel were nationalized it would, on the other hand, rise still higher. But neither change would have any of the implications for taxation that the figures suggest. If the State borrows from the market to finance investment in these industries instead of a private company doing so there is no reason why taxes should be any different.

The same criticism applies in modified form to the inclusion of investment in new housing. If part of a given housing programme is transferred from private enterprise to state-financed housing associations there is no increase in the burden that house building is imposing on the economy; and it is misleading to publish figures which – except to a few highly sophisticated Treasury officials and academics – imply that this must lead to higher taxation. The present definition inadvertently gives an alarmist impression whenever the State increases its role in the economic system. (If taken seriously, it suggests that the denationalization of electricity or the Post Office would be a painless way of raising pensions or building more hospitals.)

The official answer to these criticisms is that the Public Sector figure is not meant to be an adequate guide to the level of taxes five years hence; and that this can only be guessed from a forecast for all the components of National

Expenditure which would take into account the trend of private savings. Unfortunately M.P.s and others would not carry around long-term National Income forecasts in their head even if some Chancellor would deign to publish them; but they might well remember a single percentage for Public Expenditure and gain the wrong impression.

The question here is not merely one of presentation. It is quite reasonable, even for someone who understands what the National Income approach is all about, to ask what is likely to happen to taxation if the current Budget surplus remains around its present level, and fiscal policy does not have to move in a strongly deflationary or expansionary direction. This is not a question which the present set of figures is helpful in answering.

Appendix III : The Nationalized Industries

The Treasury does not attempt to control the spending of the nationalized industries in the same way as the spending of the Government Departments. The nationalized industries have been moving over the last half dozen years towards a more commercial orientation and the Treasury sees its relations with them as that of bankers to clients. This trend leaves ministries like Power or Transport in a somewhat anomalous position as buffer between the Treasury and the nationalized boards.

The Bible for current policy is a White Paper on the *Financial Objectives of the Nationalized Industries* (Cmd 1337, 1961). This lays down financial targets for the industries to achieve over the next five years taking one year with another. The idea is that the industries should make a reasonable rate of return on the capital employed. If they do so they will also be making some contribution to their own capital needs and will be charging prices to consumers which bear a realistic relation to costs.

The targets so far agreed include the following:

%return on net assets

Electricity	12.4*	
Gas	10.2*	
Post Office		8⬤
London Transport		5⬤
B.E.A.		6⬤

* Gross return (including depreciation)
⬤ Net return (excluding depreciation)

The Coal Board's objective is not expressed as a rate of return; the target here is to break even and make provision for depreciation. There is no target for British Railways except to reduce the deficit as quickly as practicable.

The broader background of these targets is described in Chapter 7. These financial objectives are a good deal stiffer than the earlier aim of simply breaking even, taking one year with another. They have forced the nationalized boards to look more closely into costs and efficiency, and also to reassess individual loss-making activities which were hitherto taken in their stride.

There is still, however, a long way to go. The subject requires a book to itself, but a list of a few of the inadequacies of the White Paper approach may be worth while.

1. The House of Commons Select Committee on the Nationalized Industries recommended that specific subsidies should be paid out of public funds for services which did not pay their way, but which Parliament wished to maintain. This suggestion would have clearly separated commercial judgements from wider social and economic problems which ought to be decided politically. The Government unfortunately rejected the suggestion and simply adjusted downwards the targets of industries with

social obligations. As Lord Aldington (who as Sir Toby Law chaired the Select Committee) has pointed out: 'This goes a little way to meeting the problem, but it does not – and I regret this greatly – mark a clear-cut division of responsibility between the Boards and the ministers.'* Instead of making a deliberate decision on how far to subsidize rural electrification or uneconomic transport services, the Boards are expected to 'cross-subsidize' them from their more profitable operations. This makes for bad pricing policies in the profitable sectors and tucks away out of sight what should be a conscious political decision.

2. The worst aspect of the White Paper is the concept of self-finance. Electricity's target rate of returns was originally fixed at twelve and a half per cent to limit the industry's annual capital borrowing from the Exchequer to £200m. (a hope long since vanished).

A self-financing requirement may simply be a roundabout way of laying down a commercial rate of return. As far as it is anything more than this, it might mean that the industry should reduce its investment programme. This would be absurd. Private firms without sufficient internal finance would raise funds on the capital market. Alternatively a self-financing requirement could mean pressure on, say, the electricity industry to raise its prices so as to generate a more-than-commercial rate of return. This would simply be a way of using electricity prices as a form of taxation, an imposition from which steel and cement are free, because they have the good fortune to be outside the Public Sector. There is no fixed self-financing percentage for the private sector where practice varies enormously from one firm to another.

The really undesirable part of the new approach to public expenditure is the tendency to look at all receipts and all expenditure as a whole. There is as much or as little reason to put income tax receipts together with electricity sur-

* The Select Committee on Nationalized Industries, *Public Administration*, Spring 1962.

pluses as to put them together with the profits of the whole-sale fruit trade. There may be valid reasons for wanting higher electricity prices and a higher rate of return on power stations, but they have nothing to do with 'self-finance'. The whole concept is a relic of the traditional 'finding the money' approach and it is out of keeping with the calculation in terms of real resources in which the Treasury professes to believe. 'Self-finance' is probably a transitional concept. It cannot fade away quickly enough.*

The whole point of setting a rate of return is to ensure that new public investment will go where it can make the greatest contribution to national prosperity. Other things being equal, a project which yields eight per cent is preferable to one which yields six per cent. The Treasury has done a lot of work in conjunction with Departmental ministries and the nationalized boards on the exact yardstick to apply. As a very approximate rule of thumb – to which there are innumerable exceptions – eight per cent is the minimum rate of return to which, according to current thinking, new projects should conform. (This eight per cent is not strictly comparable to the targets listed above as the latter are expressed as a proportion of total net assets after depreciation.)†

But this sort of calculation is only useful for new investment. A businessman may be landed with a factory he would

* On this point see 'Financial Control of State Industry' by A. J. Merrett and Allen Sykes, the *Banker*, March and April 1962.

† The exact rate of return to charge is an unsolved problem. Should it be what private businessmen actually get, or expect to get? Should it be the long-term rate of interest; or some 'socially determined' rate discounting the future? In practice most countries where this problem has been studied go for a compromise between the annual rate of return in private business and the rate at which the state can borrow. (Talk of a rate of return is, in fact, an approximation. Where construction takes a long time and the pattern of receipts fluctuates over the years, it is necessary to work out elaborately the rate of discount at which the present value of the total revenue accruing from a scheme is equal to the present value of the costs incurred. In the last few years the Treasury has, as part of its new look, been taking an interest in these esoteric subjects.)

never have built had he foreseen the return; but having made his original mistake it is worth keeping it open so long as there is any excess of receipts over running costs. The setting of a blanket rate of return on new and old assets only makes for confusion. It might have been better to have had two targets for the nationalized industries; a rate of return on new investment and some pricing rule to guard the tax-payer against avoidable loss on existing activities.

CHAPTER 4

Some Practical Examples

THE object of this chapter is to bring to life the general description so far given with some practical examples of Treasury men at work.

The first section is a description of what goes on behind the scenes while the Budget is being prepared. This is followed by a short attempt to explain why the tax system is not reformed.

Finally, I have not been able to resist a short section showing how the British habit of putting the most pessimistic possible interpretations on affairs is applied to national finance.

How the Budget is prepared

Mr Harold Macmillan once said that Budget Day was rather like a school speech day (adding that like speech day it was also a bit of a bore). But it is a paradoxical sort of speech day. For it is only when we are doing badly, when unemployment is uncomfortably high, or production too sluggish, that the tax-payer can expect big prizes from the Chancellor. If we are doing very well indeed and factories can hardly keep up with the demand for their goods, there is more likely to be a case for higher taxes. The object of a modern Budget is not just to raise money but to regulate the nation's spending; and it is when trade is bad that a Chancellor will want to put more spending money into people's pockets. Despite the ever-increasing ballyhoo before each Budget, this elementary principle, which in some degree or other has guided Chancellors since Sir Kingsley Wood in 1941, has still to be brought home to the public.

When does the Chancellor start thinking about next

year's Budget? If he is at all the worrying type – and most recent ones have been – the answer is: as soon as he has made up his mind about this year's. Should this year's Budget be at all a generous one, the Chancellor will be thinking to himself, even before he leaves for the House of Commons: 'There won't be much left for next time.'

Inside the Treasury itself a Budget Committee sits continuously from the end of July to the end of March. This is a high-powered and secretive body which meets under the chairmanship of the Joint Permanent Secretary to the Treasury, now Sir William Armstrong. The chairmen of the Inland Revenue and Customs and Excise, Sir Alexander Johnston and Sir John Anderson both come along, each with a deputy. The Economic Adviser, Mr Cairncross, and the head of the Treasury's Finance, Expenditure, and National Economy groups are also members, together with two or three supporting staff. A high Bank of England official is also present. Mr Heathcoat Amory made this clear when he announced in 1959 that the Bank would be represented on the main economic policy committees. It stands to reason too that the Board of Trade is represented, although a discreet silence has always been observed on the subject. It would be the easiest thing in the world for one or two representatives of any new economics ministry to be added, without otherwise changing the procedure.

The summer meetings of the Budget Committee started some years ago to take stock of the effects of the previous budget. Their main purpose nowadays is to see if taxes ought to be changed in mid year. The Chancellor's new power to vary purchase tax, tobacco, and other consumer taxes by a tenth in between Budgets (known as the Regulator) makes this very much easier.

In July the Government Departments send in to the Treasury a preliminary forecast of their spending in the following financial year, and the Inland Revenue and Customs and Excise (jointly known as 'the Revenue

Departments') send in their preliminary revenue forecasts. From these estimates, the Treasury Accountant – who is not a policy-maker, but a very senior Executive Officer – works out his first 'Exchequer Prospects Table', outlining revenue and expenditure in the coming financial year.

In autumn the pace hots up. By early October, figures for public investment – power stations, hospitals, schools, etc. – have been agreed, and in November the Economic Adviser produces his first assessment. The aim of this is to forecast the growth of demand and output in relation to the country's productive capacity, on the hypothetical assumptions that nothing is done in the Budget. This gives the

TABLE I. APPROXIMATE BUDGET TIME-TABLE

Month	Events	Information	Assessment
July	Budget Committee starts.	First National Income Forecast Preliminary 'Exchequer Prospects Table'.	'Should the Regulator be used?' Papers on long-term ob-
October		Public invest- ment figures agreed for following finan- cial year.[1]	jectives and on 'State of various taxes' come in throughout the autumn.
November	Chancellor has a few talks with	Revised National Income Forecast.	First assess- ment by Economic
December	top officials.	Revised 'Exchequer Prospects Table'.	Adviser, e.g. 'Nothing to give away'.

January	Budget Committee presents first report. Intensive discussions with Chancellor. Chancellor sees Prime Minister.		Provisional Budget judgement, e.g. Raise extra £100m.– £200m. in taxes.
February	Main Budget decisions.	Final National Income Forecast. Up-to-date 'Exchequer Prospects Table'.	Final Budget judgement, e.g. Raise £100m.
March	Finance Bill discussed. Law Officers called in. Budget speech written. Last minute changes (rare).		
Early April	Pre-Budget Cabinet. *BUDGET*	Financial Statement published on Budget Day.	
May– July	Finance Bill in House of Commons.		

1. This has usually happened in October in recent years up to the Autumn of 1963. But there is nothing to stop the Treasury from shifting this part of the time-table if it proves convenient.

Chancellor his first idea of whether he needs a hard or a soft Budget. In the course of the autumn, papers are also presented on long-term economic objectives. Ideas for changing the tax system, perhaps abolishing some taxes and introducing others, may be brought up in this context by Treasury economists, but only if they have already been considered in the past year or so and are possible runners for the next Budget. These will usually be opposed by the Revenue Departments who may have quite genuine administrative objections.

The representatives of the Revenue Departments take little detailed part in the general economic discussions, confining themselves to a remark here and there on the way they think business is moving. They do, however, put up papers in the course of the autumn or early winter on 'the state' of the various taxes. They might point out, for example, that the revenue from beer and tobacco duties, on which Chancellors have relied so heavily in the past, is not likely to grow very quickly in the future owing to changing social habits. They will have their own ideas for replacements which may be different from that of the economists, but more likely to prevail.

By 1 December, government Departments will have sent in firm estimates of their spending, and during the course of the month the Treasury Accountant will have worked out a revised Exchequer Prospects Table. The Chancellor's Budget decisions do not nowadays depend on these revenue and expenditure calculations but on his general assessment of the way business is going in the country as a whole, and on the balance of payments. According to the theory which now governs Budget decisions the news of a sudden increase in Government spending should not have any worse implications for the tax-payer than an increase in the forecast for personal spending in the shops, but it would be misleading to suggest that strict theory always prevails.

Economic forecasting is nowadays at the centre of the whole Budget exercise, whether Chancellors choose to admit it or not. Such forecasting methods are, of course, highly fallible. In 1961 and 1962 they led to a serious over-estimate of the expansionary forces in the economy; and in 1959 they failed to spot the rapid boom which was developing even without the aid of Mr Heathcoat Amory's very generous Budget. In 1963 the forecasts were, again, too pessimistic, although the error was not as large as that of many outside commentators.

These crystal-gazing efforts are too often judged by some absolute measuring rod. It is, of course, amusing to run down a list of forecast figures for exports, investment, consumer spending, stocks, and all the rest, noting all the mistakes. There are so many uncertainties inherent in the whole process that a good many mistakes are inevitable and Treasury economists are prepared for them. But with all their mistakes, forecasts can still be useful.

After all, the purpose of a short-term economic forecast is not to divine the future in all its detail, but to help the Chancellor steer the economy. If it can give him a rough idea of the direction in which the economy is likely to move, and an idea of where the risks lie, it will serve some purpose.

The real problems, as we saw in the last chapter, arise when the balance of payments forecast points in one direction and the home economic forecast in another. There are no general rules for resolving such a conflict. Much depends on the unemployment situation. My impression is that if unemployment (after allowing for the purely seasonal element) is down to one and a half per cent – about 360,000 – the balance of payments will usually be given priority; and the Treasury would not be deterred from depressing home demand by the thought of unemployment rising to say 1.8 per cent or 430,000.

But if the number out of work is much higher than this at the time of the Budget, risks may sometimes be taken with the balance of payments for the sake of domestic expansion. This happened in 1963. For at the time of the 1963 Budget the Treasury did not expect exports to rise very much over the following twelve months. (As it turned out its predictions were too pessimistic.) But armed with the still untested new international credit facilities, the Chancellor and his advisers went ahead undeterred.

As a result of NEDC's four per cent growth target, there has, it seems to me, been some adjustment of priorities. The Government's commitment to NEDC's target, however vague and watered down, was already in 1963–4 having an important psychological influence in preventing the Treasury from neglecting production for the sake of the balance of payments. This expansionary influence on official policy towards demand was worth all the physical planning in the world, and alone justified NEDC's existence.

Events will show how far the adjustment has gone. The Treasury still assumes that, whatever temporary risks are taken with the aid of international credit, a sound balance of payments is a *precondition* for achieving NEDC's growth target. The radical view (radical in an intellectual rather than party sense) that the four per cent growth target should become an overriding commitment – even if this means sacrificing the sterling exchange rate – was still as heretical as ever throughout the 1959–64 Parliament.

The main decisions about whether to increase or reduce taxation, and by how much, are taken between November and the end of February. This is known as the 'Budget judgement'. At this stage the Chancellor himself becomes increasingly involved. In November and December he will have a few *tête-à-tête* discussions with his Permanent Secretary and Economic Adviser, and he may also discuss with the heads of the Revenue Departments any specific tax changes under consideration.

In January the Chancellor receives his first set of recommendations from the Budget Committee; and from then onwards he plays a much more active personal part. He will have a few sessions with the whole Budget Committee, into which he will bring the other Treasury ministers. Informed people in Whitehall believe that the personality of the individual Chancellor has a lot to do with the individual tax changes chosen, but has less effect on the total Budget judgement, of how much to 'give away' or take back in taxation (although the second is usually far and away the more important decision).

In January and February better estimates of revenue are supplied. By mid February, the Chancellor knows the result of his battles with the spending Departments, and the Estimates of Government expenditure for the coming financial year are published. Much more important, according to modern doctrine, is the final economic assessment from Mr Cairncross, which also arrives in the first half of February.

As more and more figures come in, the 'Budget judgement' becomes more precise. In the last few weeks of the old year it is likely to be a very simple one such as 'nothing to give away and perhaps a little extra to raise'. Early in the New Year it grows a little firmer, e.g. 'some extra taxation needed'. By late January or early February the Chancellor may be advised to raise an extra £100m.– £200m. in taxation. It is about this time that in Lord Amory's words he 'begins to withdraw from society and develops unmistakable signs of going broody'.*

At some stage too, the Chancellor has to bring the Prime Minister into the picture: the exact timing will depend on the particular Premier and his mood, but mid-January has been fairly typical. The degree of interference varies, even with the same man at No. 10. My own impression is that Mr Harold Macmillan exerted himself before the 1959 give-away Budget to make sure that Mr Heathcoat Amory was sufficiently generous; but in a similar Budget of 1963, he left things largely to Mr Maudling. There are no reports of Sir Alec Douglas-Home's activities in this connexion.

One or two other 'very senior ministers' (who are unlikely to be economic balls of fire) may also be taken into the Chancellor's confidence in say February or March; but, as he is so much better briefed than they are, he is usually able to win any arguments. Other ministers are consulted on particular points affecting their Departments, but are not shown the whole picture. The procedure during the 1945–51 Labour Government was rather different, with non-Treasury ministers playing a more active part, as they

* 'Preparing the Budget', *Parliamentary Affairs*, Autumn 1961.

would no doubt do again in any Government formed by Mr Harold Wilson.

During the winter the Chancellor and the other Treasury ministers will receive a host of delegations from organizations with special interests. The motoring organizations will come about petrol duties, the distillers' about whisky duty, etc. Most demands will be shrugged off with the cynical thought that everyone is asking, to quote Lord Amory again, 'for a reduction in one or more taxes and duties, or for an increase in one or more items of expenditure – often both at the same time'. But an unobtrusive representation from Back-bench M.P.s on the Government side who claim to speak for Party opinion will have a larger effect, especially where a concession can be made at small cost to the Revenue. There are also more technical representations – for example, from accountants' organizations on Inland Revenue practice – which receive very serious attention.

The Budget Committee's work is in general treated like a military secret – except that Budget security is usually more effective. Each member of the Committee can appoint one deputy to serve in his stead, but even this overstates the number in the know (because some numbers may have a deputy in common). Until the pre-Budget printing and legal drafting – early in March – no more than two dozen people are allowed to see the whole picture; and even with the inclusion of secretaries and typists, the total number is no more than about forty.

Many other officials of course have to investigate particular points. The Inland Revenue experts have to do a lot of work on income-tax changes; but they will not know whether anything is being done on purchase tax, car licences, or anything else. Treasury economists at relatively junior levels will be asked to work out the effects of changing tax by say £100m., £200m., and £300m. on alternative assumptions about whether these take the form of alterations in the Standard Rate, in personal allowances or changes in profits tax, purchase tax, or other consumer taxes. But they do not know which permutation has in fact been chosen. The Budget Committee itself must see that the total effect of the package chosen is in accordance with the 'Budget judgement'.

An example of the pains taken to secure secrecy is the duty payable on car licence forms, obtainable from local post and tax offices. If a change is made in the licence duty, the clerks behind the counter must know how much to charge the very next day. To avoid giving any hint of the Chancellor's intentions, special sealed bags are sent to local post and tax offices every year with instructions not to open. If there is a change, the bags, which contain instructions to local offices and posters for public display, are opened on Budget night; if not the dummy bags are sent back unopened.

From March onwards, a change comes over the Budget Committee. The main economic decisions have, usually, been taken and the Finance Bill, which gives legal effect to the Budget, looms larger. The Inland Revenue may have ideas for blocking tax avoidance or improving administration; or there may be detailed anomalies to remove. At this stage, Treasury knights and economists are out, and tax lawyers are in. The Law Officers and the Parliamentary Counsel arrive on the scene; most of the Treasury men, including the Permanent Secretary and the Economic Adviser, quietly withdraw. The Chancellor, or another Treasury minister, takes the chair.

There is often no close connexion between the detailed points of tax law in the Finance Bill and the main 'Budget decisions' about income tax, profits tax, and all the rest. There is thus a strong case for an annual Finance Bill confined to the major Budget decisions, and a separate Tax Management Bill which the House of Commons might consider in Standing Committee upstairs and which would not have to be an annual event.

Such a separation would be controversial; but it might help to reduce the amount of time taken up by the Finance

Bill on the floor of the House of Commons, which is now the chief item of business from April to July.*

The three weeks before the Budget are largely spent on the Budget speech, which is put together by the Chancellor's Principal Private Secretary. The first stage is the preparation of a provisional outline or series of headings for the speech which are discussed with the Chancellor. Officials in different parts of the Treasury and other Departments concerned are then asked for contributions on their own particular subjects. Normally, the Chancellor will at this stage give out some ideas of his own to the speech writers, and perhaps mention the odd phrase or sentence that has occurred to him. He will try hard, in consultation with his advisers, to find a unifying theme to pull together the various bits and pieces. The 1963 and 1964 Budget speeches actually had paragraphs entitled 'Main Theme' (in both cases 'expansion without inflation'). The 'theme' may be genuine, more often it is concocted as a *post hoc* justification after the real decisions have been taken. Otherwise the Chancellor's main contribution lies in re-writing some passages himself, scrawling out others he does not like, asking for pieces to be rewritten by officials and raising queries, on each successive draft – there are usually about half a dozen in all.

Mr Reginald Maudling's practice has been different, as he likes to write much of the speech himself. He first tries out drafts of his own on his officials, and then considers their suggested emendations. But there are, of course, in any

---

* Even if the suggested change were made the annual Finance Bill would still often be a complicated affair, as major Budget changes can have very complicated implications for tax law and administration. It can also be argued that the amount of time actually spent on the Finance Bill at present seems to vary more with the political climate than with the length and complexity of the Bill. But on balance I think the change would still be worth making. (An 'Income Tax Management Bill' was presented to the Commons early in 1963; but this mainly affected the machinery for assessing and collecting income and profits tax and will not appreciably reduce the load on the Budget and annual Finance Bill.)

Budget speech, impenetrable lists of figures and complicated Inland Revenue points that not even a Keynes would think of drafting for himself.

Once a final draft is ready, a Treasury Principal has one last-minute check to make sure that the words of the speech tie up with the actual resolutions which the Chancellor lays before the House before he sits down. The final ritual on Budget Morning is the check by the Treasury Accountant of all the Chancellor's figures on the 'speaking copy' of his speech. This is no mere formality; the speech has been retyped so many dozens of times that something may easily have gone astray.

The Chancellor spends the last few days before Budget day partly in polishing up the odd phrases in the speech, partly in preparing his answers to the questions he thinks the interviewer will ask him on television, but mainly worrying whether he has done the right thing. And invariably he goes to see the Queen the previous night, bringing with him a short 'Royal summary' of the speech.

The Cabinet itself hears the Budget only the day before the Chancellor announces it to the House. There is a popular belief, sedulously spread by Chancellors themselves, that it is by then far too late to make any major changes. This is in my view mostly myth. It seems to me changes can be, and occasionally have been, made up to the very last minute: the Chancellor could, if he wanted to, change his mind on income tax rates up to lunch-time on the previous day, when the Financial Statement and Budget Resolutions go to press. Income tax changes do not in any case take effect until the following July; and all that would have to be altered would be the figures in these documents. The main effect of a sudden decision to take 3d. off the income tax would be that the printing of the Financial Statement would go on well into the pre-Budget night. More complicated changes – say in the tax allowances – would be not so easy, because it would take longer to work out their financial effects.

Taxes on goods would present more difficulties, but even here the Chancellor could have more scope for last-minute changes if he would arrange things the right way. A variant of the method already described for car licences might be used for sending out alternative instructions to local Customs and Excise Offices. This would be perfectly feasible for some straightforward taxes such as petrol duty, but very much harder for purchase tax, where the rate structure is extremely complicated.

The real reason why the Cabinet can do so little on Budget eve is not because it is technically impossible but because it has not been in on the key discussions and hears for the first time the Chancellor's arguments. It is then too late to thrash the whole matter out afresh.

How important is all this secrecy? It probably matters much more for purchase tax, or drink, or tobacco duties, where traders could make speculative profits at the expense of the Exchequer, than it does for income tax, profits tax, or motor duties. Might it not be worth trading a little extra security risk for the sake of consultations with people who may have a lot of useful counsel to give, but cannot now express their views until it is too late? It is just when the Chancellor goes into purdah, that he should be most involved in public and private economic arguments. As cautious an ex-Chancellor as Lord Amory thinks 'it is possible to pay too high a price for the assurance of secrecy' and maintains that economic policy should be a 'collective responsibility of the government not a proprietary product of the Chancellor's mind'.* Prior knowledge of the general shape of the Budget might, it is true, enable someone to make a little money on the Stock Exchange. But the nation may be paying too high a price to avoid a 1,000 to one risk that some unscrupulous person will make a few pounds he ought not to have done.

There might in fact be a positive advantage if the so-

* 'Preparing the Budget', by Viscount Amory, *Parliamentary Affairs*, Autumn 1961, p. 458.

called 'Budget judgement' about how much to give away or take back in tax, were to leak. There could then be public argument among experts about the Treasury's figure, before the Chancellor becomes committed to it, instead of the present system whereby he plucks it from his red box on Budget Day and then stakes his reputation on it.

The truth is that Budget secrecy has become an irrational cult, which the Press and Opposition embellish and fortify for the sake of good copy.

How Large a Deficit?

The reader may have been a little surprised to find that Budget decisions seem to hang, according to current theory, almost entirely on the economic assessment. Although there were references in the story just outlined to the tables of prospective revenue and expenditure which make up the Budget Accounts, these did not seem to play any role in the key decisions.

He may well wonder then, if he is in the mood for a technical digression, where the Budget Accounts come into the picture. Some of the more rigorous economic minds in Great George Street might say they ought not to come in at all.

It is quite true that during a recession, the Chancellor may not only cut taxes but also take a softer attitude to Government spending; and in time of prosperity the threat of tax increases is the Chancellor's most potent argument in Cabinet against exorbitant Government spending. But the battle with spending Departments is conducted quite separately from the Budget exercise, and the effects of both Government spending, and taxation at existing rates, are already taken into account in the National Income forecast.

The Treasury Economic Adviser, in the light of this forecast, produces a figure of how much to add or take off the tax bill, irrespective of the state of the Budget Accounts. It is worth quoting the current official doctrine which was published in a little noticed White Paper.

The Chancellor's budget judgement, as embodied in his tax proposals, takes into account, not only the government's own direct expenditure on current goods and services and on capital formation, but also the level of demand in other sectors of the economy and the balance of payments. These will be influenced by the government's own activities – by withdrawals of spending power through taxation and by additions to spending power through grants and other forms of assistance. If the prospective growth of productive resources in the period ahead and the growth of demand upon them at the existing level of taxation are in balance, then the budget will be a neutral one with either no changes in taxation, or offsetting increases and reductions. If the forecasts show demand to be insufficient, then the object of the budget will normally be to stimulate demand by reducing taxes. If demand is expected to be excessive, the budget will normally set out to restrict it by increase in taxation. Although forecasts of the development of the economy and calculations of the effect of particular tax changes are inevitably imprecise, a judgement has still to be made to decide the general direction of the budget. This judgement will determine the government's net borrowing or 'financing' requirement, which then has to be considered in itself from the point of view of debt management and monetary policy. (Paragraph 33 of Reform of the Exchequer Accounts, H.M.S.O., May 1963.)

The last sentence is the only deliberately ambiguous one. It hints however that the Chancellor's tax decision depends almost entirely on his economic assessment, and that the resulting borrowing requirement is considered as a technical problem of debt management.

Yet even the most sophisticated of people find it difficult to resist the temptation to look for a fixed formula, which would save them from the exercise of judgement, economic or otherwise. Neither politicians nor senior officials have been immune from this temptation, despite the brave words quoted above; and in previous years many have played about with all sorts of formulae for short-circuiting the economic arithmetic. All were devoid of intellectual foundation. The silliest was that of the 'overall Budget balance'. A more plausible sounding but equally mistaken slogan (on which Lord Cobbold was apparently very keen) was that the 'overall deficit' must be such that it could be financed from the sales of gilt-edged securities – which were identified with 'genuine savings'.*

Today's set of officials are however, mostly too sophisticated to admit that they worry about the surpluses or deficits shown in the Accounts, or that they cannot handle the resulting technical problems of debt management.

If the Budget looks as if it is going to lead to a large borrowing requirement, the more cautious officials have learnt to ask instead: 'Will it be misunderstood by the public? Will the international bankers think we have embarked on a wild spree?' They will also point out that, owing to the peculiarities of our credit system, an increase in the Treasury bill supply also provides the banks with more funds to lend to the public; and they will question whether this extra stimulus to demand has been taken

---

* Since this doctrine is still rampant among otherwise well informed people, it may be as well to list a few of the fallacies it contains:
(1) The 'overall deficit' is a purely arbitrary figure of no significance in itself. If local authorities do their own borrowing on the market, the 'overall deficit' declines. If the Government borrows on their behalf from the same source, it grows. If the electricity industry did its own borrowing on a Government guarantee as it used to do before 1956, the 'deficit' would shrink dramatically, but nothing except the mechanics would have changed.
(2) Sales of gilt-edged cannot be identified with genuine new savings. People may for instance sell equities or run down bank balances to buy them.
(3) Quite apart from this, there is absolutely no reason why 'real savings' and Government borrowing should match. The requirement for economic equilibrium is that attempted savings and investment should balance for the country as a whole.
(4) Even this requirement applies only when there is full employment (or as near full employment as the Government wants to get). Below this point production and employment will go up if people try to save less.

sufficiently into account by the Treasury economists in their normal supply and demand calculations. This last point is logically impeccable, but still basically a rationalization of the old-fashioned and uncomplicated desire of a good Finance ministry official to keep Government spending down.

But not even the most sophisticated observer can feel entirely happy at just brushing aside the Budget Accounts. Ideally one would like to use them to measure the Government's own impact on the economy in terms of Budget surpluses or deficits and not just in terms of changes in taxes – provided it is realised that the figures to be aimed at depend *almost entirely* on the general state of the economy. Indeed such an approach would have the merit of bringing expenditure and taxation together.

But an attempt to use surpluses and deficits for this kind of measurement, without falling into the howlers mentioned in the previous footnote, bristles with difficulties. Does the actual size of the current surplus and deficit matter, or is it only the comparison with the last year? Does one compare this year's estimate with last year's estimate, or with last year's out-turn? Should the comparison be of the current surplus or deficit only, or should it be of some sort of overall deficit?

No one of these measures is perfect. Each has been mentioned by different Chancellors at various times in the past when it suited their purpose.

The 1964 Budget provided a perfect example of just how confusing an attempt can be to use the Budget Accounts to assess the economic impact of the Chancellor's measures. Each of the following seven measuring rods could have been utilized by respectable economists and a good many of them were:

Increase in taxation

Change in Budget year	+ £103 million
Change in full year	+ £115 million

Current Budget Surplus

Absolute size	£67 million
Change compared with last year's *estimate*	+ £177 million
Change compared with last year's *outturn*	— £6 million

*Exchequer Borrowing Requirement**

Reduction over last year's *estimate*	— £61 million
Increase over last year's *outturn*	+ £148 million

* Allowing for changes in local authority borrowing arrangements.

These are only some of the comparisons which can be made; and they can be plausibly interpreted to show anything from a Budget with a *deflationary* impact of £177m. to one with an *inflationary* impact of £148m. If a further set of figures were published on a modern National Incomes basis, as is quite likely in future Budgets, there will be twice as many comparisons to make. No wonder most Treasury economists prefer to avoid the Budget Accounts and go straight to the National Income guesstimates.

However complicated this Note may seem, it leaves out a vast number of other subtleties which would have to be mentioned in any full up-to-date description. There is the question of whether to measure the impact of tax changes by their effect in the Budget year, when they may be only partly effective, or by their effect in a 'full year' which may be several hundred million pounds larger. Nothing has been said either of the effects on the revenue estimates of changes in the National Income brought about by the Budget itself. The Customs and Excise allows in its calculations for the effect of a purchase tax reduction on cars on the demand for them. But Customs revenue may also be affected by an expansion in the National Income resulting from a reduction in income tax, just as income tax receipts may be affected by an economic boost administered through a purchase tax cut. The calculations made by the Revenue Department do not properly allow for these interactions and this is one reason why the effects on the revenue of a tax relief Budget are almost invariably overestimated. The further investigation of these problems is a perfect recipe for intellectual constipation.

Obstacles to Tax Reform

Treasury officials have, of course, always been concerned with the *level* of taxation; and *ad hoc* suggestions for tax reform have often been made by the Economic Section before the Budget, a few of which – such as investment allowances – even survived Inland Revenue opposition. But it was a hit and miss affair, and work stopped after the Budget. It seems incredible, but until 1962 the Treasury never made a continuous systematic study of the pros and cons of different methods of raising revenue.

Since then the Treasury's new Public Income and Outlay Division has been theoretically concerned with revenue as well as expenditure. It has tried to act as an honest broker between the more hair-raising tax ideas put forward by the economists and the hardened conservatism of the Revenue Departments. But, to date, its own work on the tax structure has been 'embryonic' in the words of one very senior Treasury official.

The explanation of this startling fact is that in tax policy matters the official Treasury does not have any legal authority over either the Inland Revenue or the Customs and Excise. These two 'Revenue Departments' report independently to the Chancellor, a privilege of which they are very jealous. The only advantage the Treasury knights have is that they are personally closer to him. But as the Chancellor cannot be present at more than a tiny proportion of the meetings, the Treasury representative is normally at most *primus inter pares*.

The legal separation of powers does not today produce any overt strains among top officials, who work together on the friendliest of terms. But it does make an enormous difference below the summit. The ordinary middle-ranking

Treasury official cannot drop in on an Inland Revenue man for an informal, no-holds-barred discussion, as he can with a Treasury colleague; and representatives from the Revenue Departments come along to meetings with an agreed party line. (There are similarities between their relationships to the Treasury, and those of the Bank of England.) Many Treasury men are rather frightened of the Inland Revenue and prefer to ask through P.I.O. questions which they might well have put to the Revenue themselves.

This astonishing state of affairs could not have survived so long but for the age-old slogan 'The object of taxation is to raise revenue'. In the post-war period this slogan could even be reconciled with a simple kind of Keynesian planning. For the economy can always be stimulated or restrained simply by varying tax *rates* without getting into an argument with the Revenue about whether to have one kind of tax rather than another. The idea of using the tax structure to favour one type of economic activity (such as exports or employment in the north-east) is still a new and revolutionary one.

Until a few years ago it could be argued that the Inland Revenue used administrative difficulties as a way of blocking proposals such as a capital gains tax, which it heartily disliked on semi-political grounds. But this charge is certainly unfair on the present Chairman Sir Alexander Johnston, who took over in 1958.

One paradoxical reason why the tax system is not reformed is its very antiquity. It has emerged gradually over the centuries; no war or economic crisis has ever been strong enough to destroy it; and there has been no opportunity of starting from scratch. Company taxation emerged as an offshoot of personal taxation; surtax was grafted on to income tax, and the legal definition of income emerged long before capital gains became a problem. Unfortunately, it is much easier to build a new tax system from scratch than to rationalize an existing one.

The Inland Revenue's preoccupation with practical and

administrative difficulties is shared by most of the Establishment tax lawyers and accountants, who advise official bodies. The tax experts of the Federation of British Industrialists, so far from exercising a reforming influence, have been some of the chief obstacles to change – indeed, they have occasionally made the Inland Revenue seem radical by comparison.

But the root of the Inland Revenue's opposition to many reforms goes deeper still, to a rather limited notion of equity. Tax collection, in its view, depends on general acceptance of the system as a fair one. Europe is littered with the ruins of tax systems, undermined through lack of popular backing. The Revenue regards itself as the spokesman of equity against both the simplifiers and economists. For this reason it opposed, as unfair to other tax-payers, a tax rebate to attract back retired teachers. And if any Treasury economists want to introduce incentives to help, say, labour-saving industries and firms, or encourage exports, the Revenue will always ask: 'Will the economic purposes be generally accepted by those affected; and, if they are accepted today, will they still be accepted tomorrow?' Behind a great deal of its talk of equity is the unchallenged assumption that the *status quo* is 'fair'. Unfortunately 'let sleeping dogs lie' proves a very prudent maxim in this country, as the Ministry of Housing found out in its attempts to bring rating valuations up-to-date, an attempt that enormously increased the difficulties of the Tories in the 1964 election.

The notion of equity involved has nothing whatever to do with equality or any other view of the right distribution of income or wealth. It does not find anything disturbing in huge tax-free windfalls from the sale of land while struggling salary earners pay over a third of their income in tax. At its worst it is more concerned to prevent one tax-payer gaining a couple of months' advantage over another than to remedy the major injustices which disfigure the whole system.

Another obstacle to tax reform is the very great difficulty of establishing conclusively what effects any given tax reform has on economic efficiency and social justice. While there is considerable agreement among economists about the effects of changes in the *total tax bill*, there is no such agreement on the effects of changes in the *tax structure*. The effects of income tax on personal incentives or of company taxation on prices and profits remain extremely controversial. The sort of leading businessman who gives evidence to official inquiries tends to deny that any of the suggested tax changes put forward by economic reformers will have any impact on his own investment programme, his attitude to costs, or his export performance. He also tends to prefer the *status quo* to most proposed alterations in the tax structure other than plain reduction. These points are brought out very clearly in the report of the Richardson Committee on whether to have a form of turn-over tax instead of profits tax.*

One way out of this impasse might be to stop thinking in terms of adding or subtracting bits and pieces from the present tax system. Instead of asking in isolation 'Do we want a wealth tax?', 'Is a capital gains tax desirable?', 'Can we exempt savings?', 'Should we have a payroll tax or a tax on value-added?', we should start again from the very beginning. Is it conceivable that if a new tax system were being designed for Britain that income would be taxed heavily and effectively, and capital hardly at all?

What I am really suggesting is that a group of imaginative but down-to-earth experts should be given the job, not of reforming the existing system, but of designing an entirely new one. Having done this they should then address themselves to the second problem of how best to make the transition from the old to the new. It would be worth waiting a number of years for a solution along these lines –

* *Report of the Committee on Turnover Taxation*, Cmd 2300, H.M.S.O. 1964.

although one would hope a really good commission would throw off the odd interim idea which could be implemented without waiting. 'A Beeching on taxation' would not be a bad slogan for a reforming Chancellor to adopt.*

Presenting a Bad Image

Sometimes the Treasury, with the active cooperation of the Bank of England, seems to be bent on giving financial observers at home and abroad the worst possible impression of Britain's economic position.

One example is the treatment of Britain's gold and foreign exchange reserves. In view of the tremendous anxiety which the authorities always show when these drop, it is a little surprising that they publish figures which make them look as small as possible.

The best way to see this is to compare Britain's reserves as shown by the British Treasury in its monthly statement with a computation made by the Group of Deputies of the principal Western European Finance Ministers. A group of experts less likely to flights of fancy or carefree exaggeration would be difficult to imagine. Yet Britain has achieved the remarkable feat of quoting reserve figures hardly half as large as those put out by this highly conservative group.

* A Swedish commission, set up in 1960, practically did this. Its 800-page report recommended a big switch from direct to indirect taxation, which would involve a value-added tax of thirteen per cent at the retail stage. Second-hand cars, travel, hair-dressing and most other hitherto untaxed goods and services would be brought into the net, which would cover more than eighty per cent of personal consumption. Pensions and sickness insurance would be paid for out of employers' social insurance contributions, which would increase their share of the total tax bill. Direct taxes should fall, according to the Commission from fifty-five to forty-one per cent of total revenue. A leading Socialist newspaper has criticized the proposed switch from direct to indirect taxation for being *too mild*. So much for the conventional British prejudice that indirect taxes are retrogressive and reactionary. (See the *Economist*, 8 August 1964.)

U.K. Reserves, December 1963

	£m.
Shown by the Group of Ten	
1. Gold and foreign exchange	949
2. I.M.F. 'Gold tranche'[1] and 'standby' credit	357
3. Unused U.S. swap[2]	179
4. Dollar Securities held by British Govt	385
Total of Above	1,870
Reserves shown in Treasury's monthly statement	949

[1] The 'gold tranche' represents the portion of British credit facilities automatically available without conditions. The 'standby' credit (which overlapped the gold tranche) was already arranged with the Fund and could be drawn at any time.

[2] Under these arrangements the U.S. would hold sterling up to the amount shown at any time requested by the British Government, in return for similar facilities.

The only thing I have added to the Group of Ten's computation is the very cautious evaluation of the British Government's holdings of dollar securities published by the Bank of England.*

There were signs early in 1964 that the Treasury was thinking of counting its dollar securities as part of the official reserve, but that the Bank of England was anxious to stop this happening (probably because it wanted to have all the securities available to support the market for 'security dollars' should the premium go too high).

The Bank of England has, however, recently done a lot to increase enlightenment. In its Quarterly Bulletin for March

* It may be argued that the U.S. swap of £179 m. should not be used in the table, as it is to some extent an alternative rather than an addition to the credit available from the I.M.F. The calculations of the Ten's seem to me sufficiently cautious for all practical purposes. Moreover there are many other ways in which the table understates the true position. The value of Britain's dollar securities, for example, was calculated for the end of 1962. In the subsequent year and a half Wall Street prices rose by nearly thirty per cent, adding a good £100 m. to the value of the portfolio.

1964 it published a balance sheet showing Britain's overseas financial position in something nearer its true perspective. Quite apart from the highly liquid official reserves shown in the above table, British corporate and private investors held overseas assets worth some £8,000m. – including £3,000m. of securities which could certainly be mobilized in a crisis. The £8,000m. contrasted with a total of approximately £2,800m. of overseas investments in Britain.

All credit to the Bank for at last working out these highly important statistics. But why did it wait until nineteen years after the end of the war and countless exchange crises to do so? And why (up to the late summer of 1964) has this material not been reproduced elsewhere? So far it has hardly appeared at all in official speeches or in any of the regular monthly and quarterly bulletins issued by Government Departments on the state of the economy.

My final example is taken from the Treasury's White Paper on the reform of the Exchequer Accounts (H.M.S.O. 1963). Ever since the Sinking Fund Act of 1875 the Budget Accounts have been separated by a 'line' into two halves. 'Above the line' came ordinary Government expenditure. 'Below the line' came those kinds of spending which Parliament had authorized to be met by borrowing.

The 'line' did serve as a very rough and ready distinction between the Government's own spending, and items like loans to the nationalized industries or local authorities, where the Exchequer was simply borrowing money for other bodies to invest. In this respect its activities were similar to those of a City issuing house.

The White Paper suggested that the line should be abolished altogether. On its own terms the argument was quite logical. The Exchequer Accounts are really the equivalent of a petty cash book, and are not suited in any form to the purposes of economic regulation (although the total borrowing requirement revealed has some significance for the mechanics of monetary policy). If the Government's surpluses and deficits are to be looked at at all from the point of view of economic regulation, the right figures to look at are those prepared on a 'National Income Basis'.

Unfortunately, this reasoning left out of account the huge and growing total deficit which would be shown in the old-fashioned Budget Accounts once the 'line' were removed. In 1964-5 the overall deficit was already expected to be about £800m. With the Government doing more borrowing on behalf of both the nationalized industries and the local authorities, it cannot be long before it tops the £1,000m. figure.

All this would not matter if financial opinion at home and abroad were enlightened enough to disregard a purely cash account. But it is not, and even in the mid 1960s it would be better for foreign confidence not to arrange the figures in such a way as to show a larger deficit than necessary. On this issue the line-up has tended to be between financial journalists on the one hand, and Treasury officials and academic economists on the other. The last two groups tend to deride the journalists' fears of imaginary Zürich financiers. The record does not suggest that they are all that imaginary, even though some of them may be nearer home than Zürich.

There would seem to be two ways of avoiding this self-inflicted wound. One would be to take out all repayment and lending transactions of the Budget Accounts altogether and into a new account of their own, where they could appear as 'increase in the capital' of nationalized industries and local authorities. In this way the overall Budget deficit would have been reduced by getting on for £700m. in 1964-5, in a perfectly legitimate manner. The other more radical alternative would be to relegate the Exchequer Accounts to a minor place and present the Budget entirely in National Income terms. But until I have seen this done successfully, my own leanings will be towards the first solution, which might also be more acceptable to Parliament.

Part II
ECONOMIC STEERING

CALENDAR OF EVENTS

This list is not a comprehensive record of events or even of Treasury actions. It is simply meant as a chronological reference for the narrative in the following pages. For example, the Bank Rate changes are recorded in detail in 1960, but not in other years, because the changes made in 1960 happen to figure prominently in my text.

1947	15 November :	Autumn Budget; Budget leak; Cripps takes over from Dalton as Chancellor of the Exchequer.
1949	18 September :	Devaluation of £ from $4.03 to $2.80.
1950	19 October :	Gaitskell succeeds Cripps as Chancellor.
1951	29 January :	£4,700m. new rearmament programme announced.
	10 April :	Gaitskell's Budget; tax increases and Health Service charges.
	25 October :	Conservatives win General Election. Butler becomes Chancellor.
	7 November :	First post-war increase in Bank Rate.
1952	29 January :	Import restrictions, capital investment cuts, H.P. restrictions.
	11 March :	Neutral Budget.
1953	14 April :	Budget: 6d. off income tax.
1954	6 April :	Neutral Budget: new investment allowances.
	19 August :	H.P. restrictions ended.
1955	25 February :	Moderate H.P. controls reintroduced. Bank of England to support market for transferable sterling.
	19 April :	Budget: 6d. off income tax, etc.
	26 May :	General Election: Conservatives returned with increased majority.
	1 June :	Spaak Committee on possible European Customs Union (E.E.C.) set up at Messina.
	26 July :	Further H.P. restrictions; squeeze on bank advances; capital investment cuts by nationalized industries.
	27 October :	Autumn Budget; purchase tax increases, etc.

1955	20 December	:	Macmillan succeeds Butler as Chancellor.
1956	18 February	:	More H.P. controls; investment allowances suspended; cuts in public investments.
	23 March	:	*Economic Implications of Full Employment* published.
	17 April	:	'Savings' Budget.
	29 May	:	Spaak Committee's report accepted by the Foreign Ministers of the Six.
	26 July	:	Nasser seizes the Suez Canal.
	1 September	:	Makins succeeds Bridges as Permanent Secretary to Treasury.
	3 October	:	British outline plan for a European Free Trade Area announced.
	31 October	:	Eden's ultimatum to Egypt.
	7 November	:	End of fighting at Suez.
	11 December	:	£201m. drawn on I.M.F. and stand-by credit arranged of £264m.
1957	13 January	:	Macmillan succeeds Eden as Prime Minister; Thorneycroft becomes Chancellor.
	25 March	:	Treaty of Rome signed, establishing the E.E.C.
	9 April	:	Budget; surtax concession, special tax treatment for companies operating abroad.
	5 July	:	Closing of the 'Kuwait Gap'.
	11 August	:	French measures amounting to a twenty per cent devaluation of the franc.
	12 August	:	Council on Prices, Productivity, and Incomes appointed under Lord Cohen
	19 September	:	Bank Rate raised from five per cent to seven per cent; ceiling on public sector capital spending at £1,500m. and bank advances at £2,000m.
1958	6 January	:	Thorneycroft resigns over failure to cut Government expenditure; succeeded by Heathcoat Amory.
	15 April	:	Budget; small purchase tax reliefs.

1958	3 July	:	End of credit squeeze.
	16 October	:	Relaxation of limits on public investment.
	29 October	:	All H.P. controls removed.
	14 November	:	France formally rejects proposal for a European Free Trade Area.
	27 December	:	Convertibility announced for non-resident sterling.
	28 December	:	Franc devalued.
1959	1 January	:	E.E.C.'s first tariff reductions.
	8 April	:	Tax relief Budget: 9d. off income tax, reintroduction of investment allowance, purchase tax reductions, post-war credit payments, etc.
	20 August	:	Report of the Committee on the Workings of the Monetary System (Radcliffe Committee).
	8 October	:	General Election: Conservatives returned with an increased majority.
1960	1 January	:	Lee succeeds Makins as Permanent Secretary to Treasury.
	21 January	:	Bank Rate raised from four per cent to five per cent.
	4 April	:	Neutral Budget.
	28 April	:	H.P. restrictions reintroduced, credit squeeze.
	23 June	:	Bank Rate raised from five per cent to six per cent.
	27 July	:	Selwyn Lloyd succeeds Amory as Chancellor.
	20 October	:	London price of gold temporarily rose from $35 to $41 per ounce.
	27 October	:	Bank Rate reduced from six per cent to five and a half per cent.
	8 November	:	John F. Kennedy elected President of the United States.
	8 December	:	Bank rate reduced from five and a half per cent to five per cent.
1961	19 January	:	H.P. restrictions eased.
	5 March	:	Deutschmark revalued by five per cent.

1959	17 April	:	Budget; surtax relief, profits tax increase, fuel oil tax.
	1 June	:	New British Railways board under Dr Beeching takes over. Cairncross succeeds Hall as Economic Adviser to the Government.
	1 July	:	Lord Cromer succeeds Lord Cobbold as Governor of the Bank of England.
	20 July	:	Plowden Report on Control of Public Expenditure.
	25 July	:	'Little Budget': Bank Rate raised from five per cent to seven per cent; regulator used; Government expenditure to be checked; credit squeeze; pay pause, etc.
	4 August	:	U.K. granted I.M.F. credit of £714m.
	8 August	:	T.U.C. and employers invited to join new NEDC
	10 August	:	Britain applies to join E.E.C.
	30 September	:	O.E.E.C. becomes O.E.C.D. with U.S.A. and Canada as full members.
	16 November	:	Electricity Council breaks pay pause.
	17 November	:	O.E.C.D. agrees on fifty per cent growth target for 1960–70.
	21 November	:	Prime Minister rebukes Electricity Council for breach of pay pause.
	13 December	:	$6,000m. I.M.F. 'Lenders Club' set up.
	18 December	:	Sir Robert Shone appointed Director General of NEDC
1962	2 February	:	Two to two and a half per cent 'guiding light' for incomes announced.
	14 March	:	Orpington by-election: Government loses seat to Liberals.
	9 April	:	Budget: short term capital gains tax; other minor changes.
	9 May	:	NEDC to explore implications of four per cent growth rate.
	28 May	:	Sharpest fall on Wall Street since October 1929.
	4 June	:	Small H.P. relaxations.
	13 July	:	Maudling succeeds Lloyd as Chancellor.

1962	26 July	:	Government to set up National Incomes Commission.
	19 September	:	Maudling Plan put forward at I.M.F. meeting, opposed by U.S.A.
	1 October	:	Treasury reorganization: Armstrong succeeds Lee as Permanent Secretary.
	3 October	:	Modest measures to stimulate the economy announced.
	5 November	:	Increased investment allowances, etc.; purchase tax on cars reduced from forty-five per cent to twenty-five per cent.
	14 November	:	National Productivity Year begins.
1963	1 January	:	Minor purchase tax reductions.
	14 January	:	De Gaulle blocks British membership of E.E.C.
	6 February	:	NEDC approves four per cent growth rate target.
	3 April	:	Budget: reliefs for families and depressed regions.
	19 October	:	Douglas-Home succeeds Macmillan as Prime Minister.
	14 November	:	Reports on north-east and Central Scotland.
	18 December	:	White Paper on public spending.
1964	14 April	:	Budget: £100m. of increased taxation on drink and tobacco.

CHAPTER 5

The Measuring Rod to Use

HOWEVER we look at the British economy our slow growth rate over the past dozen years has been our main economic weakness; and its failure to give priority to putting it right has been the main charge to be made against the Treasury's past management of our affairs.

The real object of such criticisms has been neither the Chancellor of the moment nor his official advisers, but a composite body containing them both. As the following chapters show, politicians and Civil Servants have interacted to produce a much less sensible policy than either group would have produced if left to itself.

But many critics, whether on the old-fashioned Right or on the puritan Left are themselves hopelessly inconsistent when they censor Governments in one and the same breath for slow economic growth, and for concentrating too much on material affluence. When economists talk of Britain's lagging growth record, all that they mean is that output and income have not been expanding as quickly as they should have done – in other words there has been too little affluence, not too much. The nation's annual income would have been well over £2,500m. more than it is now, if NEDC's four per cent growth rate had been successfully inaugurated half a dozen years earlier. This is roughly equivalent to an average increase in real earnings of ten per cent above the present level for everyone at work, with a corresponding increase in pensions, social services, aid to poor countries, and all other state services. Even so the achievement would have been a good deal less than that of most of our European neighbours.

There are, of course, innumerable ways of using an extra £2,500m. Personal post-tax incomes might have gone up by less than ten per cent and spending on education and foreign aid by a good deal more. Alternatively we might have decided to take part of this extra wealth in greater leisure. The whole object of speeding up economic growth is to create more prosperity, in one form or another, so that we have this choice, and those who find this difficult to swallow have no right to complain about the Treasury's failure to promote growth.

There are other charges to be made against recent economic policy. We are often told that growth has had to be halted 'to protect the pound sterling'. Critics and supporters of past Government actions would nearly all agree on this point. Yet in the ten years from 1953 to 1963, British prices rose faster than those of every other major European country except France; and our gold and foreign exchange reserves were, at less than £1,000m., hardly any higher at the end of this period than at the beginning. During the same ten years, the six Common Market countries increased their reserves from less than £1,700m. to nearly £6,500m. – the climb started long before the Common Market came into existence. Britain now has to maintain the sterling area on a reserve less than half of Germany's and a good deal smaller than that of France. Yet neither country maintains an international currency, and France has a much smaller foreign trade than Britain. Britain has thus done just as badly in the 'sound finance' league of conservative bankers as in the production league of modern-minded economists. We have too often sacrificed rapid growth for the sake of a strong pound and as a result of all our pains frequently ended up with neither.

Yet even this is not the end of the indictment. Such growth as we have enjoyed has been very jerky. The foreign exchange crises with which it has been punctuated have contributed as much as anything else to the current overblown feeling of national *malaise*. And if these crises have been taken too seriously, it is largely because of the alarmist mood which the authorities themselves have deliberately created during each of them.

An added frustration has been the combination of slow growth with a highly commercial and materialistic environment. A better recipe for frustration would be difficult to find.

There might be a case for deliberately subordinating economic growth to social and cultural objectives. But there has been no such subordination. Our failures have been due to intellectual inertia and archaic procedures rather than to any conscious decisions. Britain is at least as materialistic as any other Western country (one only has to look at the issues, such as rents and rates which count in by-elections), but inefficient in its materialism. One may suspect that if wealth were increasing more rapidly the country might be slightly less materialistic.

The gap between Britain's performance and that of other European countries cannot be explained away by post-war recovery, the refugee influx into Germany, the pool of unemployment in Italy, or the reservoir of labour on continental farms. The effects of these stock explanations can be roughly measured, and they account for a small part of the gap.* The 'league table' on page 138 starts in 1955 when post-war recovery was surely over. We have had expansionist phases in the past, and the 1963–4 boom would have to go on for quite some time, with vigour but without interruption, before one could confidently throw the league tables aside.

If our rate of expansion has been so slow, how can one explain the mood of material prosperity, of 'You've never had it so good' that prevailed during most of the 1950s? Broadly speaking, the answer is that for a number of special reasons, real personal incomes were able to grow much

---

* The statistics have been documented by F. T. Blackaby in his paper to the British Association 1962 Annual Meeting, *The Recent Performance of the British Economy*. It will be obvious to those who know Mr Blackaby's paper that I have drawn from it at many points in this chapter.

faster than output for a temporary period. When the Conservatives came to office in the early 1950s they inherited a
huge rearmament programme which the Labour Government had embarked on at the time of the Korean War. This
programme, which the Conservatives reduced, reached its
peak in 1953; in the following seven years defence spending
actually dropped by a quarter (allowing for changes in prices).
The declining burden of defence spending was the main
reason why taxation could fall as a proportion of the
national income for so many years running.

The Government also enjoyed a windfall from the *terms of
trade* on two separate occasions. After the collapse of the
Korean boom, food and raw material prices fell so much
that in 1953 we could buy thirteen per cent more imports
for the same amount of exports than in 1951. The 1957–8
world recession triggered off another, and a slower slide

TABLE I Average annual increase in national product per man year 1955–63		TABLE II Share of defence spending		TABLE III U.K. terms of trade (ratio of export to import prices)	
	Percentage	Percentage of U.K. national product		(1961 = 100)	
W. Germany	4.2	1952	11.3	1952	85
Italy	4.1	1957	8.4	1953	90
France	3.8	1958	7.9	1954	87
Netherlands	2.6	1959	7.6	1955	86
U.S.	2.0	1960	7.3	1956	87
U.K.	1.9	1961	7.4	1957	89
		1962	7.4	1958	96
		1963	7.4*	1959	96
				1960	97
		*approximate		1961	100
				1962	102
				1963	101
				1964	99
				(second quarter)	

Table I shows how the growth of British production has lagged behind other countries. Tables II and III show two reasons why for much of the 1950s personal prosperity nevertheless increased fairly rapidly. After the Korean rearmament drive defence spending fell rapidly as a proportion of national output. Over the decade Britain also received a bonus from the terms of trade. The price we received for our exports rose, while import prices fell. Both the trends have now come to an end; and prosperity is limited by the growth of output.

Sources: Table I: *The Recent Performance of the British Economy* by F. T. Blackaby. Paper to the British Association, Annual Meeting 1962. (The figures here have been brought up-to-date on an approximate basis by the National Institute of Economic and Social Research.)

Table II: National Income Blue Books.

Table III: National Institute, Reviews.

in commodity prices, which eventually improved our terms of trade by another fourteen per cent, making twenty-nine per cent altogether. These two movements together were worth the best part of £1,000m. a year to the British public.

Since 1961 there have been no more bonuses of this kind. Defence spending has tended to rise at least as fast as the national income; and the terms of trade have actually moved against us. Personal spending can now rise no faster than production, taking one year with another. (In view of our commitments in Government spending, investment and exports, it cannot even rise as fast.)

It would, however, be much too facile to blame our poor growth record simply on thirteen years of Right-wing Government. The experience of Germany, Italy, and France shows that Right-wing Governments are quite capable of achieving growth. Our economic failures stem partly from the special characteristics of the particular Conservative Governments we have had, and partly from archaic modes of thought common to both political parties and the majority of people listed in *Who's Who*. The issues of financial policy discussed in this book cut across conventional distinctions of Left and Right even more than most other worthwhile topics do. Some of the most extreme monetary progressives are to be found among Tory financial journalists, while some stout Socialists are extremely cautious and orthodox whenever money is mentioned.

There are two schools of thought about what precisely went wrong. One puts the blame on a misguided financial policy. The Treasury's ideas and techniques have been inadequate, its information has been insufficient, out-of-date, and badly interpreted. Civil Servants have had too narrow a background and have not been in touch with the business world. Too high a priority has been given to the pound sterling in formulating policy. There are numerous other variants on the same theme.

The other view lays much more stress on stagnant elements in the community at large. Our trade-union movement is the oldest in the world and ill-adapted to a full-employment Welfare State. Management is often amateurish. There are not enough technologists in industry. The class and education system have an inhibiting effect. Exporters are too insular in outlook; and so one could go on.

It is not necessary to make a dogmatic choice between these two diagnoses. *If* industrial practices, trade-union psychology, and the educational system generally had been more conducive to growth, restrictionist Treasury policies could not have done the harm they did. *If* on the other hand Treasury policies had been more expansionist, out-of-date social attitudes (which were, to say the least, not unknown in France or Italy during the periods of economic miracle) would not have mattered so much, and there might have been more pressure towards an adjustment of them. Indeed the Treasury's particular defects can be regarded as one particularly important example of the wider social forces making for stagnation. It is probably arbitrary which of these two weaknesses is regarded as the most fundamental 'cause' of all the trouble.

This parity of diagnosis may not always apply. In the

1940s and 1950s world market conditions were so buoyant that a lively British industry might have been able to flourish, irrespective of financial squeezes at home. In the rest of the 1960s world conditions may not be nearly as favourable; and increased industrial efficiency could run to seed in unemployment or underemployment. This has already happened in the U.S., where the general industrial atmosphere has been extremely dynamic, but lack of demand has kept output down. In other words, it may be the demand side, financial rather than industrial, which will matter most by the 1970s.

But is the growth of output really the principal test of a 'Government economic policy'? Growthmen are frequently attacked on the grounds that the country's really pressing problems are the chaos in our cities, education, or the plight of the old; and that these are more important than a scramble for material wealth. Such criticisms, as Blackaby has explained, are based on a misunderstanding. What their authors are attacking is the use to which they think increased wealth will be put. The faster the rate of growth the easier in fact it will be to afford more town redevelopment, or better teachers' salaries or pensions.

Three provisos must be made before the usual figures of gross national product can be taken as a measure of the nation's total wealth. First the output should be of goods and services which people actually desire rather than any unwanted product that will swell the production statistics; second, healthy city environments, comfortable travel conditions, and other public amenities are – if people want them – just as much part of output as products sold over shop counters; and third, leisure must somehow be brought into the calculation.*

* Although happiness is not measurable, it ought to be possible to calculate a new index, which would be a better measure of economic welfare than the present G.N.P. series. It should be in terms of output per head, and not just output; and the index ought to go up in proportion to any voluntary reduction in hours actually worked.

Even then, it might be worth sacrificing some growth for the sake of preserving amenities; and there is a pace of change before which the most resolute growthmen would flinch.* No one has ever suggested, however, that the Treasury has pursued restrictive financial policies during the last decade to preserve the cathedral cities or to protect us from Admass. It has held back output to protect the pound sterling and secure stable prices; and it is this order of priorities from which most economic writers dissent, when they want to make the growth of output the criterion for judging the Treasury's performance.†

Mention of the pound sterling immediately takes us into the deep and turgid waters of the balance of payments. (Readers who do not want to immerse themselves too deeply at this stage might prefer to move on to the discussion of the cost of living, wages and automation on page 148 which is particularly important for the non-economist.)

The balance of payments argument is, it is important to emphasize, merely an argument against devaluation or against tampering with the exchange rate in any other way.

For the state of the balance of payments is not given in heaven; nor does it depend only on the quality of British products and British sales effort. We could readily export more and import less by the simple expedient of lowering the sterling exchange rate.

* Ideally my suggested economic welfare index ought to treat noise or spoilt countryside as negative commodities. Then it would eventually become something like a utility index. In principle this might be possible. The negative value of an electrical transmission line is the amount people would be prepared to pay for it not to be there.

† There are, of course, as economists are quick to point out, objections to those ways of encouraging growth which involve lower consumption and higher investment in the present. Whether such ways are desirable or not depends on people's preferences between present and future consumption. My main point is that there have been many occasions in the past when we could have had *both* more consumption and more investment if resources had been used more fully. Indeed in a free enterprise economy the rate of growth of investment is closely connected with the rate of growth of consumption.

If the pound were devalued a given sum of foreign currency would fetch more in sterling. (Instead of twelve Swiss francs selling for £1, they might, say, fetch £1 2s. 6d.) A British exporter could therefore lower the price he charged in foreign currency without changing his sterling price. Alternatively, he could charge the same prices in foreign currency, but make more sterling profit on each article sold. The latter alternative would give him an incentive to put more sales effort into overseas markets.

A devaluation would also put up the prices of foreign goods in British shops, as the foreign currency needed to buy them would become more expensive and both industrial purchasers and ordinary customers would have an incentive to import less.*

With sterling cheap and overseas currencies expensive, more people would take their holidays in Britain while more foreigners would visit Britain. Similarly, foreign investment in Britain would (once the shock was over) get a boost, while British investment abroad would be discouraged.

What then is wrong with devaluation? Surely the purpose of Government economic policy ought to be to promote prosperity. Is it not absurd to make a mere numerical ratio like the exchange rate into a prestige symbol and sacrifice the production of real goods and services for its sake?

---

* There are perverse cases, where devaluation would worsen rather than improve the balance of trade. This might happen if foreign demand for British goods were extremely unresponsive to changes in the prices charged. But what practical politicians and officials, who have got hold of this case, have failed to appreciate is that under these circumstances either *appreciation* of sterling, or a *more rapid rate of inflation*, would help to improve the balance of payments. If it were more generally realized that a situation where devaluation did not work is the same as one where inflation would help the balance of payments, we would hear much less of this objection. (These points are discussed very effectively in Professor Lipsey's *An Introduction to Positive Economics*, Chapter 35.) In fact recent studies have suggested that the demand for British exports is highly sensitive to price changes, and a relatively moderate devaluation would be helpful as a cure for a persistent deficit.

Yet politicians of all parties continually mouth the slogan that 'sterling must have first priority'.

The whole question is so overblown with emotion that I must make clear that I am not advocating a devaluation at the time of writing, nor at any other specific time. My argument is that if and when a growth policy led to an intractable payments deficit, we should then alter the exchange rate rather than slow down at home.

But if we had to do this, how could we know which new exchange rate would be the right one to adopt? The answer is that we couldn't. An exchange rate which is right today might be wrong in six months' time, and wrong again in another couple of years. (Indeed, the danger of our devaluing to another, and equally inappropriate fixed rate is now probably greater than of our refusing to devalue at all, if we had to face an intractable payments deficit.) There is in fact no need to fix any one definite rate. The price of pounds in terms of other countries could be allowed to float up and down in accordance with market forces. This suggestion is not an armchair fantasy, much though Central Bankers would like to dismiss it as such. Britain had a floating rate of exchange in the 1930s; without it the cheap money policy which – all too slowly – helped the country climb out of the depression would have been impossible. It is sometimes argued that devaluation is useless, as all our main competitors would follow suit. The French were at one time said to have printed instructions ready for just such an eventuality. The strength of this argument depends on the circumstances in which a devaluation was brought about. If the object were simply to convert a payments deficit into a surplus, at someone else's expense, the French would be right to retaliate. But any such objective would be both anti-social and foolish on Britain's part. An ideal devaluation would simply try to eliminate the payments deficit of the devaluing country and restore a rough international balance.

Countries in the past have used devaluation as a means of

increasing employment in their own country at other countries' expense. This is quite unpardonable now that governments know how to boost employment at home by increasing domestic purchasing power. The proper procedure for a country with unemployed resources is surely to boost domestic demand to secure full employment, and at the same time use a modicum of exchange depreciation to enable it to do so without destroying its balance of payments.

The whole problem of other countries following suit and cancelling out the effects of a British devaluation would not arise if, as has just been suggested, Britain did not have a fixed exchange rate, but adopted a system of flexible rates which moved up and down in the market.

It must be stressed that, contrary to what many businessmen fear, a floating exchange rate need not be a violently unstable one at all. After 1934 exchange rate movements were on the whole slow and smooth, yet the Central Bankers who managed the market did not have to defend to the death the pattern of rates that happened to exist at any one moment. When the relative balance of payments positions of their countries changed, exchange rates would move gradually to restore equilibrium.

As the first stage of moving to a floating rate by a country with an over-valued currency is tantamount to a devaluation, some of the arguments against devaluation and against floating can be considered together. Similar arguments, *mutatis mutandis*, can be used by those who would prefer to tackle any balance of payments obstacles to growth through import controls or export subsidies. These are really backdoor methods of devaluing. Front-door methods have fewer undesirable repercussions on economic efficiency and personal freedom of choice, but may lead to more international embarrassments in the short run.

It is sometimes said that devaluation will put prices up and that real wages will suffer. If a country's productive capacity is working full out, and it still has a balance of payments deficit, then by some means or other it will have either to send abroad more of the goods now consumed at home or import less. There is no way out of this unpleasant requirement, apart from borrowing. The usual alternative to devaluation is deflation; and deflation introduces an additional cut in living standards through lost production, over and above the temporary cut a devaluation might bring about.* More important, willingness to devalue or to float should allow a faster rate of increase in real production and income, which after a very short period will compensate for any temporary effects of higher import prices.

Another stock objection concerns Britain's international obligations. No country which holds sterling has been given any guarantee against devaluation (except when sterling has been held by Central Bankers as a form of short-term aid to Britain); and it is a fact of international life that currencies are liable to change in value, however much Central Bankers abhor this. In practice, if we were to move to a floating rate, it would be desirable to give Common-wealth and perhaps other holders of sterling balances the option of 'funding' them. This means they would be given a guarantee of the value of their balances in return for an agreement to run them down only gradually and at rates agreed between them and Britain.

A more potent argument is that the pound sterling, like the dollar, is used as a reserve currency by many other countries. This gives rise to two questions. One is whether sterling could continue as a reserve currency on the basis of a floating rate. Pre-war experience suggests that this might not be altogether impossible. The other question is whether the role of providing a reserve currency is desirable for

* The argument in the text is oversimplified. If the economy were really working flat out, some deflation would have to accompany a devaluation so as to release resources for export. But the amount of deflation would be a good deal less than if we relied on deflation alone; and there would be no need for production to fall. If there were some margin of unused resources, a devaluation would allow domestic pro-duction and incomes to rise; and this would tend to offset the effects on national living standards of higher import prices.

Britain, and whether the increased vulnerability of the British economy as a result is worth any marginal gains this might bring to the foreign exchange earnings of the City of London.

The most serious objection to any unilateral British devaluation, or decision to float, is that it would jeopardize the existing international monetary system. If 'the pound goes' the argument runs, there might then be a run on the dollar, and the result would be international monetary chaos, with unforeseeable consequences. With the improvement in the dollar's international standing this horror story is losing some of its plausibility. But even if absolutely true, it begs a whole lot of questions. By introducing words like 'system', 'order', and 'chaos', it presupposes that existing relations ought to be maintained, and that a system which might be unstable from a Central Banker's point of view would also be harmful to production and living standards throughout the world. This remains to be demonstrated.*

There are in fact various suggestions for introducing some exchange rate flexibility, which could not conceivably lead to a destruction of the international monetary system. Professor A. W. Phillips has suggested that a country might be allowed to make limited changes of up to one per cent in its official exchange rate in any twelve months' period. Such a proposal would still not permit countries to go all out for expansion and neglect monetary stability. But at least it would allow them to make some compromise between the

* All that can be shown convincingly is that a run on the dollar would probably lead the U.S. to put an embargo on the export of gold. Once this happened the link between the dollar and gold would go, and the price of gold in terms of currencies would be free to move upwards in accordance with market forces. But many international financial experts, including some of the conservative ones, would agree that a rise in the price of gold would greatly help international payments by increasing the value of world reserves. They would like to see such a change brought about in an 'orderly way'. But a change of this sort is most unlikely to be brought about in an orderly way and the choice is between obtaining it through some such route and not getting it at all.

two objectives, instead of always subordinating expansion to currency stability, as they are bound to do under the present system. This scheme, with perhaps the margin of permissible change enlarged to two per cent, ought however to be able to take care of most *changes* in relative international costs and prices, if we were starting out from a position of rough balance. It could not possibly be said to risk overthrowing the international monetary system.* If Central Bankers declare even this to be impracticable they are simply behaving like members of any business cartel who have got together to prevent prices from ever changing. The discussion of exchange roles and the position of sterling will be continued in Chapter 9, pages 282–8.

There are, of course, a number of more homely arguments advanced against flexible exchange rates. One of the most frequent is that they remove one of the biggest deterrents to domestic inflation. For once Governments and employers can no longer argue that British goods will be priced out of foreign markets, the most effective force now making for restraint will have gone. That is why, at bottom, so many sound money men loathe floating rates.

How important then are stable prices? If there were a conflict between growth and price stability, there would be in my view an overwhelming case for going for growth. The numbers appearing on price tickets in shop windows are of no great cosmic significance, although it would be

---

* In Professor Phillips's own words: 'There would, I think, be much more confidence that the country could in fact work within this rule than that it could for ever succeed in keeping the par value constant. So the fear or hope of a sudden large change in the rate, with the tremendous speculative movement it causes, would be greatly diminished. The maximum permissible change of the par rate, one per cent per year, could easily be offset by short-term interest differentials, so it need not lead to any major transfers of capital.' ('Employment, Growth, and Inflation', *Economica*, 1962.)

disturbing to orderly life if they changed at too great a speed. It is the relation between incomes and prices, and not the absolute numbers, that matter.

The main arguments against inflation are those of social justice; pensioners and those living on fixed incomes would be hard hit. But in fact the amount the country can afford to give pensioners and others in hard-pressed positions depends on its real wealth. If the country were to grow richer more quickly, it would be easier to raise the real value of pensions, even if prices rose faster as a result. A policy of rapid growth is in fact more in the interest of those who are dependent on the Welfare State than a policy of price stability at all costs. Public opinion too often confuses the cost of living with the standard of living.

People living on small investment incomes may be in a more difficult position; but even they can make adjustments for inflation by holding more of their assets in equities. Unit Trusts are an excellent medium for them to do so without incurring excessive risks.

It is sometimes argued that there is no conflict between growth and stable prices at home, that on the contrary a more rapid expansion of output helps to make prices more stable and exports more competitive than they otherwise would be. One argument is that rising demand leads to lower unit costs in the main growth industries. This is the case that Norman Macrae has put with great cogency in *Sunshades in October*. Another argument is that an incomes policy is easier to achieve if output is rising, say by four per cent a year, than if it is rising by two and a half times as fast as it was in Britain in much of the 1950s.

So long as there is any intellectual uncertainty about the issue, surely it is better to give the expansionists the benefit of the doubt? For if one restricts output on the basis of a false economic theory, at the end of the day the loss of production is a complete waste with nothing to show in return by way of stable prices or a strong pound. On the other hand, if production were allowed to expand rapidly and prices still rose, at least the country would be better off in real wealth.

But if the rate of growth of real wealth – and ultimately of living standards – is the correct yardstick for judging a country's economic performance, the rate of increase of money wages is most certainly the wrong one. Indeed, in Britain today it would be roughly true to say that the faster money wages rise the slower will real earnings grow. So long as we have a fixed exchange rate and will not devalue, wage increases too far in excess of productivity will make exports uncompetitive. As the result of the wage-spiral, again and again the Government has held back output for the sake of the balance of payments. Very often workers have suffered immediately and directly through diminished overtime, more short time, and less employment.

Even if we had a floating exchange rate, or were prepared to see occasional devaluations, some wage restraint would still be necessary (even though not enough to please those who want to stop all inflation). For while a gentle rise in the price level would not harm production, a galloping inflation, leading to a breakdown in the monetary system almost certainly would be generally disruptive. For such reasons the Treasury is given credit in the historical chapters which follow, whenever it takes a tough stand on wages. There is no contradiction in supporting at the right time a liberal, expansionist policy in taxation, credit, or government spending, and a hard line on wages. There is a great contrast between paying out an extra £100m. in, say, reduced taxes and adding an extra £100m. to industry's wage bills. Tax reductions add to the demand for goods and services when there is a slack in the economy, and creates more production and more jobs. They do not add to costs. Wage increases on the other hand raise costs but have little effect on home demand – as perhaps £80m. of the extra £100m. is eventually cancelled out in higher prices (while export demand actually falls off as British goods become less competitive).

The distinction between demand and costs does not make a good headline. Nor apparently has it always been easy to put over at Cabinet meetings. But it remains there, however tedious people find it; and thanks to NEDC some practical trade unionists are, one hopes, beginning to catch a glimmering of it.

Almost as much nonsense is talked about jobs as about wages. In a great number of political discussions jobs are treated as a scarce commodity: 'This will lose 1,000 jobs' is a dangerous war-cry from any M.P. or industrial lobby.

Such charges completely misunderstand what full employment is all about. The object of economic progress is to enable one man to do the job that ten or 100 could previously do; this is the modern equivalent of two blades of grass growing where one grew before. The men displaced should easily be able to find other jobs if the total demand for goods and services keeps rising sufficiently quickly.

In a properly functioning advanced economy it is not the jobs that are scarce but workers (apart from certain depressed areas). The amount the country can produce is limited at any one time by the size of its labour force when fully employed. It follows that measures which discourage the use of labour, whether through eliminating waste, or through automation, are normally in the best interest of the workers themselves. (I have made the argument unnecessarily difficult for myself by talking about displaced men finding other jobs. Normal retirement and wastage often take care of a great deal of labour-saving investment. In practice too, the effects on employment of more mechanized methods are often compensated for by a higher sales turn-over within the same firm. But an extreme case brings out the logic of the argument best.)

Is it not possible, however, that with the onset of automation, a small proportion of the labour force will be able to produce enough to satisfy everyone's needs and the rest will remain unemployed? Such a state of affairs is often known as 'saturation'. It is a bogey often near at hand to those temperamentally out of sympathy with economic thinking. In any discussion of the question, a distinction must first be made between real desires and what people have money to pay for.

Saturation in the economic sense would mean that, however much the Chancellor gave away in tax reliefs, people would not spend any more because they were already satisfied with what they had. It would mean that the Government itself could find no useful projects on which to spend money. All the worth-while town redevelopment, education improvements, road building, and extension of welfare services would already have been complete; and the underdeveloped countries would already be helped to the limit of their absorptive capacities. (And please let us not hear the war-cry of the economic troglodyte 'Where would the money come from?' It is real resources, not money, that are short. And if real resources – men and machinery – were in surplus, it would be the height of prudence to create as much new money as was necessary to preserve full employment.) If this state of bliss were ever to come about we could then enjoy the fruits of automation in the form of leisure.

Nevertheless the whole of the argument for labour-saving and automation collapses if the government defaults on its obligations to maintain full employment. In that case improved methods would lead to unemployment and trade unions would be right to hang on to existing jobs like grim death. We very nearly had such a state of affairs in the disastrous year between the 1962 and 1963 Budgets. The encouragement they have intermittently given to Luddite sentiments is one of the big criticisms of Treasury policies.

Having thrown down the gauntlet, I must add a final disclaimer. There is an overwhelming case for speeding up Britain's growth rate. But it would be absurd to suppose that we face disaster if we do not do so. This is not a 'state of England' book. The supposed choice between moving rapidly forward and falling steeply back is nothing more than political rhetoric. We do not stand at the parting of the ways, or on the edge of the precipice, or in any other unlikely metaphorical position. As a result of recent mistakes in economic policy we have thrown away opportunities for increasing our wealth and making life pleasanter generally. This is a serious enough charge against our financial masters to stand on its own without the aid of spurious cataclysmic overtones.

CHAPTER 6

Butskellism and Sterling

THE aim of this and the following two chapters is to have a look at some examples of Treasury policy at work in recent years, rather than to provide a full and consecutive history.

'Treasury policy' in this context is the outcome of a complicated process of interaction between Chancellor, Treasury officials, and the Bank of England, with the Cabinet in the background. Again and again in the course of my investigations, I have felt that there were many people in authority who, acting alone, could have produced a consistent and reasonable economic policy; but that when their ideas were put into the pot with everyone else's, the result was not a great British compromise, but an unconvincing muddle.

Before coming on to the controversies of the last decade, it may be helpful to start with a few fringe notes – they are nothing more – on the Labour Governments of 1945–51.

Three Labour Chancellors

The period of Dr Dalton, the first Labour Chancellor, who resigned after a minor Budget leak in the autumn of 1947, reads today almost like pre-history. He was the last Chancellor who was primarily a Finance Minister without control over economic planning; and anyone who wants a glimpse of the confusion and frustration which can result from the divorce of finance and economics could do no better than read the last volume of Dalton's autobiography, *High Tide and After*.

Dr Dalton was the most exuberant and least austere of all Chancellors. He was a colossal egotist; his great booming voice saying to someone in the garden 'Between you and me' could be heard from a twelfth-floor hotel room. Aston-ishingly enough for a Chancellor of the Exchequer, he was the author of a well-known textbook on public finance (which he brought up-to-date after his retirement) and before the war had been an inspiring and surprisingly orthodox university teacher. Yet his Cheap Money drive, which for a time brought long-term interest rates down to as little as two and a half per cent, has become notorious as a misguided attempt to do the very opposite of what the post-war situation required.

It is often supposed that this was a personal policy which Dalton embarked upon in the teeth of official advice. But just before he died Lord Dalton revealed that all his Treasury and the Bank of England advisors had supported and even encouraged him at the crucial moment. Dalton's only adviser to warn him of the dangers was the late Evan Durbin who was in the lowly position of Parliamentary Private Secretary.

Dalton's successor, Sir Stafford Cripps, knew far less about finance than people imagined from his resolute public manner. During his reign the idea of planning through the Budget first became established. The doctrines, however, were those of Sir Robert Hall and other advisers. It was Cripps who added the drive and the moral fervour.

Mr Hugh Gaitskell, who took over from Cripps in the autumn of 1950, probably understood his job better than any Chancellor we have had before or since. He was, of course, a professional economist by training, but much more up-to-date and sophisticated in his approach than Dalton. His officials had a great respect for him, but they complained that he insisted on doing other people's work for them – a complaint that may simply mean that he wanted to run his own policy.

Controls Without a Plan

It is a big myth to suppose that the Labour Government

of 1945–51 engaged in detailed long-term planning of the country's production; and most of the blame and praise directed at it on these grounds are equally misdirected. The controls and regulations which caused so much controversy were basically a hangover, which perhaps lasted too long, from wartime restrictions.

The 1947 Economic Survey contained detailed manpower and output targets for particular industries, and a comprehensive import programme, but it did not say how the manpower targets would be achieved. They were meant neither as 'an ideal distribution nor a forecast of what will happen' but as an 'approximate distribution necessary to carry out the nation's objectives if the nation as a whole sets itself to achieve them'. It is hardly surprising that these targets were not achieved, and in the 1948 Survey they were simply referred to as a 'tentative Budget'.

Subsequent Surveys became less and less specific. The 1950 Survey was described by the *Economist* as 'a humble document, meek almost to the point of being meaningless'. According to a later study by A. A. Rogow, 'had there been no Korean War it is probable that Labour Government planning in 1951 would have been almost entirely confined to Budget policy and certain balance of payments controls'.* It was towards this goal – Butskellism as it later came to be called – that the Labour Government was moving during most of its period of office.

Looking back on the documents and speeches of these years, one is struck by the extent to which economic policy was conducted on a year to year piecemeal basis. The allocation of scarce materials and of factory permits was, in Mr Rogow's words 'more often the result of interdepartmental negotiation and amateur judgement than of consistent and scientific planning'. The whole system was probably modelled on the traditional annual haggles which

* A. A. Rogow and Peter Shore, *The Labour Government and British Industry*, p. 42. Peter Shore now heads the Labour Party's research department.

the spending Departments have with the Treasury. The Five Year forward looks organized by the NEDC and the Treasury's long-term public expenditure surveys started under the Conservative Government are much more ambitious examples of forward planning than anything Cripps ever did.

The Labour Government did, it is true, produce in the autumn of 1948 one 'Long-Term Programme' to illustrate how the country could achieve 'economic independence' by the middle of 1952. Such a programme was more or less a condition of Marshall Aid, and was taken even less seriously than NEDC is today. It did not seem to have much impact on day-to-day policy and was only mentioned once in all the Economic Surveys and Budget speeches of the period.

Labour's Wage Pause

Another fact that is often forgotten is that Sir Stafford Cripps had a wage pause in 1948, some thirteen years before Mr Selwyn Lloyd. In February 1948 the Treasury put out a *Statement on Incomes, Costs, and Prices*, which said, 'There is no justification for any *general* increase of individual money incomes', although there might be exceptions in the case of undermanned industries. Many of the doctrines of that White Paper have cropped up again and again in Treasury pronouncements, irrespective of the Party in office – right down to the habit of saying 'incomes' when the writer really means wages.

The big difference between Cripps and Lloyd was that Cripps did not interfere with arbitration in the public sector. Sir Stafford said in his 1950 Budget Speech that wages had been left to free negotiations and the Government had simply put before the country its views.

As in 1961, the T.U.C. protested that it had not been consulted first; but, in contrast to 1961, accepted with a few qualifications, the principle of the pause – therefore the

Government did not have to consider interfering with arbitration. After the devaluation of sterling in September 1949, the T.U.C. General Council went further still and even recommended the suspension of cost-of-living sliding scale agreements. By 1950 the policy had begun to crumble and in June of that year the General Council sent out a circular saying: 'There must be greater flexibility of wage movements in the future.'

By the end of that year the delayed effects of devaluation and the initial effects of the Korean War had combined to push the cost of living sharply upwards, and wages and prices were shooting merrily ahead. But for a two-year period the pause had been a great success, with wages rising barely two per cent per annum. Mr Selwyn Lloyd's wage pause, by contrast, reduced the rate of increase only to four per cent, although even this was a considerable reduction on what had gone on before.

Bevanites Proved Right

The most extraordinary episode in the Labour Government's history was the cavalier way in which it panicked into an enormous rearmament programme at the time of Korea. The first programme for spending £3,400m. in three years – or fifty per cent more than was originally planned – was roughed out in ten days in the middle of the summer holidays. A few weeks later General MacArthur took it upon himself to drive his forces to the Yalu river and the West to the verge of world war. The Chinese entered the Korean War and by the end of the year had captured most of the Peninsula, save for a small perimeter around the main Southern ports. In early December Attlee flew to Washington to beg President Truman not to drop an atomic bomb; and in this mood of panic the British Government announced a truly fantastic rearmament programme of £4,700 m. for the same three-year period.

The Treasury, which is notoriously pessimistic about the

capacity of the economy to bear civilian programmes which are quite tiny by comparison, took the view that the nation would just *have* to afford this extra arms bill. Mr Gaitskell and his official advisers, who shared his devotion to the cause of Western defence, made the great mistake of assuming that sufficiently strict budgetary planning, together with the reimposition of physical controls, would produce the raw materials, machine tools, and components required for an enormously enlarged defence programme. But as Mr Aneurin Bevan pointed out in his resignation speech these 'were not forthcoming in sufficient quantities even for the earlier programme'. In the words of Mr Harold Wilson, who resigned from the Government with Mr Bevan, 'the financial programme of rearmament' ran 'beyond the physical resources which can be made available'.* This experience in 1950–1 probably lies at the root of Mr Wilson's present distrust of the Treasury as a super ministry, and his desire to put in charge of economic policy a minister who will think in concrete physical terms instead of overall monetary ones. The Bevanites, or more exactly, Mr Harold Wilson, proved right in the rearmament controversy – a fact which most politicians and Civil Servants once wanted very much to forget.

The Labour Government's rearmament programme was, of course, severely cut by the Conservatives after their return to office, but by then a lot of damage had been done to the British economy. As late as 1953 the Economic Survey plaintively noted: 'Important sectors of the engineering industries are heavily engaged in defence work when they might otherwise be concentrating their main energies on the export trade' (or, the Survey might have added, home investment). An American economist, in a recent investigation of why the 1949 devaluation did so little to

* The best full-length account of the controversy is *Crisis in Britain*, 1951 by Jean Mitchell. Some useful lessons are drawn by Andrew Shonfield in *British Economic Policy Since the War*, pp. 56–8 and 92–107.

solve the British balance of payments problem, remarks that 'at least some of the substitutions which importers were forced to find for British goods during the Korean War continued' after British goods had once again become readily available.*

The Devaluation Mistake

The 1949 devaluation does indeed look in retrospect a bad piece of tactics. The American study already quoted concludes that devaluation did not do much to improve British exports. 'Probably its strongest effect was the hidden one of softening the blow of Japanese and German recovery, since Japan remained with the dollar and Germany devalued by less than the U.K.' It might have been better, the writer goes on to say, 'to devalue a year or two later when the competition from these two countries began to make itself strongly felt'. Another argument for postponement was that 'exports could not have increased much more than they did because of the shortage of supply' induced by the Korean War.

The 1949 move also had the great political disadvantage of saddling the Labour Party with one devaluation and making it particularly anxious to avoid another. The Conservatives, for their part, became determined to avoid being tarred with the same brush.

An important body of Whitehall opinion in fact wanted a different solution to the 1949 crisis. The idea, which was believed to have had the support of the Government's Economic Adviser, Sir Robert Hall, was that instead of fixing a new exchange rate for sterling, the pound should be left to float. This would have meant that the number of dollar bills or francs a businessman or tourist received in exchange for £1 would have varied from time to time

* June Flanders, 'The Effects of Devaluation on Exports', *Bulletin of the Oxford Institute of Economics and Statistics*, August 1963, p. 196.

according to the state of the market – although the Bank of England would have intervened to iron out temporary fluctuations.

Such a solution would have dodged the whole problem of fixing a new exchange rate at a time when any figure was just a wild shot in the dark. (The actual devaluation from $4 to $2.8 for the £ was far too large; but the competitive margin we gained was quickly eroded by overseas devaluations and inflation in Britain.) Some Government economists wanted to find out if Britain could live with a floating rate in post-war conditions; and as Britain was in any case compelled to abandon the old $4 parity it seemed a good time to make the experiment.

They were defeated by the entrenched opposition of the Bank of England. The Bank has always bitterly distrusted exchange controls for reasons already discussed on page 64. It also dislikes floating rates intensely. Most traders, whether in goods or money, prefer fixed prices, whenever they can have them, to the risks and uncertainties of price competition, and Central Bankers are no exception. Their attachment to fixed exchange rates and their dire protestations of catastrophe if they are abandoned are simply a variant of the price ring and cartel mentality so common among a good many businessmen whenever the law allows them to get away with it.

Although the Bank had to tolerate severe exchange controls in the post-war years and was prepared to put up with floating rates in the early 1950s, it has never been prepared to accept both floating rates and exchange controls together; and its real aim has always been not to have either. In 1949 it argued that the extensive exchange controls, which at that time were supposed to prevent foreigners from converting their pounds into gold or dollars, could not be enforced if there was a floating rate. As no one in Whitehall was then prepared to sacrifice exchange controls for fear of a great capital flight from Britain, the Bank of England won the day.

'Butskellism'

These attitudes of the Bank of England affected economic policy both under the Labour Government and under the Conservative Government that succeeded it in October 1951.

Another link was the philosophy of 'Butskellism', a term compounded by the *Economist* out of the names of Butler and Gaitskell. Butskellism was already coming to the fore in the last few years of the Labour Government, although its progress was interrupted for a little while by the Korean War. It was an interesting mixture of planning and freedom, based on the economic teachings of Lord Keynes. Planning during this period was concerned with one global total – the amount the nation was spending on goods and services – 'the level of demand' in economists' language. If production sagged, or unemployment looked like creeping up, extra purchasing power was pumped into the system through the Budget, the banks, or the hire-purchase houses. If employment was a bit too full or the pound came under strain, demand was withdrawn through these same channels.

There is nothing wrong with Butskellism, although it may need to be reinforced by other measures. Unfortunately it was marred during a large part of the period after the Conservatives returned to office by mistakes of execution.

Conservative economic policy since 1951 has been characterized by some paradoxical features. On the one hand the Party has always treated 'the man in Whitehall' with a certain detachment. The traditional Tory attitude to Civil Servants has been one of lordly disdain; one leading Conservative politician still refers to them as 'clerks'. On the other hand policy under Conservative rule seems to have originated largely from Civil Servants. I do not mean that official advice has always been taken – far from it – but that ministers have relied on Civil Servants to provide the intellectual framework on which decisions are ultimately based.

An extraordinary feature of Conservative economic performance is that it grew worse rather than better as time went on. Some time in the middle fifties there was a move away from an expansionist interpretation of Butskellism towards safety first. Norman Macrae dates the climacteric to 1955;* my own view is that the decisive turn for the worse was taken in the sterling crisis of 1957. But whatever the precise date, a misguided change of priorities was made around the mid 1950s.†

Part of the explanation of this paradox is that there have been no less than six Conservative Chancellors. Nearly all the Tory Chancellors who held office until 1962 were highly non-expert. Not merely were they innocent of economic complexities, but they did not even have the practical financial flair that one might reasonably expect from a Party with business links. Conservative Prime Ministers, in fact, never risked putting a city figure or a big business tycoon into No. 11. Most Conservative Chancellors were impressed, and even overawed, at their weekly meetings with Lord Cobbold, who was Governor of the Bank of England from 1949 to 1961. Cobbold, who had been a disciple of the mystery-mongering Montagu Norman, Governor for twenty-four years up to 1944, had picked up from Norman some very rigid convictions, especially about the proper role of the Bank of England in the scheme of things; but he made no claim to be a monetary thinker. 'If he had been faced by someone like John Anderson instead of the Chancellors we did have,' a Conservative minister

* *Sunshades in October.*

†Mr Harold Wincott attempts to refute this charge in The *Financial Times* of 17 December 1963, by saying that real wages and salaries rose by nineteen per cent between 1948 and 1955, compared with twenty-one per cent in the following seven years. One would expect a very much larger jump in a period of excellent terms of trade and enjoying the aftermath of an investment boom, compared with the years of rearmament, Korea, and post-war shortages.

once remarked to me, 'can you imagine who would have deferred to whom?'*

It is also noticeable that after Butler and Macmillan left the Exchequer, none of the succeeding Tory Chancellors for many years after was a political heavyweight. Macmillan was long content to appoint to the Exchequer conscientious administrators, who cut no figure either at home or abroad.

When Mr Winston Churchill formed his post-war Government in 1951, he was generally expected to make Mr Oliver Lyttleton (now Lord Chandos) Chancellor. Lyttleton, a prominent city figure and industrialist, had been Chairman of the Conservative Finance Committee in Opposition. He would, he says, have taken the Exchequer 'with zest' and believed he could 'make a contribution, perhaps even a decisive contribution' to the country's financial and economic problems.† After he had broken the news of Butler's appointment, Churchill told him: 'It was touch and go, but the Chief Whip thought the House of Commons stuff was a handicap to you.'

This was the second time in his life that Lyttleton nearly became Chancellor. After the death of Sir Kingsley Wood in 1943, Churchill actually suggested to Lyttleton that he should succeed him at the Exchequer. The following day he called Lyttleton to the telephone to tell him that Sir John Anderson would be much distressed if he did not become Chancellor. 'Having started life as a Civil Servant, it would crown his career to be head of the Treasury.'

Certainly Churchill would have taken a big gamble in

* Sir John Anderson, later Viscount Waverley, was a most formidable administrative figure, who after rising rapidly in the Civil Service to become Permanent Secretary to the Home Office, later became Governor of Bengal, before entering Parliament. During Churchill's wartime coalition, he was Lord President of the Council, where he was the only successful economic coordinator without Departmental responsibilities Whitehall has ever seen. After the death of Sir Kingsley Wood in 1943, he became Chancellor of the Exchequer. (*John Anderson, Viscount Waverley*, by Sir John Wheeler-Bennett.)

† *The Memoirs of Lord Chandos*, p. 342.

1951 if he had appointed Oliver Lyttleton, at a time when he had a Parliamentary majority of only sixteen. With his watch chain dangling aggressively from his waistcoat, and his difficulty in handling the House of Commons, Lyttleton seemed to many Labour M.P.s an incarnation of the spirit of Big Business. A Lyttleton Chancellorship might have been a fiasco; if he had been able to survive the unpopularity of his early actions it might have been a big success. It is anyone's guess. (In any case, the Exchequer would probably have been more his cup of tea than the Colonial Office, or even, perhaps, A.E.I.) But of one thing one could have been reasonably sure. The triumphs, blunders, or new departures would have been Lyttleton's own.

During most of the Conservative period in office financial affairs have been treated by the Government as an incomprehensible technical exercise, divorced from the mainstream of policy. Chancellors have more or less been told to 'get on with it' in their own back gardens, and have suddenly found themselves sacked, or offering their resignations, when things have gone badly. If Lyttleton had been appointed, none of this could have happened. The most technical of Treasury activities would probably have been right in the centre of the fray; and the big issues concerning economic expansion and the pound sterling would have been forced out into the open.

Mr Churchill, having run away from the thought of Lyttleton as Chancellor, tried to keep a check on Butler, of whom he was something less than a wholehearted admirer, by appointing a 'Treasury Advisory Committee' to 'assist' him. This consisted of a small ginger group of ministers, including some of Churchill's trusted wartime colleagues such as Lords Woolton and Swinton. By all accounts, they gave the Civil Servants whom they summoned a terrible time. Treasury knights were asked what they knew about business, including some who later became successful company chairmen. But for all their bark, these committeemen had no power to bite. They had endless discussions on whether forecasting was in principle possible, discussions which were characterized by a degree of remoteness from reality of which only 'practical businessmen' are capable. They tried very hard to abolish the *Economic Survey*, but even here they failed and the Survey survived until 1962. In the end, of course, Mr Butler and the Treasury knights were more than a match for what one politician irreverently described as 'those old battleaxes'. The Advisory Committee was diluted by increases in membership and eventually became absorbed into the Cabinet's ordinary Economic Policy Committee.*

Expansion Under Rab

Indeed the faults of the system of Civil Service thinking punctured by political intrusion were least apparent during the reign of Mr R. A. Butler, who held office for the unusually long period of four years. Butler was not only the first post-war Conservative Chancellor, but probably the best (leaving Maudling out of account for the time being). Butler had probably even less technical understanding than some of his successors of Treasury operations, and one official once suggested that he would have benefited from the purchase of one of the toy 'National Income machines' used for teaching students, in which the flow of money in the economy is represented by a stream of blue-coloured fluid.

It was Butler's hunches as a political animal that enabled him to separate bad advice from good. Sometimes he would act for twenty-four hours as if he had taken a certain decision, so that he could get the feel of living with it, and then if he did not like it he would change his mind.

Butskellism is a technique which can be used in an expansionist or a restrictionist direction; and Butler himself had a consistent bias towards expansion. His first, 1952,

* See *Memoirs of the Rt Hon. the Earl of Woolton*, pp. 371–4, on which the above account is partly based.

Budget proved in retrospect too severe; but nearly all the M.P.s listening were surprised that he did not make any net increase in taxation, as most outside commentators were urging him to do.

Although many consumer goods industries were already depressed, Mr Butler had to justify at considerable length in the prevailing alarmist climate of opinion his refusal to cut personal spending further. But the most interesting thing about the 1952 Budget was how Mr Butler managed to make a Budget that made no net change in the tax burden an interesting and exciting one. He cut food subsidies and put up a few minor duties, balanced this by improved social benefits and income tax relief, and made many other off-setting changes. His Budget is still an object lesson for future Chancellors who have no net reliefs to offer. 'Restrictions and austerity are not enough,' he emphasized in his speech, 'we want a system which offers us both more realism and more hope.'

In 1953, Butler reduced taxation to take up the slack that had developed in the economy. 'The path of restriction has been so firmly fixed in people's minds,' he said, carrying on the theme he had begun the previous year, 'that it tends to be regarded as the inevitable line of conduct. But we can look to a more hopeful way. We can lighten our load and liberate our energies.' The following year was Butler's high noon. In his 1954 Budget he refused to apologize for the increase in personal consumption for which he had been criticized – 'The truth is that we must not be frightened at a little more ease and happiness, or feel that what is pleasant must necessarily be evil.' But he did supplement higher consumption by a new incentive to industrial investment. The Economic Section made a proposal that twenty per cent of the cost of all new investment in plant and machinery should be deducted from a firm's taxable income, over and above normal depreciation. Mr Butler accepted the proposed 'investment allowances' and forced them through against the opposition of the Inland Revenue, who protested that they were a 'distortion' and a subsidy – one of the few really severe defeats that the Revenue has suffered.

An idea of the deterioration which took place in the quality of British economic management in the 1950s can be obtained by comparing Mr Butler's Budget speech of 1954 with Mr Heathcoat Amory's speech of 1958. Both men were speaking during U.S. recessions; and both were speaking at a time when it was not clear whether the American economy would soon turn upwards (as in fact it did) or spiral downwards into depression. There is nothing personal in the choice of Mr Amory. Many of his predecessors and successors at the Exchequer would have said the same things if they had been in office in 1958. If Mr Amory sometimes seems more exposed to unfavourable quotation, it is mainly due to his intellectual honesty and clarity.

In 1954 Mr Butler stressed that the implications of the American decline for the rest of the world must be closely watched. If the need arose action should be taken on a national and international basis without delay. (He was speaking at a time when *discriminatory* action by full employment countries to prevent recession spreading was still regarded as a possibility.) The Chancellor warned that we must be prepared to act together with our friends. At home he would not hesitate to take more radical measures should 'later in the year circumstances so demand'. In 1958 Mr Heathcoat Amory said: 'It is no use deceiving ourselves into thinking that we can carry the world on our shoulders or stem single-handed forces which are only to a limited extent within our control.' He went on to say that the strength of sterling remains 'the primary objective of our economic policy' and later emphasized 'that we must conduct our own finances with a special caution in difficult times'.

Nothing may have seemed to the more innocent M.P. more sound, cautious, and full of common sense than Mr Amory's remarks. Yet just this attitude, if adopted by every country, could send the world spiralling downwards into depression; and it is just what did happen before the war. Every advance in economic thinking, from Keynes onwards, has been in vain if Chancellors think themselves helpless in the face of world recession. Those who believe in throwing in the towel in the face of world forces that they themselves have had a share in creating, should never be allowed to get away with the labels 'outward looking' or 'internationalist', which they so love to wear.

Oddly enough the intellectual quality of the advice reaching ministers from permanent Treasury officials and from the Bank of England (which was at that time extremely influential) reached its nadir during Mr Butler's period at the Exchequer. Monetary policy, for instance, was frequently spoken of as providing a sort of painless discipline which would not slow down expansion or be restrictive, but would nevertheless magically stabilize the economy. Precisely because Mr Butler's type of monetary policy was ineffectual, expansion was allowed to proceed; later Chancellors who received more sophisticated advice successfully brought the growth of output to a halt!

The two enormous weaknesses during Butler's period at the Exchequer, which must heavily qualify the praise already given, concerned wages and sterling. On the wages front a quite deliberate policy of appeasement was adopted. Winston Churchill still had unpleasant memories of the General Strike to live down. As Lord Woolton has put it in his *Memoirs*, 'he was determined that there should be no industrial strikes during his period as Prime Minister'.* This was the era of Sir Walter Monckton at the Ministry of Labour, when all the ministry's energies were devoted to bringing the two sides together even at the cost of highly inflationary settlements.

Appeasement did trade unionism little good, as higher wages were largely cancelled out in higher prices. Indeed the workers of this country are today still paying the price for the Monckton policy, which by pricing British goods out

* Lord Woolton, *op. cit.*, pp. 279–80.

of world markets slowed down the growth of the whole economy.

The Government walked into these dangers open-eyed. The Treasury's *Economic Survey* for 1954 – a remarkably good one – was one of the first published documents to draw attention to Britain's falling share in world trade.

The 1954 survey writer had a gift for gloomy exaggeration. 'If in present circumstances the prices of our exports generally were to be pushed up by a rise in internal costs, we should be taking a short cut to national bankruptcy' he thundered. 'Our competitive power would be disastrously weakened and the consequent worsening of the balance of payments would destroy for the time being any chances of a further improvement in the standard of living.' And Mr Butler himself repeated the point, only a shade less dramatically, in his Budget speech.

A White Paper published in 1956 showed that Treasury economists had been aware for many years of the theoretical case for an incomes policy, and Lord Woolton has written that the appeasement policy 'greatly disturbed some of us in the Cabinet'. But as the Government's Economic Adviser, Sir Robert Hall, frankly admitted to the Radcliffe Committee in 1957, 'the Cabinet,' despite Lord Woolton's strictures, 'had ever since it came to office regarded the problem of the price level as one to be solved by a change in the climate of opinion'.* Or as Butler put it in his 1954 Budget Speech, 'we do better through relying on voluntary moderation'.

In his Budget Speech of April 1955, Mr Butler listed the results of voluntary moderation. Between 1953 and 1954, output per man rose by two and a half per cent but wages and salaries rose by about seven and a half. In his speech on the emergency Budget of October 1955, he gave another progress report. Wage rates had risen by five points between December 1954 and March 1955. Between March and June

* *Volume of Oral Evidence*, H.M.S.O., 1960, 'Proceedings of Oct. 25th, 1957, Q. 1657.'

they had risen by another three points and since then by a further point, making nine points in all. In December 1955 there was a Cabinet reshuffle and Mr Butler was replaced by Mr Macmillan. But it was not until seven years after ministers had first identified the problems in their speeches that a Chancellor intervened to tackle the wage spiral at its source.

At a time when the need for an incomes policy is *the* economic fad of the hour, it is difficult to recall that until very recently it was a radical idea completely unacceptable to established opinion. Now the pendulum has swung to the other extreme and yesterday's sceptics talk of little else.

Another important criticism of economic policy during Mr Butler's term of office is that the Government tended to wash its hands of all concern for the performance of particular industries, or of problems such as industrial training, research and technology, salesmanship, and quality of management of which we hear so much today. This neglect of such down-to-earth matters served, quite unfairly, to discredit the basic Butskellian ideas. Some *laissez-faire* was an inevitable reaction to the negative post-war controls with which the Labour Government had become associated, but the reaction which took place was too long and too indiscriminate.

THE SHIFTING BALANCE OF POWER

The changes of title and position in the parts of the Government machine concerned with economic coordination shown above the line indicate the drift away from detailed economic planning. They also illustrate the movement of power first towards and then away from the Treasury.

The events listed under the ruled line show the turn of the tide towards more specific planning, and the growth of new planning bodies outside the Treasury.

May 1947	Central Economic Planning Staff set up. This was responsible first to Mr Herbert Morrison, the Lord President of the Council and later to Sir Stafford Cripps, who was for a few weeks Minister of Economic Affairs.
November 1947	C.E.P.S. moved with Cripps to the Treasury.
November 1953	Economic Section of the Cabinet Office transferred to the Treasury.
October 1954	C.E.P.S. renamed 'Home and Overseas Planning Staff' (H. & O.P.S.).
December 1958	Planning Staff dissolved. Work given to an 'Overseas Co-ordination' division and to two 'National Resources' divisions.*

February 1962	National Economic Development Council set up.
October 1963	Mr Edward Heath made Secretary of State for Industry, Trade, and Regional Development.
Spring 1964	Labour Party promises new economic planning or production ministry if elected. Conservative and Labour Parties investigate new machinery for incomes policy.

* In November 1962 two National Economy divisions were set up to take over part of the work of the Economic Section and part of the responsibilities of the National Resources division. The latter was abolished.

The Sterling Muddle

The biggest muddle during Mr Butler's reign was on policy towards sterling. The story of Operation Robot, an abortive plan for making the pound convertible to non-residents at a floating rate of exchange, and freezing certain sterling balances is already public knowledge. The plan was devised by a section of the Treasury with the support of the Bank of England, soon after the Conservatives returned to office, and was opposed by both Hall and by Sir Edwin Plowden, the Chief Planning Officer. It gained Butler's support, but was vetoed by Churchill against his original inclinations on the advice of his wartime confidant Lord Cherwell, then back in office after a short period as Paymaster General. Cherwell himself turned for economic advice to Sir Donald MacDougall, later Economic Director of NEDC. 'Robot' was put up and vetoed first at the very end of February 1952 and then again in June of that year.

If one compares the line-up on floating rates a dozen years ago with the way in which opinion is divided on this issue today, one is struck by the enormous power of fashion in economic policy. In the early 1950s the idea that we could dispose of our balance of payments problem by leaving sterling to its own devices was advocated by economists and politicians who were regarded as Right wing. Indeed, every Conservative Chancellor before Mr Selwyn Lloyd seriously considered letting the pound float up and down to find its own level in the world currency markets. If no one took the plunge it was through lack of nerve rather than doctrinal inhibitions. It was among 'progressive' and 'Left of centre' economists that exchange rate changes were violently opposed as a false solution that did not get to the root of our difficulties.

Today the pendulum has swung right back. Any thought of touching sterling is denounced in leading articles and political and City columns as irresponsibly extreme – too extreme for the official leaders of the Labour Party; and economists who believe in floating rates (mostly moderate Lib-Labs in their politics) are treated almost as bomb-carrying Bolsheviks.

Why then was the Bank of England, of all institutions, prepared to tolerate floating rates in the winter of 1951–2?

To explain this flirtation with unorthodoxy one must go back to the run on sterling which took place in the autumn and winter of 1951–2, just as the Conservatives were returning to office. The 1951–2 run on the pound was a particularly severe and somewhat mysterious one, due partly to the collapse of the Korean boom overseas and partly to overstrain caused by rearmament at home. Mr Churchill himself took a very alarmist view. 'I have seen,' he told Oliver Lyttleton, 'a Treasury Minute and already I know that the financial position is almost irretrievable: the country has lost its way. *In the worst of the war I could always see how to do it. Today's problems are elusive and intangible,* and it would be a bold man who could look forward to certain success.'*

As usual the Bank projected the outflow into the future, and worked out how many months it would be before the reserves were exhausted. In those days it had not had as much experience of sterling crises as it has since acquired and did not appreciate how easy it was to attract back hot money by raising Bank Rate and making deflationary noises.

It seemed, therefore, to the Bank during that winter as if Britain would have to devalue or float in any case; it therefore wanted to make a virtue of necessity, and gain convertibility into the bargain. There were at that time people in the Bank who had experience of working a system of floating rates in the 1930s, and this weakened their resistance to the idea. But when the reserves did not run out in the way feared, and eventually began to move back in the other direction, the Bank could see no more point in float-

* *The Memoirs of Lord Chandos*, p. 343. The italics are mine.

ing. As the 1950s wore on personalities changed, memories faded, and opinion hardened in favour of fixed rates at any price.

The idea of floating rates did not immediately die when Robot was rejected. Another secret 'plan' or series of plans for a 'Collective Approach to convertibility' emerged after the Commonwealth Conference of November 1952. These too provided for convertibility at a floating rate; but it was hoped to bolster up the sterling area reserves with an American loan or at least obtain U.S. support for an application for help from the International Monetary Fund. But when Butler presented the Treasury's idea to the new Republican Administration early in 1953, he got a pretty frosty refusal.*

These plans hung fire for a while, and emphasis shifted towards import liberalization in concert with other Western European countries. The anti-*laissez-faire* wing of the Treasury was never too keen on convertibility and wanted to make haste as slowly as possible, but the Bank of England, which was becoming more and more dominant in overseas financial policy, was gradually dismantling exchange restrictions.

From February 1955,† sterling was in practice convertible into dollars and other foreign currency for all non-residents at or very near the official rate of exchange.

By 1955 the fashion had shifted towards a 'concerted' move to convertibility on a European rather than a sterling area basis together with the rest of Western Europe; and by 1955 the Bank of England believed that it could achieve this goal. But some Treasury officials were still keen to have, if not a floating pound, at least some exchange rate flexibility;

* An account of the various plans for sterling convertibility that succeeded Robot can be found in *Britain and the Post-war European Payments Systems* by Graham L. Rees, University of Wales Press, 1963. More details of 'Robot' and how it was stopped can be found in *The Prof in Two Worlds: Lord Cherwell*, by Lord Birkenhead, Collins, 1961.

† When the British authorities decided to support transferable sterling in the market.

and as late as July 1955 the British delegation to talks on the new European Monetary Agreement, which was to come into effect after convertibility, was arguing for a three per cent margin of freedom on either side; in other words, a rate which would move from around \$2.72 to \$2.88 to the pound.

Widespread gossip on the subject during the summer of 1955, at a time when sterling was already weak, caused a burst of speculation against the pound. The Bank of England finally put its foot down against the whole idea of floating rates, and persuaded Mr Butler and the Treasury that they must do the same, if the run on the pound was to be stopped. On 14 September 1955, Mr Butler surrendered to the massed forces of financial orthodoxy under the domes and minarets of Istanbul, where the International Monetary Fund was holding its annual conference, and categorically denied all thought of a change in the sterling exchange rate. The Bank of England, for its part, had to accept a postponement of formal convertibility, which did not come until December 1958 – and then, of course, at a fixed rate of exchange. Now it has achieved both convertibility and a fixed rate without having to sacrifice one for the other, and is grimly determined to hang on to both.

With hindsight it is clear that the expansionist school inside the Treasury played its cards badly. In 1952 it had some very powerful arguments against Operation Robot. Unlike the abortive suggestion for a floating rate in 1949, 'Robot' would have made the pound convertible into dollars to foreign holders. But in 1952 the dollar shortage was still acute, and if sterling had become convertible foreign holders might well have rushed to switch their pounds into dollars at the expense of the British reserves (as happened during Dr Dalton's ill-fated experiment in the summer of 1947). A floating rate in the winter of 1951–2 would have meant a heavily depreciated rate, and a perceptible fall in British living standards; moreover, owing to the industrial overstrain caused by rearmament, British exports might not have been able to respond to the stimulus that devaluation normally brings. But in the following couple of years these arguments gradually lost most of their force; and if all the non-establishment forces inside the Treasury had really come out wholeheartedly in favour of convertibility at a floating rate in, say, 1954, the whole course of subsequent British economic history might have changed immeasurably for the better. As it was, all they gained was a period of delay, during which Britain had all the drawbacks of sterling convertibility and none of the prestige; and at the end of the day the Bank of England won a hands-down victory.

The 1955 Blunder

But I have strayed from Mr Butler and his mistakes of 1955, which were not confined to foreign exchange policy. During that year, his last at the Exchequer, Mr Butler passed through a bad period after the death of his first wife. His political intuition failed him in his April Budget, when he made a serious blunder by handing out £135m. of tax reliefs in the middle of a raging boom.

The economy was expanding rapidly; unemployment (seasonally adjusted) had fallen over the previous year from 1.5 to 1.1 per cent, and there were nearly twice as many vacancies as men out of work. The gold reserves were under strain and the economy was suffering from a demand inflation of a severity that has never since been equalled. This is a situation in which even the most expansionist of economists might have argued for a touch of the brake. The Government's Economic Adviser would not, in these circumstances, have supported a give-away Budget.

The real blame for the 1955 miscalculation lay with what might be called the Establishment wing of the official Treasury, with the connivance of the Bank of England. Incredible though it may seem, it was just those elements that are normally most cautious about expanding production when there is unemployment and slack in the economy who egged on Mr Butler to a give-away Budget, and they did so at a time of overfull employment when extra consumer spending would be sure to have the most inflationary possible effect.

One normally very mild-mannered observer of these events has described them as 'entangled and discreditable'. Some senior Civil Servants (long since departed) seemed too preoccupied with Mr Butler's political difficulties on the eve of an election. (Such a situation, it must be added, could not occur in the very different atmosphere which prevails today.) This does not mean that the officials who advised Mr Butler were cynical or dishonest. People can usually find respectable arguments for most courses of action. Having only recently rediscovered monetary policy, the Bank of England and Treasury officials overestimated the extent to which restriction in this field could cancel out the effects of a Budget hand-out. Early in 1955 Bank Rate had been raised in two steps from three to four and a half per cent; very moderate hire-purchase controls (minimum deposits of only fifteen per cent and two years to pay for both cars and durables) had been introduced; and banks had been asked to limit finance for h.p. and credit sales. There was, however, a tell-tale reference in the Budget to the 'resources of a flexible monetary policy', suggesting a slight fear that all might not be well and that greater restraint might later be needed.

There were, in fact, many excellent sentiments in the speech with which Mr Butler introduced his unfortunate first Budget of the year. He said, 'productivity should benefit from the maintenance of prosperous conditions at home and from the added incentive to effort which the prospect of rising consumption affords; and an economy in which production and productivity are rising fast, and new lines of production are continually being developed, should be in a good position to hold its own in export markets'.

If an economic writer were to utter these sentiments

today he would be dismissed by orthodox City editors as 'ultra-expansionist'. The sentiments, however praiseworthy, are very different from what Mr Butler himself was saying the previous year when he talked about steering a middle course. And it is almost the opposite of the sort of thing that Messrs Heathcoat Amory and Lloyd used to put in their speeches.

The type of Budget that is introduced must obviously vary according to the economic situation; but this is no excuse for allowing the measuring rod by which situations are judged to zig-zag around in such a dazzling fashion. At one moment all the talk is of expansion; at another we are told that easy times are gone, perhaps for ever, and that everything else will be subordinated to the overriding task of bringing inflation to an end. No wonder many businessmen, thrust into uncertainties they are not professionally equipped to handle, become resentful of the whole jargon-ridden world of politicians, officials, and economists.

Mr Butler is reported to have come back after the election full of fury with the bankers who had misled him. And well he might. By July he had introduced a package measure of further restrictions; hire-purchase deposits went up to thirty-three per cent, the nationalized industries were made to cut their investment programmes; the banks were asked to cut advances, and coal and steel prices were raised abruptly to 'mop up' spending power. But even this was not regarded as enough by the Treasury, as the pressure on sterling increased, and wages continued to soar; and in October Mr Butler introduced an autumn Budget which took back the greater part of his earlier reliefs. The damage done to Mr Butler's reputation by bad advice from permanent Treasury officials may have been at least a factor in his first failure to achieve the Premiership early in 1957 and even (through its general effect on his standing at a crucial moment) in his second failure after Mr Macmillan retired. Certainly he left the Exchequer under a cloud.

The Economics of Stockton-on-Tees

Mr Harold Macmillan, who succeeded 'Rab' at No. 11, was regarded as an 'inflationist' by Treasury and Bank officials and (after he became Prime Minister) by some of his own Cabinet colleagues. By this they meant that he was reluctant to sacrifice real wealth to preserve the figures on the price tags appearing in shop windows.

His views were coloured by his acquaintance with mass unemployment at his old constituency of Stockton-on-Tees in the inter-war period; and this was a subject of some mockery in Whitehall. Officials were rumoured to keep a mental tally of the number of times he mentioned Stockton in any one week. But the deeper wisdom lay with Macmillan. For behind his references to Stockton was a well-founded fear that prosperity and full employment could be too easily sacrificed by a one-sided devotion to 'sound money' at the expense of other objectives.

He resented the restricting influence of sterling on British economic expansion and would dearly have loved to have found a way of getting rid of the sterling area 'bank' which the family firm had inherited. He was passionately interested in the international liquidity problem, which (in contrast to most Central Bankers) he rightly regarded as a matter of generating more internationally acceptable money to finance the growth of world trade; and he kept on sending American Presidents notes on the subject. The simplest way of solving the problem, he always maintained, was to increase the price of gold; but the fetish that the American leaders have made of the existing gold-dollar parity has so far prevented a solution along these lines.

Cynics always underestimated Macmillan's economic understanding. He was intellectually unhappy at the need to exhort people to export more. The occasional speech in which he recalled the vanished mechanisms of the nineteenth-century gold standard, and wondered why there was today no automatic system of bringing exports and imports into balance, again were not the platitudes that superficial listeners supposed. Although he may not have supported 'Robot' in Cabinet, he always had a hankering after a floating exchange rate, and would have introduced one if given the slightest encouragement.

Macmillan was, it is true, rusty on the mechanics of economic control by the time he got to No. 11. He did not have any of the intuitive feeling for economic timing that Butler had at his best. Yet he often had a better understanding of the logic of the really big issues than either his Treasury or his Bank advisers; and it must never be forgotten that Macmillan was one of the very, very few Conservative politicians – Lord Boothby was another – who had been right before the war both about unemployment and about the appeasement of Nazi Germany.

Macmillan's friends might say that he came to the Treasury twenty years too late; he did not enjoy his stay and only went there because he had not hit it off with Eden in his previous post of Foreign Secretary. He more or less acknowledged this in his one and only Budget Speech in April 1956, when he began by mentioning that Churchill was said to have been quite surprised to find himself at the Treasury in the winter of 1924 – 'but not half so surprised as I was, thirty-one years later'. At the Exchequer he was no longer prepared to do the homework which would have enabled him to set forth a detailed expansionist policy of his own as an alternative to what his advisers were offering him.

But this should not have been necessary. It is a striking testimony to the domination of the Treasury and Bank of England machines that cautious sterling-first policies should have been pursued during a period of eight years when an ultra-expansionist was first at the Exchequer and then at No. 10.

The interaction between Mr Macmillan, his ministers, and the Whitehall machine has been responsible for much of what has gone wrong in Britain's economic policy. A little further on in this book there will be a discussion of

'Macmillan cycles', which did so much to harm the British economy. It is therefore all the more important to emphasize that we are talking about a period when – except for the Arctic winter of 1962–3 – unemployment hardly ever went above two and a half per cent of the employed population and was usually well below that percentage. So long as Mr Macmillan was at the helm, there were grounds for hoping that the bigger economic lunacies would never be allowed to happen. The continuous changing of Chancellors showed the Prime Minister's determination on this point clearly enough. If the danger of large-scale unemployment ever became real and not just a fantasy, it would have been very difficult for the Treasury and the Bank to deter Mr Macmillan from vigorous action by the usual lame cries of 'world situation beyond our control'. But under a Conservative Cabinet without Macmillan, one could not feel nearly the same confidence.

Mr Macmillan's one and only Budget speech, in April 1956, was by far the most entertaining in the whole post-war series. The whole mood was buoyantly expansionist. There were long passages from Macaulay to show how the country prospered in the eighteenth century, despite increases in the National Debt to may times the level that earlier Cassandras had regarded as catastrophic. The National Debt stood at £645m. on 4 August 1914, £8,400m. on 3 September 1939, £27,000m. in 1956. Its servicing, Mr Macmillan pointed out, cost at the time he was speaking £638m. a year 'or nearly 3s. on the income tax'. (Mr Macmillan was the only Conservative Chancellor to draw attention to this burden, which had been very much swollen because the reintroduction of Bank Rate – which had previously been frozen for twenty years at two per cent – as a monetary weapon was accompanied by a masochistic insistence on applying higher interest rates to the government's borrowings.)

'No one who contemplates these (National Debt) figures can fail to draw the lesson,' said Mr Macmillan. 'Whatever the temporary difficulties from which we may suffer from trying to run too fast, if we stand still we are lost.' Runaway inflation was, of course, bad, but 'we must all be expansionist of real wealth. The problem of inflation cannot be dealt with by cutting down demand; the other side of the picture is the need for increasing production. The only question is at what rate, for what markets, and how best guided our expansion is to be.'

Unfortunately, cutting down demand is just what Mr Macmillan did. A few weeks before the Budget he had introduced a particularly stiff package dose of restrictions which, among other things, tightened hire-purchase restrictions still further, cut public investment, and suspended the investment allowance for private industry – the latter move he eventually recognized as a particularly foolish decision. The Budget imposed no further net increase in the burden; but with the aid of cuts in Government spending, aimed to increase the surplus by well over £150m. The *Economic Survey* added threateningly, 'If the measures so far taken are slow in producing results they will be reinforced.'

Of all Conservative Chancellors Macmillan was the only one who really wanted a proper capital gains tax. But he was balked by the Inland Revenue and hardly encouraged by his own Party. All that happened as a result of his measure was that instead of the increased production for which he had called, 1956 was a year of stagnation. The combination of an expansionist speech and a restrictant Budget is unfortunately symptomatic of Macmillan's whole conduct of economic policy except when the fear of recession had him alarmed (which was quite frequently, but not always at the right moments).

Mr Macmillan's two main achievements as Chancellor were (a) the introduction of Premium Bonds and (b) the improvement in official statistics which he had castigated as 'last year's Bradshaw'. The fall-out from the second operation continued over many years and economic analysts are still feeling the effects today.

Macmillan's last few months as Chancellor were over-laid by the Suez crisis. A mystery still to be cleared up about this period is which ministry gave Eden the misleading advice about the supposedly catastrophic effects on the British economy should the Canal be closed.

One incident, which has not so far been revealed, con-cerns the financing of the Aswan Dam. (It will be recalled that the Western decision to cancel aid for this dam pre-cipitated Nasser's nationalization of the Canal.) When Dulles suddenly decided to cancel all U.S. aid for the pro-ject, Mr Thorneycroft, who was then President of the Board of Trade, proposed to Eden after some informal dis-cussions with the other European participants, that Britain should go ahead with her share, even without the Ameri-cans. Such a decision might well have changed the whole course of subsequent events. But Eden was furious at the mention of this idea and it was never properly examined in Cabinet.

One critical writer recently remarked that the Treasury stopped a small war in Palmerston's day by refusing to agree to the required expenditure. He asked rhetorically whether one could imagine it happening today. One could. Treasury alarm at the rate at which the gold reserves were falling had a good deal to do with Britain's decision to bring the Suez operations to a sudden halt in early November 1956, only a few days after they had begun. As was usual on such occasions, Macmillan telephoned Washington in his capa-city as Chancellor to ask for the American Administration's good offices in obtaining financial assistance for the pound. The Americans replied that there was no hope of any aid while fighting was going on in Egypt.

Macmillan had originally been the warmest cheer-leader of the Suez expedition, and had originally maintained, on the basis of a personal meeting with Eisenhower, that the Americans would not oppose it. But in a crucial Cabinet meeting in early November, he suddenly changed his mind and threw all his weight behind those who wanted to bring the operation to an end, giving as one of his reasons, 'We can't afford it'. How much then had the run on the reserves really to do with his change of front?

People's motives are rarely entirely distinct, even to themselves, in the fever-heat of a crisis. There were a great many factors involved in the final decision: the threat of rockets from Russia, Britain's fantastic isolation from world opinion, and above all, the extreme separation from the U.S. America's refusal to help Britain financially in an hour of need was symptomatic of the rupture in Atlantic relations.

Thorneycroft I and II

Mr Peter Thorneycroft, who succeeded Macmillan at the Exchequer, when the latter moved up to No. 10, has often been compared to Mr Selwyn Lloyd; and there are certain obvious similarities. Both imposed tough financial policies in the teeth of fierce opposition and eventually earned Mr Macmillan's displeasure. Neither was a man of great guile or subtlety; and both pursued their policies with a dogged determination, irrespective of the effect on their own political fortunes, which won admiration even from their critics. Neither could fairly be written off as a Tory reactionary (Thorneycroft was, for example, a keen European and a free trader; Selwyn Lloyd supported the abolition of the death penalty and had been far from enthusiastic about Suez), although both found their chief backing in the financial Right wing of the Conservative Party.

Yet there were also important differences. Peter Thorneycroft never claimed to be an intellectual high flier; but he was rarely at a loss for words and was much more interested than the average politician in general economic ideas. After his resignation he contributed to a professional symposium on the Radcliffe Report on the monetary system.* Selwyn Lloyd, by contrast, was easily embarrassed both in public speeches and in conversation, and was ill at ease in general

* *Not Unanimous*, Institute of Economic Affairs, 1960.

economic discussion. He seemed to see the world (like Bertrand Russell in the early 1920s) as a collection of unrelated atomic facts to be considered one at a time. Yet as Chancellor he had a less misconceived idea of what was wrong with the economy than Thorneycroft, and left more of value behind him.

Although Mr Thorneycroft was no intellectual heavy-weight, he had a good many sound instincts. The Aswan Dam affair, just discussed, is a case in point; and during the Suez crisis he never took seriously the scare about a world tanker shortage that obsessed many other members of the Cabinet. In the very early days of the Common Market, around the time of the Messina meeting of June 1955, when the Six were still working out the Treaty, Thorneycroft had written a paper saying that Britain should be associated with it in a free trade area. If the Cabinet had plumped for the idea then, instead of waiting a couple of years, the negotiations would probably have succeeded.

The Treasury did not suit him at all. The manoeuvring between rival knights, at which Butler had been so good, had no appeal for him. Thorneycroft was disturbed by the thought that he, as a lay minister, knew more about finance than Sir Roger Makins, his Permanent Secretary. This was very different from the Board of Trade in which he had worked together very happily with Sir Frank Lee, with whom he had a very close sympathy.

Thorneycroft's reign is quite correctly associated with the lurch towards deflation, in which the post-war objectives of full employment and economic expansion to which Butler and Macmillan had both been dedicated seemed for a time to have been abandoned. Indeed, the doctrines promoted by Thorneycroft during the 1957 crisis were far more blood-curdling than the severest utterances of Mr Selwyn Lloyd in 1961, although they were more quickly forgotten by the public. The speeches Thorneycroft made in his first six months in the Treasury were so different from those he made in his second six months that it is difficult to believe they were by the same man. Compare the following utterances by Thorneycroft I and Thorneycroft II.

Thorneycroft I: Speaking about inflation, the Chancellor said:

There are some who say that the answer lies in savage deflationary policies, resulting in high levels of unemployment. *They say that we should depress demand to a point at which employers cannot afford to pay and workers are in no position to ask for higher wages.* If this be the only way in which to contain the wage-price spiral it is indeed a sorry reflection upon our modern society. To slash production, to drive down investment, to push up unemployment to a level at which despite high world demand we have manufactured our own recession, is to say the least a high price to pay for stability.

Budget Speech, April 1957.

Thorneycroft II: After outlining the measures to limit public investment in money terms and restrict bank advances, Mr Thorneycroft went on:

Against this background, if an attempt were made to take out of the system in money income more than is put in by new effort and production the only result would be a reduction in activity and the employment of fewer men. The only other thing I would say about these measures is that I am confident they will be effective. They will be pushed to the length necessary for that purpose. If inflationary pressures grow inside the economy, other things may alter, other aspects of policy may have to be adjusted, but the strain will not be placed on the value of the pound sterling.

Speech at the Annual I.M.F. Meeting in Washington, 24 September 1957.

Thorneycroft I took the advice of Sir Robert Hall. It is not generally known that before switching over to his ultra-tough money approach, Thorneycroft did try to introduce an incomes policy. This was to have been a 'guiding light' – similar to that proclaimed by Mr Selwyn Lloyd barely five years later – giving the normal increase in wages compatible with stable prices, and stating some of the grounds for exceptions. The idea was rejected by the

Cabinet for the usual plodding, unimaginative reasons: there was a danger that the guiding light might become a minimum instead of a norm and one mustn't interfere with collective bargaining.

The three-man Council on Prices, Productivity, and Incomes appointed by Mr Thorneycroft in August 1957 to make reports to the public was the vestigial remnant of his attempt at an incomes policy. But as the one and only economist on the Council, the late Sir Dennis Robertson, was a distinguished representative of the tough-money school, there was never any chance that the Council would take upon itself the odium of producing a 'guiding light'. And so it proved. The exercise in buck-passing failed, as it deserved, and the Council contented itself with arguing the case for monetary deflation.

Mr Thorneycroft's Budget of April 1957 was quite a cheerful one. The figures worked out in such a way that he could reduce taxation by £100m. (£140m. in a full year) and yet increase his current surplus substantially. Some relief in the burden of surtax, which until then came down with a bang on all earned incomes as soon as they reached the £2,000 point, was smuggled in via the earned income relief; and this was accompanied by other reliefs of special help to lower incomes. The only big mistake was the special tax concession for companies operating abroad, which added a gratuitous strain to the balance of payments that remains to this day. The concession had been recommended by the Royal Commission on Taxation, and Mr Macmillan had given an undertaking on the subject the previous year. But he ought to have been stopped by the Treasury before it reached that stage.

It was, of course, a sudden traumatic run on the gold reserves during the summer that transformed Thorneycroft I into Thorneycroft II. In two months in the summer £186m. was lost and the sum would have been larger without some special payments. The main cause was a bout of currency speculation, triggered off by a partial devaluation of the French franc in August. Rumours were circulating that the German mark was to be revalued and sterling might be depreciated as part of a general realignment. Naturally, funds poured out of London, and traders delayed making payments in sterling and accelerated payments in other currencies. Sterling had already been weakened, first by the Suez episode, and then by the purchase of dollar securities through Kuwait by British citizens speculating against the pound. Mr Thorneycroft has publicly admitted that the Bank of England was opposed to direct action to close the Kuwait Gap,* and that this delayed action. Yet for all the Bank's 'technical' objections, the gap was closed effectively enough in July. By then it had cost the reserve £70m.†

Mr Thorneycroft responded to the run on the pound with his famous deflationary package, raising the Bank Rate from five to seven per cent. Public Sector investment was cut, a ceiling was imposed on advances, and the Capital Issues Committee was told to be more restrictive. The Chancellor, moreover, firmly announced his intention of stopping the rise in Government spending. He did not want too much attention to be paid to the Bank Rate alone and let it be known that he would like his package deal to be known as the 'September Measures'.

The curious language about stopping up the 'supply of money' which Mr Thorneycroft inserted into his speeches, had no effect on what he actually did, which was to impose another old-style set of deflationary measures to curb spending with a special emphasis on the public sector. He also threatened that any wages granted in the public sector would be at the expense of employment; but he was not long enough at the Treasury for anyone to discover whether such a policy could be implemented. It seemed to some Treasury

* Radcliffe Committee, *Volume of Oral Evidence*, Q.11255.
† *The British Economy in the 1950s*, edited by G.D.N. Worswick and P. H. Ady, p. 222.

officials that Thorneycroft had simply muddled up Government expenditure with the quantity of money.*

The Treasury itself presented a confused and divided picture during this period. Some Treasury officials saw no alternative to the September Measures even though they disliked the verbiage in which they were clothed. But the official Treasury advice which Mr Thorneycroft received from the Permanent Secretary Sir Roger Makins was opposed to what he did.

Mr Thorneycroft felt that his only consistent supporter near the top of the hierarchy was Sir Leslie Rowan who was in charge of external finance. Thorneycroft formed the impression that Sir Roger Makins was against what he was doing, but had no alternative advice to offer except to ride out the storm. There may have been a case for doing nothing, but it would have had to be argued with great clarity, force, and ruthless facing of possible consequences if it was to convince a Chancellor who had just seen a quarter of his gold reserve disappear within a couple of months.

Thorneycroft worked out the main lines of policy with the help of Mr Enoch Powell, the Financial Secretary, and Mr Nigel Birch, the Economic Secretary, who exercised a dominating influence extremely unusual for junior Treasury ministers. It was they who were largely responsible for turning the anti-inflationary policies into a crusade. Needless to say, the Bank of England sounded the alarm in the summer of 1957 and backed the Treasury ministers all along the line.

Thorneycroft's switch of policy became apparent in July when he gave instructions to the Treasury 'to consider

* The merits of what economists know as the Quantity Theory of money were never even put to the test. The money supply had been falling rapidly as a proportion of the G.N.P. for several years before Thorneycroft acted; and a table demonstrating this was rather maliciously inserted into the 1958 Economic Survey. During the twelve months after his measures the trend was, in fact, reversed. Even in absolute terms, the quantity of bank deposits plus notes in circulation rose more quickly in the year after the September Measures than in the year before.

possibilities of checking inflation by taking firmer control of the money supply'. On 7 August, before he went on holiday, he gave more precise directives that 'a study should be made in the Treasury of the possibility of bringing about a measure of deflation in the economy'.

The role of Professor (now Lord) Robbins in the affair has been exaggerated by those who believe in the conspiracy theory of history. In the period before the measures were announced, Mr Thorneycroft became very worried that neither his Department nor his Cabinet colleagues were supporting him. He telephoned to Professor Robbins, who was on holiday in Switzerland, asking him to come back to London. The Chancellor, who knew and respected Robbins, wanted to make sure that the latter thought his proposed measures were sensible. He also wanted him to speak to Macmillan, who was far from keen on Thorneycroft's proposed measures; and as the universities can now confirm, Robbins is an extremely impressive person to have on one's side.*

On Tuesday afternoon, 17 September, the Cabinet approved the Chancellor's measures apart from the Bank Rate increase. This was discussed at a 10 p.m. meeting at 10 Downing Street, attended by the Prime Minister, Chancellor, Governor of the Bank of England, Sir Roger Makins, and two other officials, but not Sir Robert Hall. After some discussion, Mr Macmillan said he 'would not make up his mind whether the Government should agree to the Bank Rate being raised, and if so, to what figure, until the following morning' – when, of course, he agreed to seven per cent.†

* Lord Robbins's actual views at the time were the subject of a great deal of newspaper gossip. Readers interested in what Robbins really did believe about the 1957 crisis are referred to his article in *Lloyd's Bank Review* of April 1958, reprinted in *Politics and Economics*.

† A blow-by-blow account of the events leading up to the Bank Rate decision has been extracted by Professor Ely Devons from the proceedings of the Tribunal of Inquiry into allegations of a leakage. It appears in a special issue of the Manchester School (Vol. 27, No. 1, Sept. 1959) which contains three highly interesting articles on the political, economic, and sociological evidence which emerged from the episode.

A Change of Priorities

The 'September Measures' of 1957 marked a turning aside from the road along which the country had travelled under successive Labour and Conservative Governments. Mr Thorneycroft's supporters saw this better than some of his critics. Although the wisdom of Mr Butler's autumn Budget of 1955, or of the curbs imposed by Mr Macmillan in 1956, is open to doubt, it could always be argued that in their time the economy was genuinely overloaded. Unemployment (seasonally adjusted) was down to 1–1.2 per cent; and there were almost two recorded unfilled vacancies for every man out of work. A deflationary policy in these circumstances did not necessarily imply sacrificing the growth of the domestic economy for the sake of sterling.

But by September 1957 the situation was radically different. During the whole of 1957 there were (seasonal factors apart) more unemployed than unfilled vacancies; despite several years of rising investment, production had only just regained its 1955 peak. Treasury economists who had supported the Butler and Macmillan squeezes of 1955 and 1956 saw that the pressure of demand on supply had already eased and they expected more slack to develop in the coming months. They feared that the Thorneycroft measures would aggravate a recession that was already on the way. Even worse was the fact that the Thorneycroft measures were imposed in response to a flight of hot money when the balance of payments itself was in comfortable surplus.

In December 1956, Government spokesmen said publicly that the best Britain could hope for was a bare current balance in the year ending mid 1957. A few months later Mr Thorneycroft told Parliament that he was looking forward to a surplus of £125m. Speaking at the I.M.F. meeting in September 1957, he announced that the surplus had worked out at over £200m. and he expected a bigger surplus in the following twelve months. By deflating the economy in the face of his own figures he was proclaiming to the world that production and employment in Britain would be held back whenever currency speculators decided to take a gamble against the pound, or traders delayed their payments – however unjustified their actions were. Public criticism of Thorneycroft's measures in Britain concentrated on peripherals and did not fully bring out the enormity of this change in economic priorities.

Supporters of the 'September Measures' often say that they were justified by the speed with which wages were rising in Britain. This can be disproved by figures published in 1958, by the Cohen Council* – who were the warmest supporters Thorneycroft ever had.

	Per cent increase Average weekly earnings	Index of wage rates
Oct. 1947–Oct. 1955 (annual average)	7.1	5.5
Oct. 1955–Oct. 1956	7.2	7.5
Oct. 1956–Oct. 1957	5.8	5.5

Not only is there no sign that Mr Thorneycroft was faced with a bigger problem of wage inflation than his predecessors; on the contrary, the pace of wage inflation was already beginning to decline when he decided to hit the British economy on the head. Indeed, most of the evidence suggests that the reduced wage inflation of 1956–7 was a delayed response to a boom that was fast fading away. As an ex-Treasury economist, Mr J. C. R. Dow, once pointed out, 'the pressure of demand twelve months ago may have an effect on the wage-price spiral that will take several years to work through'.

But the real tragedy of 1957 is the missed opportunity on the sterling side. In the sterling crises of 1961, and in other minor alarms, Central Bankers have used the state of the dollar as an argument against allowing the pound to float.

* *Council on Prices, Productivity and Incomes*, Second Report, August 1958, H.M.S.O.

or against tampering with the exchange rate in any way. If the pound 'goes', it has been claimed, there would then be a run on the dollar, and this will lead to a general flight from currencies into gold with untold consequences. This argument has carried great force with a British Cabinet which regarded the special relationship with America as the mainstay of its foreign policy. It did not, however, apply at all in 1957, as the first signs of weakness in the dollar did not emerge until well on in 1958. Thus 1957 was the last sterling crisis, when Britain could have abandoned the sterling rate fixed by Cripps in 1949 without rocking the international boat; and the opportunity was thrown away.

The Treasury ministers were not even prepared to contemplate it at the time, as they were engaged in a crusade to maintain the value of the pound at home and abroad. After the humiliation of Suez the sterling exchange rate – mere arithmetical ratio though it be – was one of the few status symbols we had left. In addition the Conservatives had had several by-election defeats, which they attributed to middle-class resentment over the rising cost of living. If the exchange rate had been freed in 1957, it would in the first instance have drifted downwards, and this would have slightly raised the cost of living (which public opinion poll respondents so often confuse with the standard of living). The September Measures probably checked living standards more than devaluation would have done; but the advocates of these Measures did not realize this; and in any case, whatever was true of the country as a whole, middle-class people of fixed income lost in the medium and short run less from deflation than they would have done from devaluation.

The P.M.'s Position

Yet this hardly explains why there was such a large gap on this and many subsequent occasions between Macmillan's own expansionist views and the policies of his

Chancellors. Part of the answer is that by recent tradition the Foreign Secretary tends to be the Prime Minister's errand boy, and the Chancellor is not.

Although, as we have seen, Macmillan had very pronounced economic views, his heart was, as the public realized, in foreign affairs. In the words of one of his ministers: 'Foreign affairs was his vocation, economics his hobby.'

Officials were never quite sure how seriously to take some of the more unorthodox ideas Macmillan expressed in memoranda or over a drink in the evening. They usually found that he was satisfied with a well-reasoned brief defending the orthodox case and explaining why his heresies wouldn't work. So long as the Chancellor of the Exchequer considered his arguments, the Prime Minister was not prepared to impose them on him – although after a while he would change the Chancellor. Moreover, for all his joy in teasing the Treasury, Macmillan did not think that Britain was doing all that badly in production and trade considering the difficulties. His own brushes with the Treasury knights had given him a slight 'thing' about them which was not very easily turned into constructive criticism.

But the most important reason for Macmillan's lack of influence over his Chancellors was his lack of a technically qualified staff to write papers for him, develop his view in detail, suggest ideas, and refute the objections of the Treasury and the Bank. The Prime Minister is the one member of the Cabinet who does not have a Department to brief him; economic policy comes up for decision through the huge machine described in Chapter 3 and, unlike foreign affairs, it looks too technical and statistical for a purely personal judgement.

There was also in 1957 an *ad hominem* point. Not having imposed a floating rate the previous year when he was Chancellor, Mr Macmillan could hardly urge this course of action on Thorneycroft. As a result some of his memoranda in the 1957 crisis were, to say the least, uninspired and were said to have raised questions such as whether there were any votes in road-building.

The last laugh, as so often in those days, was with Mr Macmillan. The three Treasury ministers played straight into the Prime Minister's hands, by their theological stress on permitting no increase at all on government expenditure for the coming financial year in money terms (which meant cutting it in real terms). The actual increase in Government spending over which they resigned in January 1958 seemed a triviality even to some of their supporters inside the Bank of England who, as usual, quickly calmed down once sterling was strong again. The ministers' resignations seemed inexplicable to many senior men inside the Treasury – although others subsequently sent private letters of support to Thorneycroft.

Shelving the Issues

The choice of Mr Derek Heathcoat Amory to succeed Mr Peter Thorneycroft seemed an ideal way out of 'little local difficulties'. Amory had acquired a good administrative reputation as Minister of Agriculture. He belonged to the liberal-humanitarian wing of the Conservative Party, and was personally popular on both sides of the House, but was intellectually very cautious and would do nothing to upset the bankers of Zürich. For Macmillan, it was a way of shelving the underlying issues.

Mr Heathcoat Amory quickly dropped the fanaticism and the monetary metaphysics, but he did not reverse Mr Thorneycroft's economic priorities. He had himself supported the September Measures, though he would have preferred less drastic action earlier. It is, in fact, doubtful if Macmillan had much idea what Mr Amory's views were when he appointed him. The Prime Minister was about to go off on a Commonwealth tour and was anxious to find a competent person to leave in charge as quickly as possible.

Indeed, it was quite exceptional for Mr Macmillan to bother about a new minister's opinions on policy before appointing him – 'That was the last thing he thought of' a leading Conservative politician once remarked ruefully to me long ago. A stress on character, reliability, and loyalty as against declared intellectual position is, of course, a fairly characteristic High Tory attitude towards subordinates. But it made it even more difficult for Macmillan to have a satisfactory impact on economic policy.

Although Mr Amory was on the Left of the Party on social matters, Treasury officials found Amory the most conservative of recent Chancellors with the sole exception of Thorneycroft II. This fact was obscured from the public because most of Amory's period at the Exchequer was spent during the upswing of the policy cycle. He had a great sense of personal responsibility and was liable to attacks of conscience, which were especially apt to come on if he thought he had gone too far in an inflationary direction.

When Mr Heathcoat Amory arrived at the Treasury, he was subjected to violent political pressure from his Cabinet colleagues and from Conservative circles in general to stabilize the cost of living above all else. He did not fail them, and he was careful not to re-expand the economy too soon for fear of starting off another wage-price spiral.* In the two and a half years he was Chancellor, retail prices rose by less than one per cent per annum, easily a post-war record.

Many people assumed that Mr Amory had to change

---

* The effects of a severe dose of deflation on the price level follows a well-defined sequence. In the first year after the measures have been taken, the results are disappointing and prices continue to rise. This is partly because the effects of earlier wage increases to which they gave rise are working themselves through the system. After that a year or two of comparatively stable prices can be expected. The early part of this period reflects recession. Wages are no longer rising rapidly, and employers are beginning to discard unwanted workers. The later and longer part of the period reflects economic recovery and the early stages of a boom, when the return of full employment has not yet begun to affect wages seriously. Eventually this period of bliss comes to an end and the wage-price spiral begins to turn again.

course gradually to avoid giving the impression of throwing overboard the Thorneycroft policies. Such a thought may have helped the Treasury knights to close their ranks after Thorneycroft, but it never, in fact, entered Amory's head. He was one of the most unscheming of politicians, and approached the Treasury almost like a very high-grade Civil Servant. He was willing to work his way through the same issues that were perplexing his knights, and he came to understand more of the language of national income forecasting than any Conservative Chancellor before Maudling.

Before the 1958 Budget Mr Amory's Treasury advisers told him, with varying degrees of emphasis, to avoid any expansionary measures that might upset foreign confidence. This advice flew in the face of the current predictions in their own *Economic Survey* of a substantial balance of payments surplus. Policy was dominated by fears of what speculators in the foreign exchange market might think of what we did. This was the heyday of 'the little men of Zürich' who were supposed to cherish a bitter hatred of the pound sterling.

Today the pendulum has swung to the other extreme and (at the time of writing) the Treasury seems confident that it can handle any speculation from the 'men of Zürich', provided the balance of payments is sound. Indeed it now gets irritated when journalists use the expression to symbolize the views of financially conservative holders of currency balances the world over.

By the time Mr Heathcoat Amory came to introduce his first Budget in April 1958, production was already known to be declining slightly and unemployment rising. In his Budget speech he predicted that these trends would go rather further during the rest of the year, although he did not expect a sharp recession.

Yet in the face of his own diagnosis he maintained: 'We are not yet strong enough to give the economy more than a minor stimulus' – some small purchase tax cuts in the context of a virtually neutral Budget. To be fair, the

Treasury in Heathcoat Amory's day did not yet have its present almost obsessive desire for *steady* expansion. The prospect of advancing by one per cent in one year and five per cent in the next did not fill it with any horror; although Mr Heathcoat Amory himself, as his tenure of office advanced, became more and more dissatisfied with the jerky methods of economic management he felt forced to employ.

An additional reason for this intense caution was the U.S. recession already discussed. But quite apart from the immediate diagnosis, the new Chancellor seemed to confirm the order of priorities introduced by Thorneycroft. He emphasized that 'provision of regular productive employment for all who are able and willing to work' was one of his main objectives. 'We want to see production and employment just as high as we can, consistent with maintaining the value of money.' Whatever else this is, it is not a full employment or a growth policy.

Kissing the Rod

The 1957 crisis had touched off a great debate on whether the sterling area was holding back Britain's growth. In the 1958 Budget speech the Treasury accepted with delight these limits on our freedom of action. The sterling area system was working well, the House was told. It would be preserved and developed, 'confidence' would be fortified, and the intention was proclaimed of 'moving gradually towards still wider freedom. 'This all means,' proclaimed the Budget speech, '*that we must conduct our finances with special caution in difficult times.*'

This passage bears all the hallmarks of the Overseas Finance Division of the Treasury. An official memorandum to the Radcliffe Committee in 1957, written before Mr Amory's Budget Speech, speaks of the confidence in United Kingdom policy which 'needs to be continuously refreshed' – i.e. by not doing anything adventurous or unconventional. Pointing out quite correctly that 'widespread and persistent expectations of a change in the exchange rate, however ill-based in the first place, can produce reserve movements on a scale which gives much more solid grounds for the initial expectation', the memorandum does not conclude that there is something wrong with the system, but reiterates the faint-hearted slogan: 'It is therefore all the more important that we should not take risks in the management of the domestic economy of the kind that affect the balance of payments.'

It is significant that the same 'outward-looking' financial statesmen who attached most value to the building up of overseas confidence in sterling, even at the cost of domestic sacrifice, were most hostile to any British involvement in the movement for European unity – and this during a period when it was probably still possible to get in on acceptable terms. Sir Leslie Rowan, the Head of the Overseas Finance Division, was asked by Cairncross at the Radcliffe Committee hearings in 1957 if there had been any suggestions about a pooling of reserves between the United Kingdom and European countries. In contrast to most other officials, Sir Leslie did not evade questions by sheltering behind ministerial apron-strings. He replied:

I think that the pooling of reserves is only another way of saying that you are going to have a common management of your currency, and if you have a common management of currency you are going to have a common management of economic policy; and if you have a common management of economic policy then you must have common legislatures, and so forth; therefore pooling our reserves is merely a way of saying federation or confederation. . . . The answer to your question is 'No'.

Here in a few forthright publicly quotable sentences is a simultaneous demonstration of what was wrong both with financial policy and policy towards Europe. Sir Leslie Rowan, to be fair to him, was keenly aware of the world shortage of reserves, as his evidence to Radcliffe shows. The Overseas Finance Division would have liked to see improvements in the international payments system which would have created more reserves, but which would not have involved any handing over of sterling balances to an international organization, or any 'funding' of them in other ways. The position of sterling as an international currency, with all the risks to which it exposed Britain, was regarded as desirable in itself, like a prisoner kissing the rod with which he is being beaten.

As 1958 wore on, the rigours of the 'sterling first' doctrines were abated, first by the growing strength of sterling and then by the fact that stagnation at home was turning into recession. The Treasury economists were warning Mr Heathcoat Amory of this by the end of May, and from June onwards Amory, whose actions were more generous than his words, began to introduce a trickle of concessions, which later broadened into a river.

There was first a minor increase in initial allowances for plant and buildings; then in late summer, the banks were granted freedom to lend as much as they liked. Hire-purchase controls were first relaxed in September, and in October – when unemployment rose above the magic figure of 500,000 – abolished altogether. During the same period Thorneycroft's ceiling on public investment was thrown off and Government expenditure was pushed up 'temporarily' to control unemployment. At about this time Mr Macmillan re-entered the economic arena with demands for vigorous anti-slump action; and was only kept at bay by the promise of a bumper Budget in 1959. At that time the Treasury did not have all its present powers of reducing taxation in mid year, short of the full paraphernalia of an emergency Budget. Perhaps, too, Sir Robert Hall deferred excessively to the 'administrative convenience' of the career Civil Servants, who wanted to wait until the Budget.*

The bankers and hire-purchase houses had assured Mr Heathcoat Amory that the free-for-all in credit would have only a very slight effect, and for a time it looked as if they were right. In January 1959, just before the annual Budget decisions were taken, winter unemployment rose to 620,000.

* See footnote overleaf.

Production had, in fact, just begun to turn upwards, but this was obscured by the effects of winter and by the time-lag in statistics. Mr Amory was told by his colleagues that he was the one man who could lose the Conservatives the election. Britain had just earned the biggest balance of payments surplus since the Conservatives came back to office. The pound had been made officially convertible in a blaze of glorious confidence, and economists inside and outside the Treasury assured the Chancellor that expansion was both safe and necessary and convinced him that £200m. of tax relief would not be nearly enough. Thus it came about that the most cautious of Chancellors was responsible for the most generous Budget ever introduced in normal peace-time conditions, which took 9d. off the in-come tax, cut purchase tax, returned post-war credits and restored investment allowances. But it was the intervention of Macmillan himself that was responsible for enlarging the income tax cut, which was to have been 6d., to 9d. and thus enlarging the hand-out by an extra £60m. to £360m.

The Budget speech itself was as cautious as one would expect from Mr Amory. He spoke about 'encouraging a steady but not excessive expansion in production'. He re-ferred to the fact that the problem of the wage-price spiral had not been solved, and this must influence his judge-ment. 'We must at all costs,' he said, 'make it our business not to return to an overload on the economy.' There were many other passages in similar vein; and until a few minutes before he sat down many M.P.s had resigned themselves to a joyless safety-first Budget.

* See the Treasury evidence to the Radcliffe Committee on 30 April 1959, Q.13319 and 13320. Hall told the Committee: 'Last autumn we thought of what was at our disposal and what we could do. There is in a sense a bit of a conflict between my interests and the general adminis-trative convenience; there has always to be a certain amount of give and take in it.' Sir Roger Makins afterwards added: 'The normal position is that major changes in purchase tax are made at the time of the budget. They could be made at other times, but it would be straining the ordin-ary practice.'

Even after he had announced his tax changes, Mr Heathcoat Amory went on to emphasize that he was not signalling 'Full steam ahead, but steady ahead with confidence. This is no spending spree Budget.' He had not changed his priorities; it was simply that his advisers had underestimated the delayed action effect of his earlier measures, and of the head of steam that was now building up in the economy.

Inadvertently Mr Amory gave a sharp upward push to a boom which was already getting under way. As a result, industrial production rose in a year by nearly eleven per cent – a rate far too rapid to be sustained for long.

Orthodox economists and officials have ever since regarded the 1959 Budget as an object lesson in the dangers of trying to go too fast. It was, however, impossible to be sure at the time that the wide margin of slack would be taken up without further government assistance, and after three years of stagnation it was understandable that the Treasury economists should want to take a risk on the side of expansion.

The real error of the 1959 Budget is surely not that it gave away too much, but that it came too late. It is apparent from the chart on page 290 that if it had been introduced the previous year, it would have alleviated or even stopped altogether the 1958 recession and led to a much smoother advance of production. The balance of payments arguments (as distinct from the 'men of Zürich ones') themselves told in favour of an earlier stimulus. As Mr Gaitskell remarked in the Budget day debate: 'A year ago during the middle of the most favourable six months for the balance of payments there was far less danger of expansion involving us in a balance of payments crisis than there is now.' The only reason for dwelling on the point is that the Treasury made the very same error in delaying re-expansion all over again in 1962; and even now the point has still to be grasped by many influential and otherwise sophisticated people in Britain and abroad.

CHAPTER 7

The Great Reappraisal

DURING the period just after the 1959 election events were moving on two different levels. In its attempts to regulate business activity, the Government continued along the old lines, perversely holding down production and employment even when it ought to have been stimulating it, and 'defending the pound' in restrictive and unimaginative ways. The same perverse interaction between officials, Central Bankers and politicians noticed in the previous chapter, continued; and the Treasury management of demand reached a low point in 1961–2, from which one hopes it has now recovered.

But, at a different level, it was a period of great change, in which traditional assumptions were challenged and many new ideas were introduced. As a result, there has already been a sea change in economic attitudes, which will prove either to have smoothed the path of a Labour Government, or prepared the way for a different kind of Tory economics from anything the country knew in the 1950s.

The year in which everything really happened but which no one really remembers, was 1960. On the surface it was an uneventful one. Businessmen were becoming more and more dissatisfied with Government policy, but neither the public nor the Cabinet gave much attention to economics. Mr Amory would make some announcement after Question Time in the quietest possible way, and discussion of it would be chiefly confined to the financial columns.

To see why the events of 1960 proved a traumatic experience for the men who make tomorrow's news, one must first take a look for a moment at the familiar dance of the brake and the accelerator.

In the first half of 1960, the post-election boom seemed

to be going too far; and the economy looked as if it might suffer from genuine overstrain for the first time since 1955–6. Unemployment was nose-diving towards one and a half per cent, unfilled vacancies were rising. The Conservative victory had touched off a spectacular investment boom, imports were soaring; and it soon became apparent from the customs returns that Britain was heading towards a large trade deficit. But the fact was hidden from many wishful thinkers among politicians and in the City by a flood of 'hot' money pouring into London from overseas – a flood which, judging by all past experiences, was bound to go back home before very long.

Ever since the 1959 election, Mr Heathcoat Amory had been worried that the economy was going to become overloaded; and in 1960 he wanted a tougher Budget than either the Prime Minister or even his own official advisers. The Treasury apparently advised him that, whatever the forecasts, it would hardly look seemly to deflate so soon after an election – another instance of the political sense Great George Street tries to develop on behalf of its masters.

1960 was the sort of year – 1964 started out as another – when the experts in National Income arithmetic want to apply a brake (for fear of stopping the vehicle altogether a year or two later), while normally cautious politicians and bankers prefer to leave well alone. This was certainly the line-up in 1960 when even the expansionist National Institute saw the case for a restrictive Budget. In such arguments the outside spectator ought to cheer on the National Income experts, as far as principles are unconcerned. Unfortunately, present techniques of forecasting seem to have a built-in bias towards projecting fast trends too vigorously, and underestimated, in both 1960 and 1964, the extent to which the boom would taper off in the following months. In any case, during the 1960 pre-Budget discussions Mr Heathcoat Amory had to change his Budget plans at a fairly late stage as a result of the opposition he was meeting from the Prime

Minister and other colleagues. The Budget itself was more or less neutral, although it raised profits tax, and contained a warning that the Chancellor 'stood ready to take any further corrective measures that may be called for in the near future in the monetary field'. The Bank of England proved very troublesome here, and put up a last-ditch emotional stand in favour of 'voluntary cooperation' with the joint stock banks, but eventually on 28 April had to restrict their credit forcibly by means of Special Deposits. The Chancellor himself imposed hire-purchase restrictions on cars and durables (twenty per cent down payment and two years to repay). Sir Frank Lee, who had become Joint Permanent Secretary to the Treasury in succession to Sir Roger Makins on 1 January 1960, after seven years at the Board of Trade, had publicly declared his opposition to hire-purchase restrictions as an economic weapon in evidence to the Radcliffe Committee. But he was alone in the Treasury on the issue, and in the prevailing political climate there was no other weapon to hand.

The possibility of a 'guiding light' for incomes was under discussion in the Treasury throughout Mr Amory's tenure; this was an idea which Sir Robert Hall had always strongly supported. Hall's opponents inside the Treasury pinned their hopes on the two and a half years or so of relative price stability which the country enjoyed during Mr Amory's tenure of the Exchequer, and which they wrongly thought might restrain wage increases.

It is not generally known that when Mr Heathcoat Amory resigned in late July 1960, a year before the Pay Pause, he gave the Prime Minister a very clear hint of trouble ahead when he came to say farewell. He warned that if he had been going to stay on – as Macmillan very much wanted him to – he would have insisted either on running the economy at a higher level of unemployment or, preferably, on the Government accepting an incomes policy. But another year was to elapse before anyone took any notice.

The Traumas of 1960

The great period of economic rethinking began before Mr
Amory left the Exchequer – unlike Mr Thorneycroft,
voluntarily and on genuine personal grounds. Following
the credit restrictions he imposed in April, production
stopped rising but, to the great disappointment of the
Treasury, there were few compensating benefits in other
directions. This simple episode had a traumatic effect on
Treasury thinking. As the months went by, it stimulated
three main lines of reflection, which were to be the source
of all that followed:

1. After all the investment of the past few years 'either
production should have increased or employment de-
creased', as Sir Robert Hall put it in an article in the
Economist after he retired.* In the event the curbs on demand
stopped production from rising, but did not cause any
unemployment or even stop the increase in the labour force.†
Hence the interest in a payroll tax to discourage the
wasteful use of labour.

2. The restrictions on home demand failed to boost exports,
even though world trade was for most of the time buoyant.
This fact, together with Point No. 1, made many Treasury
officials extremely critical of the efficiency and skill with
which industry was run. It was about this time (around the
end of 1960) that the first papers were written on the
conditions of long-term growth and that interest blossomed
in French planning methods, and in the Common Market.

* A possible explanation of this paradox has since been provided by
W. A. H. Godley, of the Treasury's Economic Section. Very roughly, in
both recessions and booms, the movement of employment lags behind
production. At the top of the boom the labour force is normally not yet
fully adjusted to the level of production; so employment may go on
expanding for some months after output has stopped rising. Conversely
employment can go on falling even after the bottom of a slump has been
reached.

See Long Term Growth and Short Term Policy; National Institute,
Economic Review, August 1964.

† 'Britain's Economic Policy', the *Economist*, 16 and 23 September 1961.

3. Soon after the Government reimposed hire-purchase controls the bottom fell out of the American car market and the consumer durable cycle turned downwards at home. Inadvertently the Chancellor had singled out for attack two industries that were already in trouble by the time his measures took effect. For these industries official action turned out to be violently destabilizing.

This was the event which turned the business community violently against 'stop-go' and made it look with a less jaundiced eye on national planning. Within the Treasury it stimulated a search for general 'regulators' that did not discriminate against one or two particular trades and which could be introduced between Budgets. It also aroused interest in a whole family of theories – the best known of which was worked out by Professor Paish – for securing steadier growth with the aid of a small and fairly constant margin of unused capacity and a slightly less ambitious definition of full employment.*

The two key figures of the Great Rethinking were Sir Frank Lee and Mr Selwyn Lloyd, who was Chancellor for almost two years after the retirement of Mr Amory.

Sir Frank Lee was mentioned in an earlier chapter as the first post-war Permanent Secretary to be fully at home in issues of economic policy. He had strong views on policy and, unlike more conventional officials, did not bother to hide them. But his own conduct was imbued with a fiery insistence on sticking to the practical and the politically possible, and woe betide anyone else who did not do so.

He understood both businessmen and bureaucrats too well to be starry-eyed about either, and both at the Board of Trade and at the Treasury, he saw more competition (he was the driving force behind the Restrictive Practices Act), rather than more planning, as the cure for British industry. The conversion of the Government to 'Conservative planning' was certainly not his work. He told the

* These doctrines are discussed in more detail in the Appendix to Chapter 9.

Radcliffe Committee, 'If I believed that you could get an overall investment plan operated by people of undoubted vision and wisdom I would agree with that concept.' Because he was sceptical whether such a plan could be achieved, he preferred a different approach.*

In the arguments between the financial expansionists and the restrainers, Lee was most often to be found on the side of the restrainers. 'I have always felt,' he told the Radcliffe Committee, 'that if the economy could be made only marginally disinflationary that would have quite an impressive effect on business psychology .. in such matters as concern for costs, attitudes towards wage claims, general willingness to fight wage claims, or negotiate longer periods for wage claims.' Lee wanted to tackle the wage-price spiral by dampening down demand and he was not enamoured of the arguments for an incomes policy when he arrived at the Treasury.

Lee had more achievements to his credit than most of his predecessors put together. As one ex-Whitehall knight privately remarked, 'Anyone who could persuade the Conservatives to become a low-tariff party must be counted a great man.' His main mistakes arose from his bias towards deflation.† He did not in practice sufficiently distinguish between making an expanding market more competitive by

* *Minutes of Evidence to Radcliffe Committee*, H.M.S.O., 1960.

† A policy of deflation means one of cutting down spending, either private spending, or Government spending, or both. For some people the word 'deflation' conjures up a shortage of spending on the pre-war scale, when unemployment varied between two and three million, and for this reason its use sometimes gives rise to resentment. I suppose it is still necessary to mention that hardly any of the people named as deflationists in this book would like to see this kind of unemployment recur. Any small increase in unemployment resulting from their policies would, they hope, be mainly people changing jobs, and is not intended to lead to personal hardship. Moreover, 'deflationists' in this sense are often in the forefront of the campaign for generous treatment for those temporarily out of work. But as the only way to avoid ambiguity in the text is to use the hideous words disinflation and disinflationist, I hope this footnote will serve as an olive branch. The argument against the present-day deflationists is not that they are callous towards unemployment but that they unnecessarily slow down growth. See Chapters 5 and 9.

cutting tariffs or curbing monopolies, and between restricting the growth of the market itself. Financial squeezes have an adverse effect on the whole climate towards risk-taking, and tend to hold back the go-ahead firm in the growth industries. Tariff cuts, on the other hand, tend to dislodge the inefficient plodders and provide opportunities in a growing market for dynamic low-cost enterprises.

The Results of Selwyn Lloyd

But if Sir Frank Lee was an unusually controversial Permanent Secretary, his political master, Mr Selwyn Lloyd, was an even more controversial Chancellor. It is particularly important to judge Lloyd by what he did rather than the way he said things. The view that he failed because he could not 'put his policies across' degrades the post of the Chancellor into that of a glorified Public Relations Officer.

Something has already been said about Mr Lloyd in the last chapter (p. 185). His faults were obvious enough. He did not have a large enough grasp to distinguish between big issues and minor points of detail, and he seemed to think about economic policy without the aid of any intellectual framework. (In this respect Mr Amory was much better.) Lloyd was also amazingly sensitive to criticism, and had a curious habit of drawing back his head in a startled manner, often when no offence was intended. Yet his sensitivity was combined with a sense of humour about himself.

But although Lloyd was intellectually dependent on his Treasury advisers, he was also somewhat suspicious of them. He sometimes gave them the impression that he did not quite grasp the full implications of what they were asking him to say, but suspected that he would not like them if he did. Lloyd had many of both the virtues and the faults of the typical Tory Back-bencher. Yet for all his defects, his period at the Exchequer was the most eventful since Cripps.

Was he a good Chancellor? On the one hand his management of the brake and the accelerator at home, and his handling of the sterling problem were pretty lamentable. On the other hand, he did far more than any other Chancellor of his Party to improve the long-term environment in which the day-to-day management takes place; and the reforms which he inaugurated will outlive his mistakes of execution. As one Whitehall man once pointed out to me, a subtler person would have seen more difficulties and snags and not accomplished as much, so curious are the workings of human chemistry.

It is worth listing a few of the reforms inaugurated during his short reign:

1. The setting up of the National Economic Development Council, which made a new kind of long-term 'planning' respectable for the private sector.
2. Long-term forward looks for the Government's own spending plans along Plowden lines.
3. Acceptance by the Government – and later by the country – of at least the *idea* of an incomes policy.
4. The raising of the surtax starting point on earned income from £2,000 to £5,000.
5. The introduction of economic regulators giving the Chancellor power to vary tax between Budgets.
6. The reform of the archaic Budget Accounts.
7. A new policy towards the nationalized industries, which has completely transformed their morale, performance, and public standing.

The regulators were due, in fact, largely to the persistence of Sir Frank Lee, and the White Paper on nationalized industries was thought out almost entirely by officials. But Lloyd does deserve the political credit for introducing both. The NEDC, moreover, is to a large extent Lloyd's own personal achievement; and to the surprise of some of his officials, Lloyd himself was also keenly interested in the reform of the Budget Accounts.

He was not responsible for the Plowden Committee which was appointed by his predecessor, Mr Heathcoat Amory. But Lloyd himself wanted to go down in history as the

Chancellor who reduced the burden of taxation. He was told by a senior official that the way to do this was to make quite sure that public expenditure, defined in the questionable way discussed in Chapter 3, Appendix II, did not exceed forty-two and a half per cent of the national product. Lloyd did not succeed in his ambition; but in his attempts he gave an impetus to the long-term planning of Government expenditure, which remains valuable even though neither political party now holds out any hope of any big alleviation in the tax burden.

The raising of the surtax starting point from its 1920 level of £2,000 to £5,000 was privately welcomed by almost everyone who knew anything about taxation, irrespective of political party. Not only did the old starting point dampen incentives, but so far from promoting equality it helped to ossify the class system. For the high surtax rates did not affect people of established wealth, or those becoming rich by capital gains, but erected barriers against young executives or professional men dependent on their own earnings.

The timing and tactics of the surtax concessions were, as readers will be reminded, a masterpiece of political ineptitude. But now that all the water has flown under the bridge, the fact remains that Mr Lloyd, unlike any of his predecessors, had the courage to make them.

The Treasury and the Common Market

Mr Selwyn Lloyd was, of course, at the Exchequer at the time of Britain's application to join the Common Market, which many people thought was a sudden response to the 1961 sterling crisis. This was a very common view on the continent, but it was completely wrong. In the first place, the principal motive of Mr Macmillan, who was personally responsible for the new European policy, was political rather than economic. Secondly, the basic rethinking of British foreign policy towards Europe was done when 'hot' money was still pouring into London and when most politicians felt no sense of economic emergency.

In the course of 1959–60, there had been a reappraisal by the Foreign Office of British policy towards Europe; and by the time Mr Macmillan came to make his decision quite a few top officials in various ministries were pleased with the way it went. But the decision was very much a personal one of Macmillan's own. There was no official *éminence grise* behind the scenes.

Mr Macmillan seems to have made up his mind around Christmas 1960 after several months contemplation. The Summit failure of May 1960 after the unfortunate U2 incident depressed the Prime Minister deeply and made him feel conscious of the need for a new role for Britain. Macmillan feared that a strong and growing continental bloc would carry more guns in Washington under a post-Eisenhower Administration than an isolated Britain. The best way to preserve Britain's influence with the U.S. might be as leader of a united Europe, although this could never be said aloud. Another factor was the changing character of the Commonwealth, which was symbolized by South Africa's withdrawal in 1961, but which was obvious long before.*

By the time he came to the Treasury, Sir Frank Lee was a convinced European. He was one of those who thought that the Common Market would give British industry a much-needed competitive impetus. But this was a personal view. The overseas coordination unit, which tries to hammer out a common policy towards Europe among all Government Departments had, as already mentioned, at the time practically a separate identity of its own distinct from the rest of the Treasury. It was on its behalf, rather than as a Treasury spokesman, that Lee took the lead, with all the zeal of a convert, in preparing Common Market briefs for the Prime Minister and Cabinet Committee. The Chancellor of the Exchequer was not during this period the minister responsible for Common Market questions.

* A detailed account of how the British Government came to make up its mind and why the bid failed can be found in *The General Says No* by Nora Beloff.

The Treasury proper was sceptical of the Common Market venture, although there were, of course, individual exceptions who were keen. The Overseas Finance Division was opposed to it partly because it did not like the idea of a common monetary policy leading to a pooling of sovereignty.* In addition it was attached to the sterling area, which could hardly emerge unscathed from an economic fusion with Europe. Its idealism took the form of support for developing the poorer parts of the Commonwealth rather than any enthusiasm for the Six.

Many academic economists, especially in Cambridge and Oxford, thought that the arguments both for and against entry were overblown. Mr Gaitskell who was, of course, an economist himself, thought the arguments were about fifty-fifty. This was also the predominant advice that ministers received from the Treasury's Economic Section during the heartsearchings of 1960 (although judging by his writings after he left the Treasury, Sir Robert Hall must have become more of a European in the following year).

Basically, however, the European negotiations were begun for political reasons by Macmillan and terminated for political reasons by General de Gaulle. The real reason for the failure was that Macmillan tried to graft the Common Market on to existing foreign and defence policies – policies which gave priority to a profoundly desired 'special relationship' with America which often embarrassed the Kennedy administration. If Britain had joined these would certainly have changed in due course, but in the meantime the General had a better justification for keeping this country out than is usually admitted (although not for deliberately misleading the whole of Europe). Again and again and again since 1945, British Governments have missed the European bus, waiting for public opinion to be ready. By the time 'public opinion' was ready to get on at one stop, the bus was already two or three stops ahead.

* See the quotation from an earlier Head of the Overseas Finance Division, Sir Leslie Rowan, on p. 200.

The Brighton Revolution

A few days before Mr Macmillan announced Britain's application to join the Common Market, Mr Selwyn Lloyd announced that he was going to set up new machinery for national planning. It so happened, moreover, that the spiritual father of the European Common Market, M. Jean Monnet, had also been the first head of the French Planning Commission immediately after the war. Later M. Monnet became chairman of the unofficial but influential Action Committee for a United States of Europe, and by 1960 he had become an active protagonist of British membership of the Common Market.

During 1960 and 1961 he was telling his many British contacts in politics, administration, and industry, that if planning was to survive in the Common Market it would have to be on a supra-national basis. He hoped Britain would throw in its weight as a pro-planning country in an enlarged Common Market, and that Britain and France together would tilt the balance against the *laissez-faire* Germans. This was certainly one of the reasons, apart from propagandist zeal, why the French Commissariat Général du Plan was so helpful during this period in arranging visits and conferences for British economists and officials to study French planning methods.

But despite these interesting connexions, the move towards planning and the move towards Europe were on the British side completely separated strands of policy, and indeed, largely the work of different people. It was mainly among some journalists that equal enthusiasm could be found for both.

'Planning' of the kind Mr Selwyn Lloyd introduced to Britain involves three basic ingredients. Different people would put them in different orders of importance:

1. A national growth target stretching over a period of several years, the possible implications of which are worked out in some detail for a large number of different industries.

2. A Council where ministers, business leaders, and trade unionists can consult each other regularly on current problems, including incomes policy, and try to hammer out solutions. This is to be supplemented by lower tier groups for particular industries.

3. An 'office' separate from the Treasury to work out forecasts and targets, and suggest ideas for removing obstacles to growth.

When Mr Selwyn Lloyd entered the Treasury, he already thought that long-term planning of Government expenditure was, like the other things he believed in, 'common sense'. He was converted to the belief that planning had something to offer for the private sector as well by a conference of the Federation of British Industries, held in Brighton at the end of November, 1960, to consider 'The Next Five Years'. At this time he had not even seen any of the Treasury's own ruminations on the subject.

The conversion of the Federation of British Industries to the idea of planning is a remarkable story. It was almost entirely the work of a tiny intellectual minority among British businessmen. Like so many other things in British life, it began with a dining club. This was started early in 1960 by a mixed group of industrialists and economists to discuss various topics, including growth. The leading spirit was Mr Hugh Weeks, the chairman of the F.B.I.'s Economic Policy Committee, whose mild manner conceals a good many rumbling heresies. Weeks was trained as an economist and had been both a temporary Civil Servant and director of several companies. But for some years he had given most of his working time to the Industrial and Commercial Finance Corporation, a joint City organization for financing small firms. He has acquired in the course of his work a way of talking about national business problems that is equally comprehensible to industrialists, officials, and economists.

The dining group was a purely private one, deliberately quite separate from the F.B.I.'s Economic Committee. Everyone who was invited in fact wanted to come, so that attendance was rather larger than the organizers had bargained on obtaining. League tables, contrasting Britain's economic performance with other countries had just come into vogue (it was, I believe, Mr Harold Wilson who first coined the metaphor). The industrialists and economists, who met round the dining table, were conscious that Britain's post-war economic record took a lot of explaining away. It was around this time too that reports that the French had a Plan first were washed ashore on these isles.* As a result of French experience a few British businessmen were beginning to realize the difference between the setting of targets and 'thou shalt not' controls of the post-war type.

The meetings of the dinner group were not sparked off, as some cynics supposed, by Mr Amory's reimposition of hire-purchase controls. Indeed, when their activities first started the economy was still in a period of 'go', which they rightly suspected would not last. What the hire-purchase controls, which hit cars and durables so severely, did do was to win them supporters among a wider circle of businessmen who would not normally have bothered about anything as long-haired as 'indicative planning'.

The Brighton Conference was held a good many months after the dining club had begun its meetings. It was attended by 121 leading businessmen and thirty-one guests, including the heads of Government Departments and of the nationalized industries, and a few economists. The conference divided into five groups, and it was not altogether a coincidence that most members of the dining group found themselves together in group III which discussed 'Economic Growth in Britain'. The group was reinforced by Mr Reay Geddes, the tall, personable managing director of Dunlops, who had not been a member of the dining club but who had himself heralded the new thinking among industrialists

* It was only after the devaluation and other reforms of December 1958 that France's neighbours began to realize that she, just as Germany, had had an economic miracle.

in a speech the previous February, which foreshadowed NEDC in a remarkable way.

In the Chair in group III was the veteran white-haired managing director of Guinness, Sir Hugh Beaver, himself a bit of an industrial radical. The group's report, presented by Sir Hugh at the end of the conference, argued that there was 'room for a more conscious attempt to assess plans and demands in particular industries for five or even ten years ahead', as already happened in the case of steel. Government and industry might also, the report suggested, see 'whether it would be possible to agree on an assessment of expectations and intentions which should be before the country for the next five years'. The report vigorously attacked rapid switches of Government policy for their effects on confidence and particularly on investment plans.

Most remarkable of all, Sir Hugh went out of his way to express his disagreement with the priorities reiterated at the opening of the conference by the ex-Chancellor, Viscount Amory, who had expounded official doctrine with his usual charm and lack of evasion. In deliberate contrast to the ex-Chancellor Sir Hugh stressed that the achievement of a faster rate of growth might be the best way of achieving stable prices, and a sound balance of payments, and not the other way round.

This report, by one group out of the five into which the conference was split, was by no means F.B.I. policy at the time. But somehow, without any specific resolution at any time, the doctrine of group III emerged as F.B.I. policy. To use language normally to be distrusted, a sort of general will arose in the early 1960s towards merging sectional interest into a wider national purpose.

Soon after the F.B.I. Conference, Mr Selwyn Lloyd mentioned the planning idea to Mr Macmillan. The Prime Minister, who was well known since the 1930s for his belief in planning, welcomed the idea with alacrity. He may even have suggested something like it himself to Lloyd earlier on, in one of the many *tête-à-tête* conversations they used to have together in those days. But there is no sign that Macmillan ever tried to initiate anything himself on these lines before his Chancellor took up the idea, and it is Lloyd who must be given the credit for it.

During the course of 1960, some of the more active minds in the Treasury had, quite independently from the F.B.I., become interested in new ideas for adding some zip to British industry. A very popular conclusion from the disappointments of 1960 was 'how little the Government can do' and that everything depended on a change of habit and outlook on the part of both management and trade unions. The tendency for the Treasury to blame industry for British economic shortcomings, and for industry to blame the Treasury, is regrettably still alive.

Officials who thought in this way were looking above all for an effective channel of communication with both sides of industry, and were often just as sceptical about 'planning' itself as Sir Frank Lee. Too many of them simply jumped at the idea of a so-called 'planning' body as a possible way of involving the unions in an incomes policy. During the course of the negotiations with the T.U.C. the Treasury in fact played this point down. It was confident that any impartial investigation of the obstacles to growth would bring the question on to the agenda without any forcing. Its confidence was justified, partly as a result of NEDC's own inquiries, and partly because Mr Lloyd's successor, Mr Maudling, insisted again and again that incomes policy was central to the whole exercise.

There were it is true, a very small number of officials who thought that it was worth putting together the forecasts and plans on which individual industries were already working to see if they fitted together. At the very least, they thought this might throw up problems and suggest methods of tackling them. In the course of 1960, some Treasury officials made unpublicized visits to Paris to study at first hand what the French were doing. On the whole the officials most interested in studying French planning were neither the economists nor the mandarin types, but a handful of career Civil Servants who happened to be concerned with – and also interested in – economic questions.

There had been in existence since the days of Sir Stafford Cripps a small so-called Planning Board, on which a few Treasury officials and business and trade-union leaders discussed economic subjects once a month, with very little follow through. After the F.B.I. Conference, the Planning Board discussed 'conditions favourable to growth' at four of its meetings in the first few months of 1961. A paper on the motor industry and another very good one on chemicals helped to liven up the proceedings of the Board (which was, of course, afterwards dissolved when NEDC was established).

At these Planning Board meetings, one well-known official, speaking for a large section of Treasury opinion, strongly opposed the creation of an independent office. He thought that the best way to embark on long-term studies was to expand the Economic Planning Board and enlarge its staff – a recipe which, in the prevailing climate of opinion, would have made sure that no one in industry took the slightest notice of what happened.

Mr Lloyd ran into a great deal of opposition to the NEDC concept from other ministers. Most of the Cabinet was, in fact, opposed to him on this issue. Among Lloyd's few supporters were Lord Hailsham (now Mr Quintin Hogg) and Mr Hare, the Minister of Labour (now Lord Blakenham). Some ministers said that contacts already took place with industry through existing channels, and Mr Lloyd should work through these. Another argument was that NEDC might duplicate the work done by Government Departments and even cut across the responsibilities of the Cabinet. The feature which gave rise to as much opposition in the Cabinet as in the Treasury was the independent Office.

On this point Mr Lloyd rightly dug in his heels. He thought, as he wrote later,* that an independent body was

* 'NEDDY and Parliament', *Crossbow*, October–December 1963.

much more likely to be successful in bringing together the view of people inside and outside Government. An independent office, he maintained, would give its studies a value and authority which they would not have were they just another Government Department. Last, but not least, Mr Lloyd is believed to have wanted another source of advice to which he could turn as an alternative to the Treasury. The constitution of NEDC cannot be understood in isolation from the mood of profound distrust which had gathered round the Treasury by the time of the 1961 sterling crisis. From the day it was set up the NEDC office consciously tried to establish a different order of priorities from Whitehall. Members of the Office in their off-guard moments jocularly refer to the Treasury as 'the other side'.

One of the main opponents of the NEDC concept at the time was Mr Reginald Maudling, then President of the Board of Trade. He was, it should be said, a great advocate of more and better coordinated industrial forecasting. He regarded the investment and stock cycles as the greatest defect of the capitalist system and welcomed anything that would lessen them. On the other hand he could see little point in an independent office distinct from the Whitehall machine, and was suspicious that too many get-togethers by industrialists would lead to market sharing agreements and other restrictive practices.

If matters had been left to the slow machinery of Cabinet and Civil Service Committees, NEDC might have been buried beneath delicately balanced memoranda. There was still no Cabinet agreement on the subject until the sterling crisis forced the issue. When Mr Lloyd introduced his 'Little Budget' on 25 July 1961, something had to be said in desperation to show that the Government had some long-term ideas apart from 'stop-go'. A fortnight later Mr Macmillan allowed Mr Lloyd to invite both sides of industry to join a national planning council, on the grounds that his statement of 25 July had in practice committed the Government. Cabinet rumblings continued for a long time afterwards, but to little effect.

It took several more months of delicate negotiations before the Council and Office were finally established. From the outset Lloyd had intended to make Sir Robert Shone, the former head of the Steel Board, whom he had known for years, Director General, and he was appointed on 18 December. It was not until 24 January 1962 that the T.U.C. agreed to serve. During these months of delay, it would have been very tempting for Mr Lloyd to have gone ahead without the unions, as many commentators advised him to do. Now that NEDC has become one of the few bodies involving the Government which the T.U.C. likes and trusts, one can see how wrong this advice would have been.

In the end the real weakness on the Council was on the employers' side. The six industrialists chosen were far above average in quality, but because of the division then prevailing between the three employers' organizations, they were chosen simply as individuals and had no power to commit anyone else.

Without Sir Frank Lee, NEDC would have remained a paper dream. He was ill in Paris during the July crisis; when he came back to London and found that the planning 'decision' had been taken, he spared no effort to make it work, whatever he might personally have thought about 'planning'. Lee was fully behind Lloyd's insistence, against the advice of many senior Treasury officials, that the NEDC office must be distinct from the Treasury if the unions were to have confidence in its independence.

The New Look for State Industries

Another rather different product of the economic rethinking of 1960 was the New Look in the nationalized industries.

A great many of the changes since 1960 have of course

been due to developments in the nationalized industries themselves; all the same, the Treasury has never received the praise due to it for its undoubted share in this revolution. Of course a minister like Mr Marples must be given the credit for finding Dr Beeching and no one would suppose that the Treasury suggested his £25,000 salary. But the prelude to the new personalities and policies was a piece of Whitehall rethinking in which the Treasury took the lead. This saw the light of day in July 1961 in a White Paper whose very title *The Financial and Economic Obligations of the Nationalized Industries* ensured that it was buried away on the inside pages of the few serious newspapers that bothered to report it at all.

The basic principle of the White Paper is that State industries are not a form of social service, but must earn a return on their assets to justify their existence. This is what has led to the closing down of high-costs pits and uneconomic rail services. A few of the shortcomings of the White Paper policy have already been discussed.* But compared with what went on before it was an immense change for the better. In 1960 most state concerns were demoralized and uncertain of where they were supposed to be going, like animals in a maze. The most important thing was to give them a visible goal: the rest could come later.

The new policy was achieved in spite of, rather than because of, the committee of ministers which asked for the study to be made. The ministers were chiefly interested in organizational forms. Politicians chronically pay too much attention to the question of who should take decisions ('the chaps'); and to whom they should report, rather than the criteria on which decisions should be based. For a long time many Conservative M.P.s had an obsession with geographical decentralization as a short cut to commercial principles, a misleading doctrine, as Dr Beeching has shown. But ministers and M.P.s found it easier to talk of geography and lines of command than of the pricing

* See Chapter 3, Appendix III.

policies and rates of return which were implied by the free enterprise principles in which they professed to believe. Before 1960 most of the nationalized industries had been reorganized over and over again; and it was the Treasury that managed to give the discussion a constructive and less organizational twist.

The Search for Regulators

Although the new thinking on economic planning and the nationalized industries showed the need for longer horizons, there was also a pressing need for better short-term weapons. The last six months of 1960 were accordingly taken up with the search for fairer ways of regulating consumer spending between Budgets than the hated hire-purchase restrictions.

The subject is inevitably a little more complicated than some of the other topics treated so far in this chapter, but is nevertheless worth unravelling. Good regulators are important for steady growth and – of more direct interest to the ordinary tax-payer – some of the tax suggestions that failed to make the grade in 1960 may well turn up again in one form or another.

The characteristics of a tax which is to be moved up and down as an economic regulator were simply stated at the F.B.I. Brighton Conference by one of the groups (*not* group III) of which Sir Frank Lee happened to be a member. Such a tax should be, according to the group, speedy in its effects; it should cut right across the board; it should cause the minimum disruption to business plans and, if possible, should attack or at least 'be inimical to' the rigidities which hamper change in British economic life.

One of the most interesting suggestions was for a 'PAYE regulator'.* The idea was that income tax rates might be

* Most of the ideas for economic regulators in the air at that time were discussed by Mr J. C. R. Dow in the *Westminster Bank Review*, August 1960.

varied part of the way through the year if economic conditions changed. One simple method, which would not required fresh tax tables, would be a straight percentage change in everyone's tax bill from the date at which the regulator is applied. But the suggestion never got as far as a definite proposal. The Inland Revenue predictably objected on the grounds of administration and equity, and politicians disliked the idea, ostensibly because income tax changes by Order in Council would detract too much from the authority of Parliament.

Another idea, and one on which Sir Frank Lee had always been keen, was a uniform sales tax in place of purchase tax, over a wide range of consumer spending, which could be varied up or down by a point or two as the economic situation changed. This idea was defeated partly by the Customs and Excise, who made great play of the difficulties of taxing services, and partly because of the embarrassments of taxing food. A Value Added Tax (VAT) was also considered as a possible substitute for a sales tax. This would have been a tax on business turn-over minus purchases from other firms. This was fiercely resisted by the Customs and Excise on the grounds that it would have meant several hundred thousand points of collection.

Finding its bright ideas repulsed, the Treasury understandably asked the Customs and Excise for its own suggestions for regulating consumer spending, and, surprising though it may seem, the Customs produced a device within a very few weeks. This was accepted the first time round with very little argument and was included in the 1961 Budget. It has since become known as the 'Regulator' or (inaccurately) as the Purchase Tax Regulator. It is simply a power that the Treasury renews every year to vary all consumer taxes – drink and tobacco duties as well as purchase tax – by up to ten per cent in between budgets. The ten per cent does not, as is often supposed, refer to the taxes themselves, but is a percentage of the previous rates – for example, a fifty per cent purchase tax is raised by five per cent to fifty-five per cent when the Regulator is brought into full operation.

Whenever the Regulator is raised it puts up prices and thus reduces the amount of goods bought. This might seem a clumsy way of fighting inflation which even the textbooks define as rising prices; and the same disadvantage would apply to a sales tax and similar weapons. It might therefore be supposed that politicians would be happy to use the regulator in a downward direction, when they might gain popularity from reducing prices, and reluctant to use it in an upward direction. But so great is the unconscious masochism of English public life that the opposite has so far proved to be the case.

Another concept very much in vogue in the Great Rethinking of 1960, and of which we have certainly not heard the last, was the payroll tax. Two different ideas, with different histories, were involved here, although this was not sufficiently appreciated at the time. One was a 'surcharge' on payrolls as a temporary economic regulator to stimulate or restrain private spending. The other was for a payroll tax as a permanent part of the tax system, which would not add to the tax burden, but replace other imposts.

The latter idea arose from a study of the structural weaknesses of the British economy during the Great Rethinking of 1960. Sir Robert Hall's disappointment, expressed in his *Economist* article, that the 1960–1 investment boom had had so little effect on productivity, has already been mentioned. In the short run, he attributed it to labour hoarding. But he also diagnosed deeper defects. A great deal of new investment, he suggested, had been of the wrong kind. Too much had taken the form of simple additions to productive capacity and too little took the form of modernization or new processes. As a result there was not enough labour to man the new plant and equipment; and in a time of boom, overfull employment of labour was reached (apart from depressed regions) when there was still a great deal of unutilized industrial capacity. Sir Robert concluded that labour hoarding should be discouraged and investment given a more labour-saving twist.* In other words, instead of putting up more and more factories, offices, and shops of an existing kind, there should be more concentration on automation and other techniques which cut down labour requirements. Hall's warning was as valid in 1964 as it was when he wrote the article.

The supporters of a permanent payroll tax hoped it would stimulate labour-saving investment. It was pointed out that in other European countries, especially France, a far higher proportion of the cost of the social services fell as a charge on employers' payloads. The more thorough-going supporters of the payroll tax, such as Sir Robert Shone, saw it as a reform of company taxation.†

The idea of a permanent payroll tax was, in fact, put up by Treasury economists. It was much less radical than Shone's. It was simply to impose a payroll tax in exchange for a reduction in purchase tax and other indirect taxes, and the main incentive to labour-saving was expected to be a psychological one. But it was rejected by ministers on the grounds that it was 'a tax on employment' which – in a full employment economy – was what it was intended to be.

The other idea of using payroll tax variations as a way of regulating the business cycle has a long history of its own. As long ago as 1944 the wartime Coalition Government's White Paper on employment policy contained a scheme for varying both employers' and employees' National Insurance contributions, to increase purchasing power in a slump and reduce it in a boom. The variation in the *employees'* contributions in such a scheme would be most effective in both directions. If anti-inflationary action were desired, workers'

* I have paraphrased a long argument here. The *Economist*, 16 and 23 September 1961.

† The arguments against a value-added tax instead of profits tax put forward recently by the Richardson Committee (H.M.S.O. 1964), are also relevant to the payroll tax proposal (unless perhaps it is re-drafted as a highly selective regional measure).

spending power would be immediately reduced and in a way that did not put up prices. The increase in *employers'* contributions on the other hand would take a long time to affect consumer spending, and this would only happen to the extent industrialists passed on the higher contributions in the form of higher prices.

During the search for regulators in 1960, the Treasury was asked by Lee to take another look at the 1944 idea, which the National Insurance authorities had insisted was impracticable. The result of its researches was the 'Second Regulator' which gave the Treasury power to impose a surcharge of up to 4s. per week on employers' National Insurance contributions. As a regulator it had all the wrong qualities. It was very slow acting. There would be delays of nearly three months before the surcharge could be introduced, and the choice of the employers' contribution showed that the whole scheme had either been misunderstood or distorted to make it politically acceptable – probably a bit of both. In any case, the only way it could work would be through pushing up industrial costs, including export costs.

The Second Regulator had only one strong supporter among senior officials; the rest were either strongly opposed or at best lukewarm. Yet to everyone's astonishment, Mr Selwyn Lloyd accepted the idea, and asked for the necessary powers in his 1961 Budget Speech. The main argument in its favour that appealed to the ministers was that two regulators were better than one. The hope of its official supporters was that if it had a trial run as a regulator, it might later become more acceptable as a permanent tax.

Just how misguided their hopes were became clear within a matter of hours. The very, very slight discrimination it introduced against firms which were heavy employees of labour in relation to their output was enough to set off a howl of protest from industry. An embarrassed F.B.I. was deluged by telephone calls and telegrams and had to back-pedal very quickly on its earlier sympathy for the idea. Once again the lesson was learnt that those who lose from any change in industrial taxation always make far more noise than those who gain; equity is always judged in terms of the *status quo*. Mr Selwyn Lloyd himself lost faith in the Second Regulator within a few days of his announcing it; and the concept of a permanent payroll tax was retarded rather than enhanced by the attempt to combine two different ideas.

Great George Street Panics

All the new thinking about Britain's industrial structure and on economic regulators was taking place against a gathering sterling crisis, which was itself handled by the worst of the old school methods.

The story, like everything else in this chapter, really started in 1960 when Britain had the worst balance of payments deficit for a whole decade. There was something to be said for softening the blow by attracting some foreign footloose funds to London by high interest rates. But in 1960 so much hot money was attracted to London that the gap was filled to overflowing and the reserves rose substantially. On a modest estimate, some £500m. of 'hot money' was attracted into London during 1960* – almost exactly the amount that went out again in the sterling crisis of the following year. Can there be any doubts that we would have been much better off if the bulk of this money had never arrived and never left? It is a sad, but well-established paradox of international finance that an inflow of funds does much less good than an outflow of the same

* The current account deficit in 1960 was £258m. (it looked even worse in the April 1961 balance of payments White Paper). Taking capital payments into account, the overall payments deficit came to the gigantic figure of £445m. Faced with a gap of this kind, one might expect to have seen a big fall in reserves; instead they rose by £177m., largely due to an inflow of 'hot' money. The inflow was swollen by the distrust of the U.S. dollar, in front of the Presidential elections, and by the barriers that Germany and Switzerland put up against the entry of short-term funds into their own money markets.

amount does harm – because bankers and speculators will always project the outflow to the point where a country's reserves are completely exhausted.

The Treasury and Bank of England were both involved in this dangerous game. Neither deliberately wanted to attract so much 'hot money'. Bank Rate was raised from four per cent to five per cent in January and to six per cent in June, to reduce demand at home. But the British authorities were seriously at fault in not realizing soon enough that they were playing with fire; and the issue of a new Government stock, tax free to foreigners, aggravated the situation. Bank Rate did go down by half a per cent in October and again in December, but by then it was far too late to repair the damage. The cavalier attitude towards the risks involved was epitomized by Mr Cameron Cobbold (now Lord Cobbold) the Governor of the Bank of England, at the Lord Mayor's Banquet in 1960 when he said: 'I see no cause to cheer when these short-term money movements cause our reserves to rise; nor shall I see any cause to complain if our reserves fall because they go the other way. This is what reserves are for. And a good deal of what now looks like short-term money may in fact turn out to be more permanent investment.' Famous last words, in no way redeemed by the preparatory escape clause: 'Provided that movements do not get too big and that there is no underlying disequilibrium.' The movements were too big and there was an underlying disequilibrium.

The signal that reversed the hot money flow was the five per cent upward revaluation of the German mark, announced on 5 March 1961. Many people thought that this was only a first stage and that sterling would be devalued as part of a general realignment of currencies. Rumours of this kind were responsible for a big run on the British reserves which began as soon as the German revaluation was announced. The outflow was hidden for a while by the Basle arrangements under which the Continental Central Banks stockpiled over £300m. of sterling. Towards the end of June the Central Banks made it clear that they had stock-piled enough and in July came Mr Selwyn Lloyd's crisis measures.

The 1961 crisis was practically a repeat performance of 1957. On both occasions the hot money exodus was touched off by speculation in favour of the mark. On both occasions, by the time the Chancellor acted, the underlying balance of payments was satisfactory and rapidly improving – a fact which was apparent at the time from the trade figures. And on both occasions, the economy was in any case coming off the boil and the Chancellor simply made sure that an easing of business activity turned into a recession.*

There was just one difference between 1957 and 1961 of which the public was unaware. Whereas in 1957 it was the Treasury ministers who panicked, in 1961 it was the officials who lost their nerve and put pressure on Mr Selwyn Lloyd. Part of the explanation may be that the Treasury was in the process of changing Economic Advisers. Mr Cairncross arrived only in June 1961 and could not possibly have acquired enough power in the following few weeks to stop the deflationary package even if he had wished to. Then again, the chance of securing a margin of excess capacity, in accordance with the prevailing intellectual fashion, was too tempting for some Treasury officials to

* The following table speaks for itself:

Current balance of payments (seasonally adjusted)

		£m.			£m.
1960	3rd quarter	—94	1962	1st quarter	+37
	4th quarter	—71		2nd quarter	+43
1961	1st quarter	—35			
	2nd quarter	—17			
	3rd quarter	+30†			
	4th quarter	+12			

† Emergency measures taken
(The July measures came too late to have accounted for more than a very small part of the improvement shown.)

resist, whatever the circumstances in which this came about.

But even these explanations are too complicated and too flattering. The fact is that normally staid Treasury officials are prone to panic whenever there is a run on the reserves – which they interpret as 'the money running out of the kitty'.* Sometimes papers are drawn up in deliberately strong terms to alarm ministers and the official authors become infected by the atmosphere they have themselves created.

Mr Selwyn Lloyd's Little Budget of 25 July raised by its full ten per cent the consumer tax Regulator and put a fierce squeeze on Government spending and bank advances. And of course, it raised the Bank Rate to seven per cent. These measures caused enough outcry when they came and helped to ensure almost two years of near stagnation in production. Yet it is not generally known that the Treasury, and even more the Bank of England, considered them not nearly severe enough (one judges the Treasury more severely, because it ought to be (a) more detached from market-moods and (b) less exclusively concerned with sterling, than the Bank).

The Bank calculated that the reserves would be worth —£150m. by Christmas. The Treasury concluded a little more cautiously that they would just have run out com-

* The alarm they display on such occasions is very unsophisticated. For in a country with Britain's volume of overseas payments, a tiny acceleration of payments due to foreigners, and a tiny delay by foreigners in making payments for British goods, can cost the reserves many hundreds of millions. The slightest speculative flutter can set up these movements, known to monetary technicians as 'leads and lags' and their volume is a very poor guide to the state of the British economy. Ultimately these movements must be reversed. Mr Maurice Parsons of the Bank of England pointed out to the Radcliffe Committee in 1959 (*op. cit.* Q.13383) that if current sterling area transactions with the rest of the world were accelerated by just one month and sterling area receipts of foreign currencies were delayed by a similar period, the cost to the reserves could theoretically be somewhere between £800m. and £900m.

pletely.* The Treasury originally wanted to raise income tax in addition† to all the other measures. When it failed to sell the idea to the Government it then tried to persuade Mr Lloyd to use the Second Regulator – the 4s. levy on payrolls – as well as the first, to take another £200m. of spending power away. A levy on payrolls (even though extracted from employers) on top of a pay pause would have been a nice combination indeed. At this point the Home Office should have been brought into the consultation to give its advice on Public Order.

Mr Lloyd resisted this extremism doggedly; and the last stage of the drama was fought at Chequers the week-end before the Little Budget. An *Express* photographer managed to obtain a picture of Macmillan and Lloyd. An observant person looking at the photograph would also have noticed the back of a third person's head. No one realized at the time that this was the Earl of Cromer, the new Governor of the Bank of England, who had arrived to put the case for sterner measures. Mr Lloyd had also at the time to fight off even more extreme advice from Dr Per Jacobsson, the Managing Director of the I.M.F., who was muttering darkly about cutting government spending by £500m. Although Mr Macmillan's main thoughts were elsewhere, he would certainly have encouraged Lloyd to fight the financial extremists.

There was, in fact, nothing in the July Little Budget that could not have been enacted with less subsequent

* If this had really happened we would have then have had a practical demonstration that the reserves are not our life-blood, and that we could trade and pay for our food and raw materials without them. Gold and foreign exchange reserves are used by the Bank of England to reinforce the demand for sterling, and keeping the exchange rate during periods of pressure. If there were no reserves the exchange rate would fall. Admittedly this would make imports more expensive in terms of sterling, but life would carry on.

† This would have meant putting up rates for the whole of 1961–2, and would not have involved any mid year regulator of the kind rejected.

damage to the economy in the proper Budget in April.

The Treasury would then have preferred the tax increase to have reached £100m., and would have been happier if the increase had been levied on consumer spending rather than fuel oil. But it is difficult to see these small differences as a timely warning to Lloyd of the dangers ahead.

The public is entitled to expect the Treasury and the Bank to have a better idea of what to do than a lay politician with no economic pretensions, and not a worse one. In retrospect quite a few of the people involved recognized that they had been wrong to cut demand in July 1961. Contrary to what was claimed at the time demand was not rising at all quickly in the middle of 1961 and unemployment would probably have risen even without the July measures. Yet no one in the Treasury or the Bank voiced dissent from the severity of the advice given, which if accepted would have made the July measures even more harmful than they were.

The Cabinet did not cut a much more impressive figure than the officials. Many ministers intensely disliked the July package, but they could think of no alternative. The crisis came to them as a bolt from the blue. The Treasury was afterwards full of misplaced indignation with journalists who suggested that the measures had been forced on Britain by Dr Jacobsson of the I.M.F., or by the Basle bankers. But this was how it seemed to a good many members of the Cabinet, who would never otherwise have accepted the July measures, and I have since heard the general thought confirmed by a high and unimpeachable financial authority. The whole attitude of senior ministers to economic crises over the last ten years can be summed up in the exclamation, 'Oh dear, what shall we do now?'. Like Eisenhower, they reacted to events which constantly came as a surprise. The idea that men can be masters of their fate or that events can be anticipated would have struck them as pious idealism.

Pay Pause in Perspective

Popular reaction to the July measures concentrated on the pay pause, which was the only justifiable part of the whole package. Having said this, one must immediately add that there was little in the timing and tactics of their handling of the wages situation in the months leading up to the pause of which either Mr Selwyn Lloyd or his advisers could feel proud. Indeed during the early period it is the Bank of England that emerges with most credit. Very early in 1961, long before the April Budget, the Bank gave the Government a warning that the wage settlements already in sight would give Britain an overvalued currency, and that the only cure for an overvalued currency was devaluation. This, it was said, would set off a train of unpredictable events outside Britain's control. Whenever it gave such a warning the Bank was shrewd enough to point out that devaluation would weaken our foreign policy. Of all the possible consequences, the one that could be relied upon to inhibit the Prime Minister most was the effect on Britain's relations with the United States of any move that affected the dollar, as a devaluation of sterling was bound to do.

The fact that wages had got out of control was obvious well before the April Budget. The *Economic Survey* pointed out that earnings per head in the second half of 1960 were six and a half per cent higher than in the previous year – a rate far higher than productivity can ever be expected to rise. The Budget Speech itself mentioned the Treasury's fear 'that the cost inflationary process will speed up further. That I feel is the principal menace at present, and one which it is impossible to exaggerate.'

Yet in the face of this menace the Chancellor did nothing but warn and more precious months were lost. Not merely did he take no action, but his whole Budget showed no recognition that he might have to deal with wages later. It is facile to criticize the surtax concessions as badly timed. If Mr Selwyn Lloyd had not made them then, they would have been quite impossible during the rest of the 1959–64 Parliament. But they should have been balanced by some other measure to redress the social balance, preferably a proper capital gains tax, which was being widely advocated at the time on its own merits, and not only among Socialists. How any set of politicians can have been so ham-fisted as to do one without the other and then introduce a wage pause three months later passes belief.* As the political corres-pondent of the *Financial Times*, Ronald Butt has written: 'The seeds of the slump in the Tory fortunes seem to have been set' in the period of the pay pause. 'For all Mr Lloyd's denial that he had singled out one portion of society for sacrifice; for all his insistence that the "pay pause" was part of a "comprehensive national approach" the public con-trasted it with Mr Lloyd's surtax concessions and many were not convinced by the national arguments for the con-cessions, nor by the fact that they did not come into force straight away.'†

Sir Frank Lee, it will be remembered, was in hospital in Paris when the crisis measures were prepared – which helps to explain their very poor public presentation. It was a Civil Servant at a middle level who deserves the credit for per-suading the Government to grasp the wages nettle.

A report‡ by six economists to the Organization of

* There were in fact two clumsy attempts at a *quid pro quo*. One was the promise of a tax on short-term gains realized within six months. Whether a good idea or not, it was a minor measure which the unions were right to ignore. A hint of it was introduced into the April 1961 Budget Speech as a result of a revolt by the Left wing of the Govern-ment at the pre-Budget Cabinet involving Maudling, Macleod, and Heath. The other was a further increase of two and a half per cent in profits tax to fifteen per cent in the 1961 Budget, following a similar increase in 1960. But the very impersonal and obscure nature of such a change defeats its own object. For the public hardly know that it has happened and do not weight it in the balance at all when judging surtax reliefs which have a spectacular effect on individual people.

† *Financial Times*, 20 September 1963.

‡ *The Problem of Rising Prices*, O.E.E.C. 1961, obtainable from H.M.S.O.

European Economic Coordination, supporting the wage-push theory of inflation, published between the Budget and the July crisis, meanwhile helped to convince many sceptics in the Treasury and elsewhere of the need to tackle wage inflation at its source in industrial settlements, and not rely exclusively on financial policy.

Another key to the conversion of the Government to an incomes policy in July 1961 was a change of front at the Ministry of Labour, which had previously been the main source of resistance to the idea. After a long line of Permanent Secretaries who mostly saw the job in terms of conciliation, the ministry now had Sir Laurence Helsby, a former economics don with a Treasury background who later became Head of the Home Civil Service.

Under his reign the ministry decided as a conscious act of policy that it could no longer automatically step in to conciliate irrespective of the economic damage it produced in the process. This new view still prevails despite some unfortunate backslidings in 1964, for which the responsibility is as usual diffused among different ministries and politicians.

Equally important was the fortunate accident that the Minister of Labour, Mr John Hare (now Lord Blakenham) was a personal friend of Mr Selwyn Lloyd's and willing to listen to the Treasury point of view. When Lloyd was dismissed by Macmillan in July 1962, Hare offered his own resignation, pointing out to the Prime Minister that he too was involved in all Lloyd's actions on the wages front.

Why, as the T.U.C. so bitterly complained, did not Mr Lloyd consult the unions before acting? His reason was that he could not put them in the picture without mentioning his other measures, including the seven per cent Bank Rate. There is nothing more in it than that. If he could have had his time over again, Mr Lloyd would probably have announced his package in two stages. He would have introduced the financial measures first and then held emergency talks with the unions over wages. But why did not someone in the Treasury suggest this course of action to him? Where were the general qualities of common sense and under-standing that the non-specialized Administrator is supposed to bring to Government Departments?

The extreme rigidity with which Mr Lloyd tried to enforce the pause in the public sector was not a personal policy. He, for example, wanted to make concessions to the univer-sity teachers. But in each case the Treasury insisted that if he gave way on any point the whole front would collapse.

On the other hand, Mr Lloyd was violently opposed to the electricity pay settlement of November, which was the first major defeat for the pause. The Prime Minister was in Scotland and Mr Lloyd in Paris. The chief negotiator for the Electricity Council telephoned Mr Richard Wood, the Minister of Power, who told him: 'You must take the responsibility,' which he did. Later Mr Macmillan gave the Electricity Council his famous rebuke in the House of Commons. But the breakthrough showed quite clearly that relations between the Chancellor and ministers responsible for particular industries are not organized in the way that would be necessary to make an incomes policy work.

The fact remains that, for all its inept handling and occasional breaches, the pause had some notable achieve-ments to its credit. It shocked people into an awareness of the problem, in a way that a whole decade of ministerial ser-mons had failed to do. Most of Lloyd's critics accused him of trying to achieve an incomes policy in the wrong way. But before the pause only a small intellectual minority believed in an incomes policy at all, compared with its near-unanimous acceptance today.

It is probable too that the pause, which ended on 1 April 1962, had some effect in slowing down the wage-price spiral for a few months,* and that, together with an even

* This statement is to some extent guesswork, as the Treasury's own calculations to show the success of the pause cannot withstand any sort of rigorous sceptical scrutiny. In particular they cannot refute the hypothesis that the slow-down was entirely due to the trend of unem-ployment.

bigger contribution from the Continent of Europe it has helped to make British exports less uncompetitive than they would otherwise have been. The experience of both Cripps in 1948–50 and Lloyd in 1961–2 suggests that an occasional pause in the inflationary process is possible, and may be more successful than an attempt to limit wage increases, year in year out, by means of a guiding light.

The Cabinet, in fact, had endless difficulty in agreeing on an incomes policy to follow the pause. The incomes policy statement which was issued in February 1962, and which set forth a guiding light, stating that money incomes should not rise by an average of more than two and a half per cent per person each year, had been in existence for well over five years and draft after draft had been sent back to ministers for rewriting. The document which appeared was a triumph of obscurity and an object of derision even in the Treasury corridors. The evasion and double-talk arose from the very British refusal of the Cabinet to choose between unpalatable alternatives.

To Macmillan the White Paper was not a policy. He wanted, above all, an institution which would help decide priorities among different kinds of workers, and different kinds of income. All sorts of ideas were in the air. Some officials hoped to find a way of introducing national economic considerations into the actual processes of wage negotiations or conciliations. The idea did not prove a runner. Others wanted ministers to pronounce in public on wage settlements which were against the national interest as soon as they were made or even before. But this was too forthright a solution for a Government which much preferred to pass the buck to outside bodies headed by distinguished lawyers. In the end Macmillan lost his patience with the argument and delay and himself summoned a group of officials, including Sir Laurence Helsby, to Admiralty House in the spring of 1962 to hammer out the main lines of NIC – an extremely unconventional kind of initiative for a British Prime Minister to take.

There is a curious tailpiece to the story. Mr Selwyn Lloyd was holding talks in the summer of 1962 just before he was dismissed, with Mr Victor Feather, the Assistant General Secretary of the T.U.C., on the establishment of NIC. Some misunderstandings seem to have arisen at this stage. For although Feather was non-committal, it seemed to the Treasury that the talks were going reasonably well, and there seemed no hint of the furious T.U.C. objections which were later to develop. Later on in July, Mr George Woodcock came back from a meeting of the International Confederation of Free Trade Unions and treated the project as a personal affront. By then the Prime Minister was determined to introduce it in the Vote of Censure Debate of 26 July, and the Whitehall preparations had acquired a momentum difficult to stop.

It can certainly be argued that Macmillan would have done better to wait for the National Economic Development Council to come round to incomes policy as one subject of many rather than set up a twin organization against bitter union opposition. But early in 1962 NEDC was in no condition to deal with the subject, and the unions would have left, if it had tried.

The Story of Four Per Cent

The National Economic Development Council, in fact, held its first two meetings in March and May 1962. An expanded version of the Treasury's earlier papers on obstacles to growth was placed before the Council at one of these early meetings. It was abruptly turned down without consideration on the grounds that the Council wanted to hear from its own office and not the Treasury; and it was incidentally one of the employers present who took the lead in this. The words 'Treasury trash' were heard to cross the table.

Some Whitehall officials feel rather bitterly about this incident, and claim that their own documents made nearly all the points in NEDC's own report on *Conditions Favourable To Growth* which appeared a year later.

There were undoubtedly many points in common; both sets of documents put considerable emphasis for example on the need for incomes restraint. The Treasury papers put the emphasis on the obstacles and the difficulties; the NEDC papers started with the assumption of a growth programme and looked at the problem in that perspective – psychological differences of this kind can be important, however similar the points of substance. The main triumph for the NEDC office came, however, in the acceptance of the four per cent growth target – a masterpiece of diplomacy on the part of Shone and his energetic Economic Director, Sir Donald MacDougall. Where, the question is often asked, did the four per cent target come from?

A figure that provided a gleam in the eye was the target of fifty per cent growth in ten years (equivalent to four per cent per annum) set for the West as a whole by the Kennedy Administration soon after taking office at meetings of the O.E.C.D. (the Organization for Economic Cooperational Development, the successor to the Marshall Plan organization which included the U.S. and Canada as well as Western Europe). This target was based partly on the assumption that the U.S. would move nearer to full employment under Kennedy than under the Eisenhower Administration and partly on the Common Market's growth record (allowing here for some slowing down).

The main thing, however, was that from NEDC's point of view, four per cent also suited Britain's particular requirements for the period 1961–6. On the basis of statistics derived from the past the Treasury then thought that Britain's productive capacity was growing annually by three per cent. This was obviously not good enough, both because Britain ought to be able to do better in the future than in the economically uninspiring recent past and because it came from the Treasury. Because of its concern for Government spending and the balance of payments, it is simply not the Treasury's job to take any very optimistic view of the future.

How much faster than three per cent? NEDC was looking for a target high enough to be a challenge, but not so high that it would be doomed to disappointment. Three and a half per cent was not very much above the figure to which the Treasury was prepared to raise its own 'realistic target on the basis of recent investment booms in British industry'. For NEDC it was too unambitious. On the other hand, four and a half per cent had to be ruled out because it would have meant too rapid an acceleration at the end of the period to make up for the ground lost since the beginning of 1961. Between these two limits four per cent seemed about right.

Some Treasury officials were in favour of using four per cent as a basis for NEDC's studies because they thought that a figure higher than was likely to be achieved would bring out all the objections and snags they wanted to see discussed. Too late they realized that once the magic figure of four per cent was announced it would inevitably become a target from which it would be highly embarrassing to draw back.

At NEDC's second meeting in May 1962, four per cent was accepted as 'a reasonably ambitious figure likely to bring out problems that have to be solved if faster growth is to be achieved and as a help in focusing thinking on the problems of faster growth'. Long before the Industrial Inquiry was completed near the end of the year, the four per cent figure was prematurely treated in the Press as a target, an error which the Office did not over-exert itself to correct.

This insistence on a four per cent growth target, obscure and statistical though it may seem, was Mr Selwyn Lloyd's own greatest personal achievement as Chancellor, and right up to the time of going to press is NEDC's own greatest success as well.

This central goal was important for several reasons. It was not a balance of payments target (such as the Treasury had issued on previous occasions), nor a prices target, but a production target. In other words it was concerned with real wealth and living standards rather than paper symbols. Its existence and the political pressure behind it makes it several degrees more embarrassing for Chancellors to hold back output for the sake of other objectives than it was before.

This achievement had little to do with 'planning' even in a fairly loose sense of the term; and it would never have been possible without the popular disillusionment with the Treasury which led to the establishment of an independent office. If the office had started inside Whitehall, as many Socialists were initially inclined to argue, the central goal would have been buried beneath compromise and qualification.

An Unfortunate Budget

At the time of the 1962 Budget, the Government was not yet formally committed to the four per cent target. The Treasury was still laying down an ultra-cautious short-term policy, completely opposite in spirit, which led to stagnation and unemployment in the following months. A few commentators hoped the 1962 Budget would produce some ingenious device for stimulating exports; some thought it would provide incentives for private investment, by then obviously on the downturn; others thought that it would give some stimulus to purchasing power. Hardly anyone believed that the Budget would contain none of these three things and that the only innovation would be a tax on confectionery and ice-cream.

There is no need to dwell on the fact that the Budget judgement proved a gross blunder. So far from foreseeing the unemployment that was to come, the Chancellor in his Budget Speech actually worried that total spending would make 'too great a call on our resources'.

The buoyant forecast was mainly due to an extremely

optimistic view of exports, which emanated from the Board of Trade. The Treasury in its own analysis of what went wrong* puts most stress on the nasty surprise it received when, contrary to expectations, exports levelled out and then fell slightly after the middle of the year. As a secondary factor it blames the fall in private investment which was much steeper than it thought it would be. These two set-backs helped to generate a typical deflationary cycle, which led to lower employment, shorter hours, and a fall in industrial stock building.

An important contributory factor was that Mr Selwyn Lloyd was led to think that Britain would know that she was in the Common Market by July 1962, and that everything would be cut and dried by September. This news, he thought, would stimulate a big investment boom.

The Treasury economists overestimated the growth of demand just at the time when they were most entranced by the idea of maintaining a margin of spare capacity. (This doctrine will be examined in the Appendix to Chapter 9.) They also took no account, moreover, of the more cost-conscious atmosphere which they themselves had striven so hard to create, but sceptics would argue that on this last issue they were right.

Mr Lloyd became personally worried about the Treas-ury's 1962 forecast a week or so after his Budget Speech. So in time did the Board of Trade and the Ministry of Labour, but the Treasury stuck to its guns. In June Mr Lloyd allowed hire-purchase deposits on durables to be reduced from twenty per cent to ten per cent, a relaxation which the Treasury considered unnecessary.

The April Budget was very badly received by some of Lloyd's colleagues, and the promise to abolish Schedule 'A' at some future date was inserted after the pre-Budget Cabinet as a sop to critics. During the months after the Budget a number of ministers wrote personal papers for the

* *Economic Report for* 1962, published as a supplement to *Economic Trends*, March 1963, H.M.S.O.

Cabinet voicing concern about a possible recession and attacked the Treasury's complacency. The critics included Lord Mills, the Prime Minister's confidant, Sir David (now Lord) Eccles, Mr Marples, and, to some extent, Mr Macleod and Lord Hailsham. Yet despite these dissatisfied voices, Lloyd's dismissal on 23 July came as a bolt from the blue, both to Lloyd himself and the Treasury.

CHAPTER 8

Some Chinks of Light

ON 11 July, the day before Lloyd heard the news of his dismissal, a Treasury minister (not Mr Lloyd) gave the Press a 'Lobby briefing' which showed no change of heart whatever. *The Times* headlines ran:

NO ECONOMIC STIMULUS LIKELY YET
TREASURY CONFIDENT OF STEADY GROWTH
OUTPUT, EXPORTS, AND HOME DEMAND ALL RISING

Normally it is hitting below the belt to sneer at economic forecasts for going wrong. This happens just as much to the National Institute and to other radical critics as to the Treasury. But there was something unpleasantly Panglossian in the Treasury's misinterpretation of the existing situation. Stock Exchange prices had just slumped after a Wall Street crash; industrialists were nervous, uncertain, and deferring investment plans; retail sales had been stagnant for eighteen months running, and unemployment (adjusted for seasonal changes) had already been rising for a whole year. It was difficult to remember a time when business and Whitehall were so far apart in their economic assessments. The Bank of England, to give it its due, was far more conscious of the dangers of recession than the Treasury and (sterling being fairly strong) was pushing for more expansionist policies.

The most unforgivable part of this briefing was the view reported in the *Financial Times*, 'Fears of repeating the 1958 error of stimulating the economy too soon out of fear of recession still sway the Government more than the doubtful outlook for the American economy, or the failure so far to get any steam behind a revival of business confidence in Britain.' As one City editor wrote at the time, 'Too soon!

How it can seriously be suggested that after three years of stagnation the economy was re-expanded *too soon* in 1958 I find utterly bewildering. After all the Treasury has never done anything too soon (nor probably has any other Government department for that matter). Its actions fall neatly into two categories, too little too late and too much too late.'* So it proved both in 1958 and 1962.

As the minor post-Budget relaxations showed, Mr Selwyn Lloyd had himself been champing slightly at the Treasury bit. At a meeting of the Cabinet Economic Policy Committee, during his very last week as Chancellor, Mr Lloyd heard for the first time of a new forecast that winter unemployment would reach 525,000 instead of 450,000 as originally expected. This new estimate probably came from the Ministry of Labour grass roots investigation rather than from the Treasury's own back room. The news came as a shock to Lloyd, and he told Macmillan that if the economy really proved to be running at a standstill during the summer, he would want in the first few days of October, the earliest Parliamentary rules allowed, to move the Regulator downwards. This would have reduced all purchase tax and other consumer taxes by a tenth and injected an extra £250m. or so of extra spending power.

On the eve of his dismissal, Lloyd had made tentative plans for a Bank Rate reduction to four per cent for early August (this did not in fact happen until 3 January 1963) and a release of another one per cent of Special Deposits (which did not happen until October). Mr Lloyd also authorized an extra £70m. of public investment, over and above what he had originally planned, which would mostly take effect in 1963–4. This he regarded as making a virtue of necessity.

As soon as Mr Lloyd had gone, the Minister of Labour, Mr Hare, became terribly worried that the change of Chancellor would delay measures to fight unemployment. At his request Lloyd sent a letter to a member of the

* Nigel Lawson, *Sunday Telegraph*, 15 July 1962.

Cabinet outlining all the plans just listed, as examples of the sorts of action which he would *not* regard as a repudiation of his own policies.

Why Lloyd Went

The reasons for Lloyd's dismissal have never been adequately explained. It would be consoling to report that it was because he was too late and too timid in switching over to re-expansion. Unfortunately, most of the evidence suggests that any such feeling was, if it was there at all, only a minor element in a much more general belief that Macmillan had gradually acquired that Lloyd was (a) not up to his job, and (b) a political liability. The dismissal came not very long after Orpington and a whole series of really shattering Conservative defeats.

The unfairest of reasons given for Lloyd's dismissal, but one that is all too likely, is the two words 'pay pause'. Lloyd paid the price for an unpopular policy which quite a few eminent men of a Labour and trade-union background privately believed to have been absolutely necessary—'saved the nation' was one, albeit exaggerated, remark actually made.

Another factor was that Lloyd could not take part to Macmillan's satisfaction in ruminative general economic conversation. On complex Treasury matters Lloyd seemed to the Premier and to some of his colleagues to be too dependent on his brief, and looked at a loss when unexpected questions turned up. Whether these criticisms did justice to Lloyd as a minister or not, they were perfectly predictable when he was moved to the Exchequer after five years as Foreign Secretary. This deficiency was, however, aggravated in Mr Macmillan's eyes by the Wall Street crash and renewed talk of the difficulties of the dollar. These events had revived the Prime Minister's concern with the liquidity problem, i.e. the inadequate amount of gold or alternative types of international money to finance world trade. He wanted a Chancellor who could force the Treasury and Bank into taking some initiative on the question.

Probably a more important reason was Macmillan's extreme irritation that Lloyd carried on talking about an incomes policy, after the end of the pay pause, without, as the Prime Minister thought, doing anything practical about it. If there was one specific incident which turned the balance against Lloyd it was the inaction which led Macmillan to set up NIC himself.

It is far from clear in retrospect that Macmillan was right to insist on setting up an unpopular twin brother to NEDC, which the T.U.C. loathed, and with which it refused to cooperate. Very little would have been lost if the Government had waited for NEDC to come to grips with the problem, and in the meanwhile had taken upon itself the job of investigating and pronouncing on wage settlements which worried it. But this last suggestion was hardly one that would appeal to conventional political wisdom.

Someone Who Understood

Unlike Mr Selwyn Lloyd, Mr Reginald Maudling, who succeeded him at the Exchequer, had never been personally close to Mr Macmillan. The Prime Minister brought him in at a low point in Conservative fortunes, when he wanted above all someone who could understand economic policy and was able to express himself on the subject in public.

Mr Maudling had these qualities. The intellectual framework within which policy is discussed both by Treasury economists and their critics proves extremely difficult for those new to the game; but once they have been grasped, the underlying ideas are if anything too simple. Maudling got hold of these ideas many years ago, and as a result found his job neither as agonizing nor as time-consuming as most of his predecessors. When in good form, Maudling, who is known universally as 'Reggie', sparks off an endless stream of ideas in the hope that if his own are not practicable they will at least provoke someone to think of something better. His speed of work and his casual conversational manner mislead some people into thinking that he is lazy. Rows and showdowns are not, however, his cup of tea; he is either too good-natured or too sceptical towards life to be a ruthless administrator steamrolling his way through colleagues and advisers.

The new Chancellor did not attempt to turn the Treasury upside down as MacNamara did the Defence Department in Washington. He was relatively independent of his officials, because he could absorb what they had to say before they finished speaking, and could often guess what they would be worrying about in a few months time.

Although he was appointed Chancellor at the age of forty-five – a precocious child by British standards – in one sense he was appointed several years too late. He had been around the Treasury in one capacity or another for the best part of a decade. He had been Economic Secretary under Butler, and had supported successive Chancellors of the Exchequer in economic debates, first as Paymaster General then as President of the Board of Trade. He had seen too many policies tried and failed.

Then too, he came to office after his Party had been in power for eleven years and was hardly in a position to repudiate the heritage of his predecessors. He was appointed in the second half of a Parliament – never a good time to introduce heretical ideas, which in the first instance usually lose more votes than they gain.

The month of July 1962 saw not only the announcement of a new Chancellor, but a new Permanent Secretary as well. The appointment of Mr William Armstrong, who was whisked up from the ranks of Third Secretaries over the heads of his superiors, after the retirement of Sir Frank Lee, was in its way even more surprising than Lloyd's replacement by Maudling. Armstrong was not even a knight when his appointment was announced.

Armstrong, who has already been referred to on page 52, is a medium-sized sparsely built man, and is as strong a contrast to Lee as anyone could imagine. Lee was an expansive extrovert, while Armstrong is more of an introvert but a friendly and approachable one. While Lee would take charge of an investigation from the beginning, Armstrong would let his subordinate officials pursue their own course before coming in with his comments.

Unlike Lee, Armstrong has not become associated with any strongly defined policy attitudes. He dislikes humbug and insists on basing policies on facts and logic. His favourite motto is Leonardo da Vinci's 'He who controls the weather controls the world'. But he has not tried to arrogate to himself the choice of policy goals. Although he has still to achieve Lee's pre-eminence in inter-departmental committees, he is probably the first Permanent Head of the Treasury to have a thoroughly sophisticated and contemporary approach to economic management.

Armstrong, who took over on 1 October, presided over the big Treasury reorganization described in Chapter 2, of which he himself was one of the key architects.

There never is any direct connexion between Cabinet and Civil Service changes in the lifetime of a government. Armstrong's appointment had certainly been approved by Mr Selwyn Lloyd before being confirmed by Mr Maudling. But at a deeper level the two sets of changes had a common origin in a strong feeling of dissatisfaction that the Prime Minister and one or two of his close personal advisers had long had with the workings of the Treasury. As so often, dissatisfaction with *policies* made itself felt in a demand for organizational changes. Politicians can never free themselves of the hope that better information, or improved administrative machinery, can prevent the policy dilemmas which they so much dislike from emerging. Maudling himself knew too much to have such illusions, but he certainly did not want to face these dilemmas earlier than he could help it. What can one say of his reactions after two years at the Exchequer?

There are several issues on which the economic performance of any Chancellor in recent years should be assessed. First and foremost is the priority he gives to expansion when it comes into conflict with the needs of sterling or the balance of payments. Secondly there is his detailed management of the domestic economy: when exactly to inflate or deflate and by how much. Third are his efforts to improve efficiency in his capacity of economic coordinator and guardian of the Exchequer purse strings. Fourth comes incomes policy – a post-1961 innovation. Fifth, there is his conduct of international financial negotiations. On the first two issues the Chancellor has a remarkably large element of personal discretion. But on the third and fourth, responsibility is shared with other ministers. On the fifth count, his powers to act are strictly limited by the attitude of foreign Governments.

On the first crucial issue, whether to give priority to expansion, the testing point for every Chancellor comes during his first big sterling crisis when he must choose between slamming down the brakes (usually signalled by a seven per cent Bank Rate) and breaking with established orthodoxy.

Radical economists should on no account hold Mr Maudling to blame for the size of the 1964 trade deficit, despite the temptations of party politics. Measures to improve the grass roots efficiency of the economy take a long time to have any effect, and nothing that he or Mr Heath could possibly have done here in the year or two before the end of the Parliament could have acted quickly enough to prevent deficits emerging at this particular stage of expansion. The real test will be the handling of the deficit after the election.

There were signs however of an all-important change in Mr Maudling's 1964 Budget speech when he said:

I do not object to import controls on doctrinal grounds, but on grounds of practical policy. Certainly there could be occasions when their use would be justified and permissible under international agreements, that is, if we should be facing severe balance of payments difficulties which could not be dealt with in better ways.

Whitehall has always had stand-by schemes for re-imposing import controls. They are on a limited range of goods, mostly finished manufactures, and about two months' notice is required from the time a secret internal warning is given in Whitehall to the time the controls come into operation. An alternative scheme – which would be greatly preferable – is also available for temporary import levies on broad classes of commodities.

These schemes had been examined in previous crises, but pigeon-holed in the end. Mr Maudling's Budget speech indicated a new willingness to use them which he must have made clear inside Whitehall considerably earlier.

No liberal-minded person can be fond of import controls; but under fixed exchange rates they may sometimes be the only alternative to holding back expansion for years at a time. On the most important issue of all then, Mr Maudling, one can fairly say, seemed to have moved a little away from the blinkered orthodoxy of his predecessors.

This digression from strict chronology is necessary to give perspective to Mr Maudling's management of the home economy. The popular view is that he handled this very well, doing much less than outside economists urged in both slump and boom, and turning out right in the end. In his second year of office, from the summer of 1963 to that of 1964, the Chancellor did indeed prove far shrewder than his critics; but it still seems to me that he got off to a slow start in his first year, and that this had repercussions over a longer period.

Making Haste Slowly

For all his achievements, the idea of an expansionist Maudling replacing a restrictionist Lloyd was a popular delusion, as far as the months immediately following Lloyd's dismissal are concerned. All Conservative Chancellors have loosened the purse-strings when unemployment has risen and production stagnated, but have waited too long before doing so. The transition from Lloyd to Maudling actually delayed re-expansion by several months.

Although Mr Maudling is sometimes a bold conversationalist he is cautious in his actions. As President of the Board of Trade, he was quite an influence for moderation during the 1961 crisis. As Chancellor a year later, he was equally moderate about re-expansion, and was again very moderate in the Budgetary restraints he imposed on the 1964 boom.

Up to about July or August 1962 the delay in re-expanding the economy must to a large extent be blamed on the Treasury economists. But from that point onwards the main responsibility lay with the new Chancellor personally. The Treasury cannot be exonerated completely as until well into the autumn it took far too rosy a view of the situation. Yet the fact remains that it was for action and the Chancellor for delay.

The Treasury, to do it justice, had by the summer of 1962 an expansionary package in reserve, which could be introduced very quickly should its view of the situation change. At the very same time as the Lobby correspondents were being given the ludicrously optimistic briefing already mentioned, officials at a middle level were already revising their forecasts downwards – an illustration of the drawbacks of the lengthy 'processing' and discussion through which ideas go before they are placed in front of ministers.

But by the late summer the Treasury was already advising Mr Maudling to use the Regulator – as Mr Lloyd had contemplated. It wanted him to announce this at his Mansion House speech on 3 October. To give Parliament time to discuss the move within twenty-one calendar days, as the Finance Act then demanded, the House of Commons would have had to be recalled one day early. Unfortunately Mr Maudling came back from the I.M.F. meeting feeling that too early a reversal of Mr Lloyd's policy would be bad for sterling. His initiative had been rebuffed; sterling had taken a short, but nasty knock after a Telstar broadcast by

President Kennedy in defence of the dollar, and Maudling was in a very cautious mood.*

All that was announced at the Mansion House was a small release of post-war credits, the increase in public investment that Mr Lloyd had already approved, and the end of the credit squeeze. But as Lord Plowden pointed out in the House of Lords in a speech the following February 'Cheap credit is no help when there is a short and declining order book. It is like a fuel that will catch fire only when the fire is burning well.'† The same remark could also be applied to the improved investment allowances announced a month later.

As the business situation worsened during the course of the autumn, Maudling still refused to use the Regulator. His main excuse was that more than half its effect came through lower drink and tobacco prices. This was not a strong argument, as a surcharge imposed by the Regulator does not change the existing distribution of taxes between different items, but simply lifts the whole scale up or down. In any case a reduction in the price of tobacco and drink would simply have compensated for the earlier increase when the Regulator was used in an upward direction in July 1961. The use of the Regulator was also disliked by Macmillan, who found it difficult to believe that 'making a glass of sherry a bit cheaper' could do much to restore prosperity.

Mr Maudling eventually decided to act on purchase tax. A separate attack on all the different rates proved an extraordinarily complicated affair, so in the end the Chancellor

* As usual an overseas publication provides the best clue to what was going on inside the U.K. Treasury. The *Annual O.E.C.D. Survey of the U.K.* published in July 1963, explains that in 1962 '*reflationary action was more gradual than many people were urging*', partly due to the difficulties of diagnosis, but also to '*the Government's judgement*' that faster growth on a sustained basis 'would be impeded more if an over-rapid expansion of demand had subsequently to be restrained than by a *policy of hastening slowly, even if such a policy resulted in an undue slack in the economy persisting rather longer*'. P.5 (my italics).

† *House of Lords Hansard*, 19 February 1963, column 1284.

and his advisers came to the conclusion that it would be better to reduce all tax rates in the highest forty-five per cent category to twenty-five per cent. (The special stimulus to the motor industry was mainly a *post hoc* justification.) The total value of the purchase tax cuts was about £90m., much less than half of what the Regulator would have been. Yet even these modest relaxations were staggered in two stages. The cuts for cars were announced on 5 November (together with increased investment allowances) and the reductions for cosmetics, records, radio, and T.V. were held over for two months until New Year's day.

Mr Maudling did however have at least one very good idea just before Christmas 1962. This was to pay out the higher pensions and other National Insurance benefits which the Government had promised for 1963 several months before the increase in contributions. If Maudling's idea had been accepted, a large temporary stimulus worth several hundred million pounds a year would have been applied when it was most needed. Later, when contributions were raised, the stimulus would have been cancelled out in a way that everyone would have regarded as fair, and could not possibly be denounced as 'stop-go'. The Chancellor asked the Ministry of Pensions officials to his room to argue the matter out, but he was defeated by 'administrative difficulties' of unbelievable obscurity. Somewhere in the background, one feels sure, was the moralistic belief that if the link between contributions and benefits was broken only for a few months, the whole myth of an insurance scheme would be shattered beyond repair.

In January the Chancellor was still being urged by his economic advisers to use the Regulator, but he insisted on waiting until the Budget. This introduced tax reliefs, to take effect in July 1963, when production and employment were already well on the mend. (The graph on p. 290 illustrates the point.) What Mr Maudling failed to see was that whatever the faults of the Regulator, it was, as

Mr Butler might have put it, the best Regulator we had.

A gradual step-by-step approach may often be good politics, but economic policy is in this respect different. For the golden rule in trade cycle control is to act with maximum speed as soon as signs of slump or excessive boom appear. The longer the Chancellor waits, and the greater the time-lags in the actions he takes, the more likely he will be to aggravate the fluctuations he is trying to cure. Part of the trouble was that the public, and perhaps the Chancellor too, had been, as Lord Plowden put it, 'mesmerized' by the expression stop-go.

Sir Robert Hall, who was the Government's Economic Adviser for fourteen years up to 1961 has put in print his personal doubts about the timing of the Chancellor's measures. He has criticized the delay in adopting measures of expansion during the period of rising unemployment in 1962 and the character of the expansionist measure actually adopted. In Hall's view Mr Maudling appeared to be losing a valuable opportunity in the Budget of 1963 when he refused to withdraw the increase in indirect taxation resulting from Mr Selwyn Lloyd's regulator, at a time when it would have been very valuable to give the public confidence in this instrument: if it is used upwards again, people will tend to think it is a subterfuge for increasing indirect taxes. Hall adds that a substantial increase in public expenditure however justified from a social point of view, is a method of expansion notoriously slow to take effect and has tended to get out of phase and exert a destabilizing influence throughout the post-war period.*

During the winter of 1962–3 many people refused to listen to any explanation of the high unemployment in these terms at all. The popular view was that there was something wrong with specific areas. Of course there was. These were weak areas that felt the brunt of any recession and did not

* 'Incomes Policy – State of Play', the *Three Banks Review*, March 1964.

quite fully share in any recovery. Their problems certainly needed tackling. But the *cause of the recession* was inept management by the Government of the business cycle. The following table shows that the regional problem was hardly any worse than in the previous recession four years before (the north-east was very much a special case). The trouble both in 1958 and 1962 was the movement of demand in the country as a whole, difficult though this was to demonstrate over the T.V. screen.

	Thousands of Workers	
Unemployment	December 1958	December 1962
Northern Region†	40.7	64.9
Scotland	95.5	100.6
Wales	39.5	36.6
N. Ireland	39.7	36.9
Total Depressed Regions	215.4	239.0
Total U.K.	571.4	603.0
Depressed Regions as Percentage of the Total	37.8%	39.6%

† Mostly north-east.

These initial errors of timing in economic management must be set against a number of individual and specific bright ideas. A good example is the introduction of free depreciation in high-unemployment areas. This allows an industrialist to write off against tax all he spends on new plant in the first year of its life – the equivalent, according to one very large firm, of a ten per cent subsidy on new capital expenditure in the development districts. It was Maudling himself who pressed the idea on the Inland Revenue. Originally he thought of it for the country as a whole, but was put off by its cost – perhaps £400m. per annum.* He

* This shows how skin-deep is the conversion of even the most sophisticated of politicians to the Keynesian approach. In terms of real resources the extra load on the economy might have been very much less.

then thought of giving it a trial run in the development districts. The Inland Revenue was so horrified by another idea it was asked to consider – profits tax discrimination in favour of development districts – that it gratefully seized on free depreciation as a lesser evil.

Quite apart from his special help for unemployment areas, Maudling enormously increased tax incentives for capital development for the country as a whole, first in November 1962, and then in the 1963 Budget. Britain's fiscal incentives to investment are now about the best in Europe, however much business accountants have striven to hide this fact. British industry would have benefited greatly if these concessions had been applied in the middle 50s when it was demonstrably suffering from too little investment compared with its European competitors – much more so than today. Here is another reason for asserting that Maudling arrived at the Treasury several years too late.

A minor triumph for Maudling was the £75m. Exchequer loans for shipowners willing to place orders in British yards. The loans were just enough to tide the ship-building industry over a trough and bring into operation labour and capacity that would otherwise have lain unused, but not enough to put the industry on a permanent subsidized basis. The scheme which was announced by the Minister of Transport was a personal notion of Mr Maudling's, which ran into great scepticism from both officials and other ministers.

But the scheme of which Maudling was most proud was the special aid for poor developing countries that were willing to place contracts in depressed areas in Britain. Loans have been given, to a modest total, for example to India for the purchase of steel plates, to Pakistan for sugar machinery, to Ghana for cargo ships. The scheme appealed both to Maudling's humanity and his logic, and he insisted on it even though it ran counter to all his Department's traditional doctrines of 'untied' aid which it preached at endless international gatherings.

Does Nature Move in Leaps?

Although the Treasury rightly wanted Mr Maudling to be more expansionist than he was in the summer and winter of 1962–3, its views on the country's longer-term possibilities were still extremely pessimistic and conservative – 'realist' would be its preferred word. As we have seen in earlier chapters, it has all along been extremely sceptical of NEDC's four per cent growth target for 1961–6. This disagreement between Treasury and NEDC is very important for an understanding of the events leading up to the 1963 Budget and of the way in which it was presented.

Among the ministers and career Civil Servants involved, the real doubt was whether exports could rise by the five per cent a year necessary on average to achieve this target. NEDC's industrial inquiry showed little hope among the firms questioned about expanding overseas sales in line with this requirement – a point glossed over in its first Report. But the Treasury economists who argued with NEDC at ground level did not, it is most important to understand, base themselves on the export argument at all, but on the historical figures of productivity mentioned in the last chapter. These showed that the trend of output per head in the past was insufficient for much more than three per cent growth, even if sufficient goods could be sold abroad.

The long-term trend of productivity reflected in their view the fundamental working habits and pace of innovation of the whole nation and could not be changed overnight, least of all by stoking up the flames of demand. The motto which governed their reactions appears on the title page of Alfred Marshall's *Principles of Economics*, first published in 1890: *Natura non fecit saltum:* Nature does not move in leaps. Here, in this symptomatic quotation, there was a welcome point of contact between the economists and Treasury officials with a classical background.

The NEDC economists on the other hand believed, on the

basis of their own statistical studies, that the underlying trend of productivity had speeded up in recent years, and that this had been hidden from view by the depressed conditions of 1961–2. Technical conversations between the two sides failed to clear up the differences.*

The statistics were not conclusive on either side. But the subsequent statistical analysis has definitely shifted towards the Treasury camp. The real reasons for giving NEDC the benefit of the doubt lay in the physical changes that had taken place in British industry too recently to show up in a long run of figures, for which the Treasury then failed to make sufficient allowance.

The very high investment of 1960 and 1961 had not yet found expression in the output figures because demand had been held down. Civil spending on research and development trebled over the previous six years; but again the benefits were likely to be in the future. It was moreover quite obvious from actually looking at industry, reading company reports, or talking to businessmen, that most firms had had a big competitive shakeout. Many of them had launched drives against the wasteful uses of labour. All over the country industrialists were insisting that they could increase output by very large amounts with very small increases in their labour force.

The big weakness of the whole Treasury attitude to growth was that it was tied to the past. The novelty of NEDC was that it tried to find out from industrialists what they could actually do in the present and the future, if the demand were there for their products and the different sections of the economy moved in phase. Its first inquiry, completed near the end of 1962, was admittedly a crude and pioneering affair. It did suggest, however, that on the basis of businessmen's estimates, cross-checked for consistency with each other and with the probable growth of the

* The NEDC target involves a 3¼ per cent average annual growth in output per head. The Treasury insisted that statistical studies over the past few years showed a trend increase of only 2¼ per cent.

labour force, a four per cent growth rate was (when translated) regarded by industry as physically possible.

The Treasury view minimized by implication all the Government's own efforts to improve labour training, squeeze profits, introduce more competition, and all the rest. This is a refreshing cynicism, but it should be only one element in the advice reaching ministers.

Mr Maudling did not lose much sleep over any of this statistical theology. As has been explained earlier, he had not been a great supporter of the NEDC organization in Cabinet, and at its early meetings some Council members had the very strong feeling that (like the Regulator) it was 'not his baby'. On the other hand he personally quite liked the four per cent growth target. Although Maudling is a cautious man, he is also temperamentally an optimist; and looking at other European countries, four per cent did not seem too absurd as a bench mark at which to aim. Long before the NEDC formally approved the four per cent objective on 4 February 1963, the Chancellor was supporting the target in his public speeches. He made it quite clear inside the Treasury that the four per cent target could not be quietly dropped without inducing a national mood of frustration and disappointment. He determined to go on as long as he could playing it by ear and not attempting to define too closely over what period the four per cent average was to be measured.

But he was a little slow to follow through the far-reaching implications of the NEDC target for everything the Treasury was doing. There was, for example, an unfortunate incident early in March 1963 when the Government's Economic Adviser, Mr Cairncross, defended a 2–$2\frac{1}{2}$ per cent guiding light for wages in front of the National Incomes Commission, on the basis of evidence prepared some time before – only to be repudiated in the Budget Speech when the Chancellor proclaimed a new guiding light of 3–$3\frac{1}{2}$ per cent which fitted the NEDC target.

An Unusually Secret Budget

Maudling's relations with NEDC as an organization went through several phases. After his early scepticism, he seemed suddenly to realize that the Council, with its representatives of both sides of industry, gave him an opportunity to mobilize support for the Government's objectives, above all for an incomes policy; and in the Council discussions around the beginning of 1963 he suddenly came to life. His Budget Speech of that year followed very closely, almost in the order of contents, the NEDC *Report on Conditions Favourable to Faster Growth*.

The Budget itself aimed to give away an extra £250m. in reliefs. It did so through higher income tax allowances for married couples and families with children. It abolished Schedule 'A', introduced further improvements in industrial investment incentives, and reduced stamp duties.

The main aim of the Budget was to obtain union support for an incomes policy. The tax reliefs Maudling gave were equivalent for many workers to a wage increase of two per cent. For the same cost he could have reduced income tax by well over 6d in the £; if he had done this the Chancellor would have obtained better headlines and pleased many Conservative supporters a great deal more than he did. Instead he achieved the satisfaction of having his Budget praised by the T.U.C. Economic Committee – probably the first time ever for a Tory Chancellor.

Although Mr Maudling made a great song and dance about the £250m. figure being a personal judgement, it was in fact little different from the recommendation he had been given by the Treasury's Budget committee. There had been some slight dissension around the figure – the Treasury economists might have been happier to see it topping £300m. and some of the veteran officials were worried at seeing it above £200m. But within the large margins of error inherent in the exercise, £200m.–£300m. was regarded as a pretty good consensus. No one who counted in the

. Treasury wanted to give away in reliefs the £400m. urged by the National Institute, but the Chancellor and his advisers were delighted with this recommendation, as it made anything they did seem moderate by comparison.

The decision to give away only £250m. (£280m. in terms of detailed arithmetic) turned out right in the end, as the National Institute itself subsequently admitted. Yet the actual assumptions surrounding the Budget judgement were, at Maudling's insistence, surrounded in mystery at the time. They eventually emerged in a little noticed *O.E.C.D. Report on the U.K. Economy*, published during the summer holidays. If they had come out at Budget time they would have caused an outcry, because of the leisurely pace at which the Treasury envisaged the return to full employment. In fact the economy was recovering more rapidly before the Budget's stimulus took effect than either the Treasury or its critics realized; and production rose and unemployment fell in the closing months of 1963 with unexpected speed.

The one unfortunate aspect of the Budget was its timing. We have seen that Mr Amory's expansionist Budget of 1959 came too late, and added fuel to the flames of the next boom. But in some ways, Mr Maudling's Budget was even more perverse in this respect. For while Amory's reliefs had their full impact straight away, Maudling's reliefs were not expected to have anything like their full effect until the financial year 1964–5, when the economy was much more likely to need restraint than stimulation. The main tax reliefs were not paid out until July. The following table sets out a comparison.

Tax Reliefs
£m.

	Estimated Value in Budget Year	Estimated Value in Following Year
Mr Amory in 1959	366*	361
Mr Maudling in 1963	269	446

* including £71m. of postwar credits.

Although demand was not *increasing* at all excessively in

the opening months of 1964–5, its absolute *level* was too high for comfort – certainly higher than anything the Treasury would have deliberately chosen. There was at least a case for supposing that once employers had taken on all the labour they needed, unemployment would fall to well below 1½ per cent seasonally corrected – overfull employment by any standards.*

Avoiding a Clash

In the course of 1963–4, the centre of gravity of economic policy began to shift slightly away from the Treasury. More and more ministries approved schemes for the modernization of Britain – there were the Robbins Report on Higher Education, the plans for the North-East, Scotland and the South-East; and although the Buchanan Report on urban traffic never really became a 'Government commitment', it did influence the whole climate of policy discussion. A big innovation was of course the appointment of Mr Edward Heath in October 1963 as President of the Board of Trade with the additional resounding title of Secretary of State for Industry, Trade and Regional Development.

The Board of Trade was supposed to be responsible for promoting industrial efficiency as well as for the Government's relations with particular industries; and it was also in charge of Britain's overseas trade policy. Yet until an ex-14th Earl appointed Mr Heath, the President of the Board of Trade, however able a person, was treated by Prime Ministers as if he sat below the salt. 'Who can be interested in things like GATT?' one Civil Servant super knight once remarked to me (referring to the international agreement laying down the trading rules which so vitally affect British exporters). The title of Secretary of State, of which only a limited number can be created without a special Act of Parliament, greatly enhanced the President of the Board of Trade's standing in the innermost circles of the

* National Institute Review, August 1964, *op. cit.*

Cabinet and Whitehall. This, together with the appointment to the post of an able and energetic politician who enjoyed a special relationship with the new Prime Minister at long last put industry and commerce at the top table.

It must be said, however, that much of Mr Heath's influence on policy arose from his high position in the Cabinet, rather than from operating the Board of Trade itself. The Board is an administrative machine more than a planning unit and most of its key officials are engaged in running services or agencies (for example Bankruptcy or export information). Characteristically all its pronouncements about the state of business – including the much-publicized monthly trade figures – emanate from statisticians rather than from economists, or officials concerned with policy. Whether fairly or not, the Department has a slightly musty air in the eyes not only of some really top Civil Servants but of industrialists as well.

Putting one man in charge of regional development was a very good idea. Quite the worst way of treating the problem was the earlier expedient of giving each regional pressure group a spokesman inside the Cabinet. The really important job is not to spread bribes fairly between constituencies, but to hold a sensible balance between different regions – to encourage development, for example, where there is unused labour, and to discourage it where there is congestion and overful employment. Mr Heath has had a much bigger impact on regional policy than the public realizes. But his experiences have not convinced those reformers who doubted whether the small group of officials from different departments who served Mr Heath could do the job, and who believed a complete new Ministry was required.

When Mr Heath was first appointed every political columnist speculated about a coming clash between him and Maudling. The two are, of course rivals for the Conservative succession and – although they do not differ all that much from each other on policy – are temperamentally poles apart. The stock witticism was that the Conservatives would now provide a preview of the fight confidently expected between Mr George Brown and Mr James Callaghan, who were being groomed for the Economics Ministry and the Exchequer respectively in the next Labour Government. Alas for the columnists the promised Maudling–Heath clash failed to materialize, largely due to the painstaking diplomatic efforts of the two men's Permanent Secretaries to keep them from wandering into each other's gardens.

The price of this contrived Apartheid was inevitably a loss of coherence and overall direction. There was no one man who was clearly in charge of economic policy as a whole. Sir Alec Douglas-Home's best friend could hardly expect him personally to provide the economic keynote for his Administration, and the Cabinet Office was in no position to give him independent advice.

There was one other missing element. The three Ministries bestriding the key areas of economic policy were the Treasury, the Board of Trade and the Ministry of Labour. An astonishing number of Britain's problems, from incomes policy to the wasteful use of manpower, are in the Ministry of Labour's sphere, yet it was never in the period covered by this book a top political office, worth holding for its own sake rather than as a stepping stone to higher things. Sir Alec if anything reinforced this unfortunate tradition by appointing Mr Joseph Godber, an amiable man who had made a very good impression as Britain's disarmament negotiator, but was hardly a heavyweight as a Minister of Labour.

Added to this was the widespread feeling amongst people in both business and Whitehall that they were dealing with a lame duck Government. Worse still was the national hypocrisy about modernization and change. The fashionable belief among Left and Right alike is that if a country is to get moving, it needs not a new financial policy but more fundamental changes in its industrial and business structure. Indeed it is a fair bet that reviewers will criticize this book for not stressing the point enough. Yet whenever any such structural change is proposed all hell is immediately let loose, as Mr Heath found out when he brought in his famous Bill to abolish resale price maintenance. The Labour Party, to its discredit, simply abstained and enjoyed the fun, while large numbers of Conservative M.P.s – Cabinet colleagues as well as Back-benchers – made no attempt to conceal their opposition. 'They have no loyalty, no philosophy and no guts', was one comment of someone who saw the battle at very close quarters.

It was not Mr Heath's fault that the R.P.M. Bill came to take on an exaggerated importance as an isolated measure. Mr Heath originally regarded it as part of a wider policy for making the economy more competitive and cost increases less easy for employers to pass on. These wider aspects were the real casualty of the political storm which caused the issue to be treated mainly as a Conservative Party row.

Quite a number of other worthwhile reforms were introduced in the last year of the 1959–64 Parliament. Industrial Training Boards were set up, much more generous grants were provided for training in the high unemployment areas, 'Little Neddies' were set up for individual industries and new agencies were formed to promote industrial building. Indeed Whitehall connoisseurs suggested that the change of outlook in favour of greater planning was a precursor of a later change of party – just as the shift away from detailed controls after 1949 was a sign that the public was moving towards the Conservatives.

In most of these areas the Government was doing some of the right things, but often too slowly and with insufficient vigour. Too many ministers relied too much on consultations with trade associations and other established channels and were reluctant to force the pace themselves. Government purchases, running into many thousands of million pounds a year, could be a first-class instrument for promoting automation and amalgamation in industry, but an official committee on this subject was marking time.

There were too many conferences and not enough action.

An additional difficulty was that neither Maudling nor Heath was much enamoured of NEDC which might have been a channel for a more vigorous economic policy. But both had to accept what they found. Members of the NEDC staff itself, unfortunately, began to run out of steam as a result of the failure to agree on an incomes policy in the early months of 1964, and the long-drawn election wait. From the day NEDC was set up the Treasury thought of it far too exclusively in times of restraining income, and not nearly as much work was done in Great George Street on how it could be used to boost productivity.

An incomes policy is a never ending series of tactical engagements. To have any hope of even partial success against the powerful forces ranged against it, every trick has to be used; probes into price increases, the threat of unilateral tariff reductions, special investigations into monopoly profits, and the willingness to sit out strikes, are a few of the measures which should be used as the occasion demands. These are not crankish dreams but are listed in a sober report by responsible officials from several different Western countries published in 1964 by the O.E.C.D. entitled, *Policies for Prices, Profits and other Non-Wage Incomes*. Such a policy demands a central nerve centre, considerable support from public opinion, and probably cannot be carried out by a Government in its last year of office which has the public opinion polls running against it for most of the time.

Early in 1964 Mr Maudling tried very hard to secure a joint statement urging responsibility on all sides; and the employers offered a price review body as a sweetener. With an election approaching, the Union leaders refused either to cooperate with the Chancellor or to suggest an alternative policy of their own.

Mr Maudling thought of an incomes policy too exclusively in terms of a deal with the T.U.C. Even if such a deal had been made it would still have had to be reinforced by the kind of measure mentioned in the last paragraph.

There were one or two errors of timing at these NEDC sessions. For example the unions' representatives were handed the Government's ideas for a *quid pro quo* on the side of profits and prices two days after the T.U.C. Economic Committee had already met and decided to refuse a deal. But I doubt if better timing would have made the outcome any different.

In the course of these talks the employers' representatives offered to set up a Price Review Body which would investigate and comment on controversial price increases in basic commodities. Seeing that no deal was forthcoming on wages, the Federation of British Industries understandably withdrew its offer. The Government should then have taken over their idea itself as worthwhile in its own right. Many Continental countries, listed in the O.E.C.D. Report, have such bodies which work quite successfully despite unanswerable theological question such as 'what is a commodity?'. These bodies have discouraged employers from granting wage increases in the expectation of passing them on in higher prices.

No vague general statement, even if the Union leaders had agreed to sign one, could have been a substitute for imaginative generalship on the Government's own part. When, for example, the engineers settled for five per cent it took the Chancellor a couple of weeks before he announced that this was only $3\frac{3}{4}$ per cent at an annual rate; and he failed to pounce indignantly, as Dr Erhard might have done in his place, on the employers' statement that the settlement would lead to higher prices.

An increase in engineering prices did in fact follow the wage settlement with suspicious smartness and uniformity. Perhaps its size could be explained away as a delayed response to a whole series of cost increases going back some time. But if the habit of granting wage increases with the expectation of passing them on in higher prices was ever to be broken, the best place to start was with prices;

and it is here that the Government may have missed an opportunity.

Worst of all was the return to the policy of industrial appeasement which Whitehall had foresworn in the 1961 pay-pause crisis. By the summer of 1964 top officials no longer bothered to pretend that an incomes policy existed. The Public Sector had played a leading role in the inflationary breakthrough – postmen, electricity workers and busmen all received increases which were above the $3\frac{1}{2}$ per cent guiding light; in the case of the busmen the Ministry of Labour returned to the bad old habit of appointing a Court of Inquiry.

No doubt these were special cases – we all have a special case for higher pay. In none of the negotiations did the Government urge the nationalized industries to break with the custom of across the board increases and insist on offering differential increases in areas where labour was short. The undefined seniority of the Chancellor over other economic ministers was not sufficient to push through radical changes in wages policies. Nor did the Government try to improve the supply and demand position in overloaded areas by a selective immigration policy. This would have meant choosing newcomers according to the skills they possessed (as the Germans did), but was prevented by the 'Commonwealth first' tradition. And the familiar incomprehensible Ministry of National Insurance objections prevented Mr Maudling from thinking about a selective payroll tax areas such as the south-east where the demand for labour was particularly high.

The Post Office dispute was a classic example of how to get the worst of all worlds. The pace was made at first by the Treasury knights, more in their capacity of guardians of the Civil Service than as economic advisers. The Civil Service had just accepted a $3\frac{1}{2}$ per cent pay increase and the Treasury was terrified of the unrest that would be caused by a higher award in the Post Office which, by some anachronism, come under the Civil Service pay arrangement. The Treasury's attitude would only have made sense if the Cabinet had been prepared to sit out a Post Office strike, which it clearly was not before the election. Well-placed observers in other parts of Whitehall are convinced that the Government could have settled for less than the eventual 6½ per cent if its offer had been made earlier in the year.

Even the 6½ per cent offer was put in an unnecessarily bad light. For when Mr Maudling presented the settlement to the Cabinet, with all its face-saving clauses, he ran into opposition from a redoubtable possé including the two ex-tough Chancellors Messrs Selwyn Lloyd and Peter Thorneycroft. By the time Mr Maudling, reinforced by a thoroughly infuriated Mr Heath, had worn down their opposition, the postmen had called a strike and the offer looked like an abject surrender to the threat of force. The whole episode is a perfect case of the recurrent thesis of this book that all sorts of different people, politicians, officials and others, acted together to produce a much worse policy than any one of them would have produced left to himself.

Budget Vindicated

The 1964 Budget was a much happier story than the incomes policy. In contrast to 1955 the Treasury excluded all electoral considerations from its policy thinking. The likely pace of the boom (going ahead at the turn of 1963–4 at the unsustainable rate of six per cent per annum) was uncertain and the official advice was to increase taxes by something in the rather wide range of £100m.–£225m. Mr Maudling was warned, however, that if he plumped for the lower end of the scale he might have to add on a bit more tax in the summer – at a time when his Cabinet colleagues might have objected to anything which jarred with the run-up to the election. This may help explain why Mr Maudling was such a keen advocate of an early election.

Nevertheless the Chancellor personally suspected, in the

face of almost all published comment, that the boom was flattening out of its own accord, and he produced a surprisingly mild Budget collecting only the minimum figure of another £100m. in higher drink and tobacco duties. Sir William Armstrong (and one or two other senior Treasury Administrators) were also anxious to avoid giving a shock to business confidence by too high a tax increase and they wanted to persuade sceptical industrialists that stop-go had at last been abandoned in favour of steady growth.

By the summer there were unmistakable signs that the growth of the economy had slowed down to four per cent or less. The boom could, of course, accelerate in 1965; but for the period for which the Budget was designed Mr Maudling was right and his critics wrong.

Something has already been said about the large trade deficit which arrived with the 1964 New Year. It gave rise to a fierce statistical haggle, with many political overtones, about whether it was due to stockpiling or more basic weaknesses. The row was pretty pointless. A deficit of this kind is a cyclical phenomenon which had a pretty close parallel four years before. It could be expected to narrow automatically with time. The real question was how much it would narrow and how quickly. History provides little guide, as previous booms had had their heads cut off at this stage.

A similar argument applies to productivity. We simply do not know how fast productivity will be able to grow in a sustained boom, as in previous cycles a boom has never been allowed to go very far before it has been severely checked to protect sterling.

Export Enigmas

There was much speculation as this book was going to press about the poor performance of British exports in the first half of 1964. It presented quite a paradox. Wage and productivity statistics suggested that as a result of Continental inflation the *costs* of British exporters were rising much more slowly than those of our main competitors. Yet *prices* of British exports continued to rise more rapidly than any of our principal rivals and our share of world exports and manufactures continued to drop rapidly. (The failure of exports to grow was incidentally one, but not the only, reason why the domestic boom flattened out before the middle of the year.)

Quite possibly the very new look at productivity which many British firms took in the early 1960s, and which both Whitehall and the economic world were so keen to encourage, led many firms either to devote less attention to some of their less profitable export markets, or at least to give top priority to raising profit margins.

Another big factor which may have been holding exports down, was the tendency of many firms to invest in new factories in the 'white' Commonwealth countries at the expense of their direct exports. If a levy or other means of control were ever imposed on imports, it would be right to consider on a cold-blooded national interest calculation a similar levy on capital investment in developed sterling-area countries. Such a levy would create a barrier equivalent to the one already imposed by the 'dollar premium' in the non-sterling markets, and would not be all that different in principle from a similar tax imposed by the free enterprise American Government. It would have to be weighed in the balance against the possibility – which would certainly be exaggerated – of increased restlessness among Commonwealth holders of sterling balances.

There was considerable evidence too, that British industry was at long last beginning to suffer from her exclusion from the Common Market, where tariff discrimination was becoming serious. One of the first questions to be answered by the new Government was whether we could sit down meekly and let this happen with no thought either of retaliation or of attempting, despite all previous reverses, to strike a purely economic bargain with de Gaulle.

For all these difficulties there was nothing in the state of export order books (in the late summer of 1964) to prevent British exports from suddenly shooting ahead just when everyone least expected it. If there is one lesson to be derived from past experience it is that exports are unpredictable. The surge of imported manufactures, above all machinery, was in many ways more worrying than the, possibly temporary, failure of exports to rise. The import upsurge suggested the *possibility* that at current exchange rates Britain was still not competitive enough to support a four per cent growth rate. In other words the devaluation argument first launched by the National Institute 3½ years before may still have been valid.

I make no apology for using words like 'possibility' and 'may'. The task of policy makers is not to usurp the role of soothsayers, but to hope for the best and prepare for the worst. If the National Institute turns out to be right a Chancellor of either party who devalued the pound would deserve not opprobrium but gratitude for saving us from a far worse fate – provided he did not repeat Cripps's error and attempt to fix another rate too quickly.

As the storm clouds gathered over the pound, with the approach of the 1964 election, the official doctrine was that future difficulties with sterling, whether due to speculation or to temporary stockpiling, would be met by international borrowing. This is a story we heard before in 1959, when the present head of the Treasury's Finance Group, Sir Denis Rickett, told the Radcliffe Committee that he thought and hoped that Britain's drawing facilities at the I.M.F. would be enough to deal with unforeseen contingencies. Two years later Mr Selwyn Lloyd was persuaded to bring the growth of the economy to a complete halt.

Will history repeat itself? My own guess is that if a big deficit persists the result this time will be a compromise between the old fashioned deflationary approach, and less orthodox expedients such as import controls. In other words, from the point of view of expansionists, it will be neither black nor white but an indeterminate shade of grey.

One other prediction can safely be made. The Government installed after the 1964 election will have to take a very tough line with a trade-union movement which has shown little sign of being able to put its own house in order. Egged on by the Post Office settlement, extravagant, mischievous and ill-reasoned wage claims were tabled in the summer which, if met with weakness, would sabotage all hopes of a more rapid rise in *real* living standards. Even a devaluation would have to be accompanied by a firm policy on wages to have full success. Mr Maudling, if he got back, would probably threaten that without some wage restraint, expansion would just have to be brought to a halt by old-fashioned methods. Mr Wilson's message might amount to something not very different. But he might have the advantage of a much canvassed, though not very blissful, honeymoon period with the unions.

The issue goes beyond wages. Bad management and bad unions have fertilized each other for too long. In attitudes to manning of machines, training, redundancy, union structure, and company profits, the British union movement has – for too often repeated historical reasons – claims to be regarded as the worst in the world. Paradoxically, one of the strongest economic arguments for a Labour Government is that, beneath layers of velvet, it might be more prepared to face a showdown in dealing with the unions.

Appendix: In Place of Gold

A final word on a very technical subject. One of Mr Maudling's first actions on becoming Chancellor was to put forward to the 1962 Conference of the International Monetary Fund a plan to improve 'international liquidity' arrangements – in other words to find a new form of international reserve to supplement gold, dollars and sterling. The Chancellor agreed with those who thought the lack of man-made international currency was the main basic threat to world economic expansion.

This was very much a personal move on the part of Mr Maudling, who was strongly and insistently backed by Mr Macmillan. The actual scheme presented by the Chancellor was largely worked out by Mr Lucius Thompson-McCausland, a forward-looking Bank of England adviser who had been secretary to Keynes as a young man. This does not mean that the Bank approved of Maudling's initiative; but it was well aware that if it did not have a plan ready on occasions such as this, someone else would come out with something which it would dislike a great deal more.

The British Chancellor's initiative was in fact much derided at the time by orthodox financial opinion throughout the world and he received an offensive public snub from Mr R. V. Roosa, the U.S. Under Secretary of the Treasury and key figure in American overseas financial policy.

Later on in 1963–4, many of those who originally derided Mr Maudling's 1962 initiative, including Mr Roosa himself, became convinced that something needed to be done to improve the world's financial system; and even the inadequate and tentative proposals put forward at the Tokio I.M.F. Conference in 1964 for enlarging world credit might never have emerged without the British Chancellor's initiative.

All the same it is difficult to feel entirely happy about the negotiating attitude adopted by the British Treasury. In 1963 Mr E. M. Bernstein, the well-known American expert and former Director of Research at the I.M.F., came out with a plan for 'international reserve units'. These were to be composite bundles of the main world currencies and would be issued in agreed quantities to supplement gold and the existing international reserve currencies, the dollar and sterling.

Mr Bernstein's suggested reserve unit was taken up in later negotiations by the six Common Market countries, and with particular alacrity by the French. The British side, however, gave it a pretty dusty reception and preferred different devices for creating new international reserves. There were some genuine technical snags about the plan, but the real difficulties went deeper. The French, under de Gaulle, were pretty obviously interested in doing down the dollar – in finding ways of disposing of their own dollar holdings, and dethroning the dollar from its position as principal world reserve currency.

Moreover, many Continental countries believed that there was 'too much international liquidity'. Unlike Mr Bernstein himself, they envisaged the creation of reserve units to replace rather than supplement existing holdings of dollar and sterling. The French plan actually involved an annual repayment of sterling balances, which the British balance of payments would be most unlikely to stand. The net effect would have been to destroy reserves rather than to create them.

All the same, Britain might have done better to have considered the French proposal as a basis for discussion. Granted its political motives – granted even that the French might have withdrawn it if the Anglo-Americans had taken it seriously – the reserve unit idea did have in it the seeds of a new and less vulnerable international monetary order. Britain should have welcomed the plan and suggested practical modifications to give it a less deflationary bias.

The really disquieting feature was that the British attitude was still influenced by the Bank of England's dislike of anything that might throw the slightest doubt on the continuation of sterling as a reserve currency. For many years past very senior British Cabinet Ministers insisted privately that sterling's role as a reserve currency was a burden of which they would only be too pleased to be rid, if only they knew how. One wondered whether this attitude had been made at all effective at the official level. For although ministers might use four-letter words about the prestige aspects of sterling as a world currency, these prestige considerations had certainly not been banished from the minds of many of those with practical responsibility for formulating the British attitude. Sir Leslie Rowan's passionate defence of the sterling area quoted on p. 200 still reverberated through some corridors in Great George Street and Threadneedle Street.

On the political level the British attitude was also coloured by the top priority given to preserving a specially close relationship with America on as many issues as possible. A book on the Treasury is not the place to discuss whether this priority – which, arguably, kept us out of the Common Market – has been misguided.

But I cannot end the most recent of the historical chapters without noting the growing danger of Britain retreating further and further away from Europe into a cosy English-speaking world; a danger which was not reduced either by the Commonwealth emphasis of Labour Party propaganda, or by the reaction among the Conservatives to two successive snubs from France in negotiations with the Common Market.

CHAPTER 9

What Went Wrong

THE previous three chapters have shown that Britain's economic steering over the past decade was hardly a triumphant success. The aim of this chapter is to draw the threads together and summarize what went wrong. It contains inevitably a fairly hard economic core. The question of why it went wrong, which brings in broader questions such as national psychology, political attitudes, and traditional institutions will be discussed in Chapters 10 and 11.

The sad story of British export performances is summarized by the following table.

1953—1964 (1st Quarter)

	% Change in Price of Manufactured Exports	% Change in Volume of Manufactures exported
U.K.	+19	+48
U.S.	+18	(+16)*
W. Germany	+ 7	+233
France	+ 3	+136
Italy	−18	+303†

* Base is average of 1952–4.
† All exports.

The table covers a long span and conceals the improvement in the American position and the deterioration of the Italian one near the end of it; but it alas gives a fair picture of the U.K. over almost the whole of the eleven-year period. Even if Britain's competitive position should begin to improve very soon, the eleven-year deterioration will have exacted a very heavy toll in lost economic growth.

Speculation about why Britain's European competitors secured a price advantage over Britain is less important than the fact that they did so. One reason why Germany and Italy may have secured a competitive start in the buoyant export markets of the early 1950s is that Britain was then bogged down in a rearmament drive.. There were also deeper sociological causes connected with the aftermath of war and the presence of a large pool of unemployed refugees in Germany's case and southern workless in Italy's. Having gained this lead, the two countries became caught up in what is often called 'a virtuous circle'. High export demand led to a rapid general rate of growth, which in turn led to high investment, not only in machinery but in research, new products, and overseas sales promotion. In this atmosphere productivity grew quickly and for years export prices remained extremely competitive.

For one reason or another the British economy did not benefit from any such 'virtuous circle', and it was therefore the responsibility of the Government to do something about it. What could the Government have done? Today the main moral the Treasury would probably draw from the table is: 'Need for an incomes policy.' A good debating reply would be to say that German wages rose much faster than British (from a much lower level) but were more nearly offset by rising productivity. But it would be silly to deny that a temporary slowing down in the growth of British *money* wages during the years of Monckton appeasement in the early 1950s would have been beneficial to exports and ultimately to real earnings. It is incredible that throughout the period covered by the table, even the statement of a guiding light by the Government was regarded as an unwarrantable interference with free collective bargaining. Certainly a Government which stood idly by, while this deterioration was recorded every month by the O.E.C.D. in Paris, and which neither devalued, nor introduced an incomes policy, nor thought of any other alternative, demonstrated a remarkable level of incompetence in the conduct of economic policy.

The Government's policy towards the taxation of income

and wealth certainly made an incomes policy no easier. The charge here is that a double system was allowed to flourish. Nominal rates of taxation on incomes and on estates passing at death were if anything too progressive, and allowed too little opportunity for encouraging people to increase and pass on their wealth. On the other hand, for those who knew the ropes the high rates were just a farce. Until 1961–2, surtax started at £2,000 a year and together with income tax took away nearly half of all extra income earned beyond that point. Yet there was no tax worth mentioning on capital, capital gains, or land values; the five-year rule and discretionary trusts made estate duties a voluntary tax, and Top Hat pension schemes and educational covenants introduced further huge loopholes for the financially smart. Indeed many Left-wing economists wanted *lower* taxes for the wealthy but wanted to make them *effective*.

The public did not understand the details of these abuses, and its resentment, naturally exploited by the Opposition, often took the form of anti-economic and illiberal demands for rent controls, fixed land prices, dividend controls, and of a primitive dislike of speculators. But it rightly sensed that something was wrong. The hypocritical attitude to untaxed wealth 'it's all right if you can get away with it', must have poisoned the atmosphere in talks with the unions more than an honest Tory policy of lessening redistributive taxation through the front-door would have done. Irrespective of its side effects, the double system was indefensible.

But whatever opportunities had been lost earlier on, by the time of Mr Lloyd's 1961 pay pause it was too late to expect an incomes policy to do the trick alone. For by then Britain's export costs had clearly become uncompetitive.

This is only another way of saying that the pound was overvalued. The National Institute was howled down for pointing this out at the beginning of 1961, six months before Selwyn Lloyd's emergency measures. But as has been shown, its diagnoses were not all that different from warnings that the Bank of England was giving at the time; and when two such different bodies are even remotely near agreement, there is usually something in what they are saying. Since, however, devaluation or any other kind of tampering with exchange rates was ruled out of court from the mid 1950s onwards, we had to endure several years of stagnation, and below-capacity growth, hoping for continental inflation to restore our competitive position. This is essentially what is meant by the familiar but justified change that domestic growth has been sacrificed for the sake of sterling. (The following remarks should be read in conjunction with the discussion of exchange rates in Chapter 5, pages 142–8.)

As the Federal German Chancellor, Professor Erhard, once wrote: 'I come repeatedly to the same point: it is an odd, not to say a grotesque position that, in spite of different trends of prices in the individual national economies, the rates of exchange have remained immovable, as if between these two factors there existed no inner relation. Out of such a contradictory policy a considerable shift in the opportunities for export must inevitably result.'*

The one country whose exchange rate had not remained immovable when Professor Erhard wrote these words was France. French industrial psychology is even more home market-oriented than Britain's, and suffers from many of the ills diagnosed in this country by the sociological school of writers. By the late 1950s, France had also landed itself with an overvalued currency. But unlike Britain, France devalued twice (as well as using all sorts of export-promotion and import-discouraging devices while her payments were in the red) and as Frank Blackaby has put it, 'was able to resume rapid growth with a firm basis in increasing exports'.†

This has nothing to do with national character. In 1963–4, there were signs that inflation had eroded France's earlier competitive advantage. But de Gaulle was enforcing

* *Prosperity Through Competition*, p. 241. Professor Erhard wrote these words just before the Deutschmark revaluation.

† F. T. Blackaby, *The Recent Performance of the British Economy*, British Association 1962 Annual Meeting.

a new order of priorities which gave priority to a 'strong franc', and all the much vaunted 'planning' did not prevent a deliberate policy of cutting back the growth of output below the *Commisariat*'s targets.

The fact that all the World's Central Bankers and Finance Ministry officials have become more and more firmly committed to fixed exchange rates should not deter anyone from advocating an alternative policy. It is a good generalization that just at the moment when all the leading authorities shout most vociferously in favour of a fashionable dogma and try to make their opponents feel unrealistic dreamers, the dogma itself is not very far from breaking down.

Some writers when attacking Chancellors for putting sterling first have in mind an allied but different criticism. The policy with which they find most fault is that of maintaining sterling as a world currency. This policy can for convenience be divided into three aspects: (1) the sterling area system under which most Commonwealth countries and one or two others hold the bulk of their international reserves in pounds in London; (2) the policy of encouraging foreign Governments, banks, financial institutions, and commercial firms to hold large working balances in sterling; (3) the fostering of London as an international financial centre with gold, foreign exchange, and commodity markets, where world trade that does not touch Britain's shores can be financed, and where loans can be negotiated for overseas borrowers.

It is quite true that maintaining sterling as a reserve currency for the Commonwealth is nowadays an unrequited burden; and pride rather than self-interest has at times made the British financial authorities too suspicious of plans for transferring these balances to an international institution. But these plans would present both political and technical difficulties, to put it mildly, even if Britain were less equivocal towards them. Moreover sterling area balances were relatively quiescent for a very long time.

European- and American-owned balances under heading (2) above have been the most volatile over the last few years. It is these balances that in the words of the 1963 O.E.C.D. Report on Britain 'make the pound sensitive to doubts about U.K. economic policies in a much more acute fashion than is the case for most other currencies'. The O.E.C.D. Report adds pharisaically 'in itself, it is no bad thing that a country's policies should be under constant scrutiny in this way'. One does not have to be an old-fashioned believer in untrammelled national sovereignty to feel that an international bankers' House of Lords is quite the wrong group to exercise a scrutiny of this kind. Still the fact remains that for the time being we could not afford to lose these short-term funds. For if they were withdrawn, while the exchange rate remained immutable, the reserves would fall catastrophically.

The effects on Britain's freedom of manoeuvre of the private financial activities of the City, listed under heading (3), vary a great deal. Many of them, as conducted in 1964, are pretty harmless and perhaps even beneficial as far as the effects on the reserves are concerned. The speculation that develops against sterling in the foreign exchange, gold and commodity markets in times of crises, would simply be transferred to other centres if the London markets were shut. The raising of foreign loans in the City is unobjectionable provided the subscriptions also come from overseas.

These activities, however, do not depend on sterling being a reserve currency. Amsterdam and Zürich are more than purely domestic financial centres, without the florin and the Swiss franc being international currencies. Unfortunately the Bank of England always itches to go beyond these strictly entrepôt activities and has campaigned very vigorously for the freeing of capital movements into and out of Britain, both for residents and for foreigners. To allow concessions to the Bank on this issue would expose the reserves to quite unjustifiable additional risks.

Even if sterling had not been a world currency in any of

the senses listed, the sheer volume of inward and outward payments from Britain to the rest of the world – £13,000m. a year, thirteen times the value of the published reserves – would have been enough to set off enormous speculative movements whenever traders felt the slightest doubt about the pound.

Could, on the other hand, sterling survive a change in its exchange rate and remain a world currency? I do not know (in the 1930s it managed to do so). But the belief that it could not has inspired innumerable financial restrictions on domestic output. During past sterling crises British diplomacy was a masterpiece of self-abnegation. The handling of the 1961 crisis, for example, was vitiated by a complete failure to use the considerable bargaining power which Britain then possessed. One did not have to be a confidant of the Banque de France or the Federal Reserve to appreciate that over the last few years Britain's main allies were just as anxious not to see sterling devalued as the British Government and would have gone to considerable lengths to avoid this happening. In fact the main reasons advanced for not touching sterling the last few years have been primarily those of good world citizenship. Sterling devaluation, it has been said by leading bankers, would start an uncontrollable run on the dollar, destroy the world's monetary system, disrupt the Commonwealth, etc.

If these arguments are right, then Britain was doing the world a service by not devaluing and might expect to be rewarded. If instead of cringing before the prospect, British negotiators had actually threatened to devalue, we might well have been able to get more financial aid in the past without having to introduce a big deflationary package. It is extremely doubtful if Britain used even a fraction of its potential bargaining power in the crises discussed in earlier chapters. The Treasury and Bank thought it necessary to deflate in any case, and most Cabinet ministers did not have a clue what the arguments were all about.

Not only did the Government put sterling first during this

period, but it systematically deprived itself of nearly all other weapons for influencing the balance of payments apart from internal deflation. The movement to free world trade from import controls was, of course, a desirable one and it was in Britain's interest to give a lead. Yet GATT – the world-wide trade agreement that sets the rules of the game – has always allowed temporary exceptions for countries in balance of payments difficulties. Until Maudling's heretical utterances in 1964 British Governments do not seem to have thought of using these escape clauses.

As Professor Austin Robinson has pointed out, 'We have appeared to assume that we can follow policies bound to increase our propensities to import in the simple faith that exports can be left to balance our imports whatever they may be.'* The authorities were neither willing to contemplate any variation in exchange rates, nor did they have what Professor Robinson calls a 'fail safe' foreign trade policy in the background.

British policy was also extremely high-minded about providing any tax or other special privileges for exporters. Most European countries introduced special export promotion laws as part of their post-war reconstruction efforts. As a result of international agreements many of these special laws were done away with in the 1950s; the German one expired on 31 December 1955 – after it was no longer needed. Britain had no law to abolish. Such devices were for lesser breeds. Even minor inducements such as higher investment allowances for whole industries with a good export potential, or permission for successful exporters to maintain small personal private bank accounts abroad, were firmly eschewed.

This self-abnegatory attitude to our trade and financial problems coincided with the years of Suez, of a bared-teethed determination to preserve our position in Kuwait by force, and of an obsession with an 'independent' nuclear deterrent. British policy was tough where it should have been

* *Three Banks Review*, December 1963.

conciliatory, conciliatory where it should have been tough; nationalist where it should have been internationalist, internationalist where it should have been nationalist. Perhaps there was a *folie de grandeur* consistency about the whole combination.

The criticism made so far is that Britain was playing the wrong economic game during the last dozen years or so. There is also another criticism to be made of a different kind. This is that even if the chosen game is the right one, it has played it badly.

If a policy of putting sterling first, and protecting the balance of payments purely by operating on internal demand is to have a chance, the most delicate economic management is required. The Cabinet must be interested and knowledgeable enough to act in time, for in controlling cycles delay is fatal. Officials need to be highly expert, to possess a sound flair for the business situation, and iron nerves; and the same politicians must stay in their post long enough to give continuity of policy. (It is not I who am dictating these highly idealized conditions; they are dictated by the strait-jacket of assumptions in which British economic policy has been confined.)

Instead, bad tactics, political fears, intellectual mis-understandings, and failures of timing all combined to reduce Britain's economic performance even below what was necessary to protect the pound. These highly critical words apply not to any single individual but to the resultant of all the conflicting forces that went to make up the official Treasury line.

In the 1950s and early 1960s the Treasury behaved like a simple Pavlovian dog responding to two main stimuli: One is 'a run on the reserves' and the other is '500,000 unemployed'. On the whole (although not invariably), it was officials who panicked on the first stimulus, and ministers on the second. Each side usually managed to communicate its alarm to the other. Officials instinctively regard a rapid fall in the reserves as 'money running out of the kitty'. Politicians feel alarmed by unemployment figures, which they never adjust for seasonal factors (not that the Ministry of Labour does either in public), and which as a consequence always come to them as a nasty surprise.

With a response system as crude as this, Government stabilization policies are pretty well bound to have the reverse of the effect intended. Government stabilization policies have more often than not tended to aggravate the fluctuations they have been meant to correct. Mr Butler started on this perverse path in his 1955 Budget when he inflated in the face of a boom; and the course was confirmed by Mr Thorneycroft in 1957 when he deflated in the face of a slump. The chart shows on page 290 how frequently the economy was given a downward shove on the eve of a recession and an upward thrust as a boom was gathering force.

The root of the trouble is that economic life is subject to time lags. On the upward phase, the boom in home demand, the balance of payments deficit, and the run on the reserves, although inter-related, do not coincide in time. Instead they often come in three successive phases. Similarly in the downturn, by the time unemployment has risen above 500,000 it is far too late to stop a recession.

Government policy has in fact been subject for many years to a remarkably regular four-year rhythm of mixed political, psychological, and economic origin. This rhythm fitted in so well with some of Mr Harold Macmillan's own temperamental characteristics that one is tempted to label it the Macmillan Cycle.*

But I do not want to stress the personal aspects. The cycle was working both before and after Macmillan's Premiership, and in any case reflects closely the instinctive reflexes of the whole Government machine. A stylized picture of such a cycle runs as follows: It begins with a period of recovery and

* See 'Too many Regulators', by Samuel Brittan, *the Banker*, September 1962.

boom. By eating into a large margin of unused resources businessmen are able to push up output at a much faster rate than they can hope to sustain in the long run. Wage increases are first held down by unemployment and then offset by the exceptional rise in output. Butler's golden age

STOPS AND STARTS 1954–64

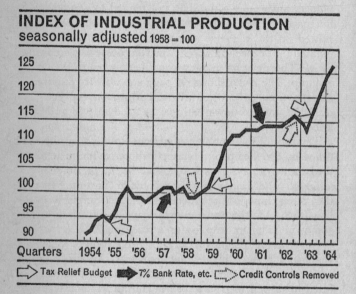

INDEX OF INDUSTRIAL PRODUCTION
seasonally adjusted 1958 = 100

⟹ Tax Relief Budget ➡ 7% Bank Rate, etc. ⟹ Credit Controls Removed

Crisis restrictions, involving a seven per cent Bank Rate, were imposed in 1957 and 1961, as the economy was about to move into a recession. The big tax relief Budgets of 1955, 1959, and 1963 were introduced after production had already begun to climb rapidly upwards. The major credit relaxations (accompanied in late 1962 by a purchase tax cut on cars) were not quite so badly timed, but nevertheless delayed until long after business had become very slack.

The normal trend of production is upwards in any advanced economy enjoying full employment. A steep rise is a sign of boom; a levelling out, or period of marking time is a sign of stagnation.

was in 1953–4; Amory's in 1958–9. Maudling's would have been in 1963 and early 1964 were it not for memories of the past and the political troubles through which his Party was then passing.

During the golden age, with an election either just past or just ahead, the Government hesitates to put a brake on the expansion of demand. Eventually the slack in the economy that has made the golden age possible is taken up, symptoms of labour shortage appear, and the underlying balance of payments begins to weaken. The reserves are probably still all right at this stage, either because 'hot' money is flowing into London (as in 1960), or because the sterling area is piling up reserves in London (as in early 1964) or just conceivably because overseas Central Bankers are granting credits to cover the gap.

At this stage events vary slightly from cycle to cycle. The Government may, as in 1956 and 1960, deflate enough to bring the rise in output to a halt, but not enough to convince the hard money school that it has eliminated inflationary pressure. This may be followed by a false dawn, as in 1957 and 1961, when production is allowed to rise again for a brief spell. But by now, we are in a stage of the cycle when anything can touch off an outflow of short-term funds. Holders of sterling have become aware of the size of the previous year's balance of payments deficit – even though the gap may already be narrowing. The abnormally rapid increase in wages, which is causing such alarm in financial circles, reflects a labour shortage that may already be waning. Meanwhile the investment boom has almost run its course. The same politicians who opposed the smallest degree of restraint when the economy really was over-strained now work out in hushed whispers how long it will take to exhaust the reserves completely. A particularly strict dose of deflation is announced in a mood of panic – including, of course, a seven per cent Bank Rate.

The economy now begins to go downhill. Early action which might do something to arrest the fall in investment is not taken, as a new and permanently tougher policy is supposed to be reigning. The Cabinet insist that the crisis measures have 'worked', but later forget the new tough policy and manage to dispense with the services of the Chancellor who introduced it. The first re-expansionist measures are furtive and inadequate. But by this time sterling is strong; and as stocks are more than adequate, the first few stages of re-expansion have little effect on the import bill. Months or years too late the Government plucks up confidence to reflate in a very big way. By this time however production is rising fast enough unaided and we are back where we came in.

For a country bent on preserving its exchange rate on a slender margin of reserves this cycle is a disaster. To begin with it takes the economy into inflationary regions that could be avoided if progress were smoother; the process of cost inflation operates like a ratchet. Money costs are pushed up during a boom, but do not fall back again during a slump. This makes it particularly important to avoid extreme peaks.

The other side of the coin is that for far too many years at a time output is sluggish, stationary, or sagging. In periods such as 1955–8, or 1960–2, output not only marks time but the Government is seen to be hitting it on the head whenever it shows any sign of rising. This creates the worst sort of environment for encouraging labour-saving investment, redundancy schemes, or modernized industrial training.

The economy has been stopped in its tracks so often in the past that businessmen have become extremely sceptical of all talk of sustained growth and react with hyper-sensitivity to any suggestion of even the most moderate application of the brake to prevent a genuine overstrain. Such reactions may not show British businessmen in too good a light compared with their German opposite numbers who still seem to react to a slowdown at home by going all out for exports; in this way they recreate their own boom without Government stimulation. But British Chancellors were not dealing with

German industry. British manufacturers, just like their French counterparts, need a sustained increase in home demand to spur them to activity.

The failure to introduce an incomes policy until very late in the day has already been mentioned. Restraining the rise in incomes in a free full-employment society is bound to be a never-ending series of tactical engagements; and for these successive ministers showed neither zest nor skill. One factor has been that for all the proliferation of inter-departmental committees there have been no unifying political figures linking the acts of the Treasury with other economic ministries. The President of the Board of Trade has never threatened to suspend tariff protection for industries where inflationary wage claims threatened. Nor have the spending ministries ever hinted that they might refuse to take excessive wage increases into account in placing government contracts.

Another factor here – which went right through Conservative economic policy – was the extreme unwillingness to mention specific industries, let alone firms, by name. Chancellors have never up to the summer of 1964 expressed views on specific wage claims or on the action of particular employers in passing on awards in higher prices. There were loads of exhortation but of a deliberately unspecific kind. It is significant that NIC was (a) outside the Government, (b) headed by a lawyer, and (c) reported on settlements long after they had been made. One cannot help comparing this lack of gumption with the activities of Professor Erhard when he was German Economics Minister. Erhard was far more of a doctrinaire opponent of State intervention than any British Conservative, yet he had not the slightest hesitation in letting particular industries and firms know exactly what he thought of their activities. He was perhaps also aided by the habitual respect with which many Germans invest the words of either ministers or a Professor, let alone a man who is both.

A different fault of British economic policy was the

neglect for so many years of what economic theorists call the supply side of the equation. By this they mean absence of measures for improving the efficiency and responsiveness of British business. This type of thing is today on every-body's lips. Examples are: encouraging science and auto-mation; improving industrial management; education; the training of skilled labour; redundancy; regional develop-ment and the new look in the nationalized industries. This is not to speak of the failure to do anything about the state of industries such as ship-building and machine tools early enough in the day. State interest in such fields is a normal part of any mixed economy; and a government that neglects them is not being pro-free enterprise, or anti-dirigiste, but simply asleep.

The Treasury cannot be blamed for the wasted years here. In fact from 1960 onwards it stepped in to give a lead in some of these areas, because no one else was doing so, even though they were quite outside its ordinary scope. I shall return in Chapter 11 to the question of why so little was done to remove the industrial and social bottlenecks stand-ing in the way of growth.

As far as the nationalized industries are concerned, the Labour Party bears a share of the responsibility for starting them in such an unenterprising, uncommercial mould, with boards full of retired generals, trade unionists, and safe figures of all kinds to reassure middle-of-the-road opinion. While the French State Sector formed the spearhead of the modernization drive, Britain developed a Morrisonian form of socialism modelled on the London Passenger Transport Board.

Appendix: An Influential Doctrine

During the last few year some policy thinkers in the Treasury have developed a doctrine of their own, which they think could help steer Britain off the rocks described in the preceding chapters. The doctrine is not, of course, a rigid orthodoxy and if any Chancellor were to put forward alternative policy criteria, he would naturally receive full cooperation. But it is a sincerely held framework of ideas which lies behind a great deal of Treasury advice.

Outside writers often label it the 'Paish Theory' on account of its resemblance to a theory put forward by Professor Frank Paish of the London School of Economics.* The label irritates some Treasury men beyond endurance, partly because many of the Department's own economists developed these ideas quite independently of Paish, and partly because there are notable differences between the Paish theory and their own doctrine. A better picture would be that of a whole family of ideas, developed simultaneously by various economists, to which the 'Paish' and 'Treasury' variants both belong.

This family of ideas is ingenious and persuasive, and it certainly deserves to be stated fairly. But I must make it clear that the following brief summary is very much my own interpretation and cannot claim any sort of official backing.

Perhaps the simplest way of starting is with the observation that small differences in unemployment percentages are associated with quite large changes in the demand for labour and in the size of the annual wage round. When unemployment is down to one and a half per cent of the labour force (or 360,000 men) the competition of employers for labour is so brisk that, it can be argued, a wages policy would have little chance of success. (There may also be a tendency then to suck in imports and deflect exports to the home market but the evidence here is less convincing.) Unemployment has reached this level, or even fallen below it, in most of the post-war booms.

The exact relationship between unemployment and the

* See Chapter 17 of *Studies in An Inflationary Economy*, by F. W. Paish.

size of the wage round has been the subject of a great deal of technical discussion.* Published studies suggest that if unemployment were consistently maintained at a level higher than one and a half per cent but not as high as two per cent, money wages might rise very much more slowly than they have done in the past. For ease of exposition this optimum level is taken at 1.8 per cent, but this is not intended to bring into the argument a precision that its exponents would not claim. An unemployment level of 1.8 per cent is in fact no higher than the average of the last few years, even leaving out of account the heavy unemployment of the 1962–3 recession. The Treasury house doctrine suggests that something like this should be the target level and that government financial policy should try to prevent it going as low as 1.5 per cent in future booms.

An increase in the unemployment percentage from one and a half per cent to 1.8 per cent is associated with a much bigger difference in production. For when the demand for labour is lower, less people are drawn into the labour force and less overtime worked. Professor Paish has calculated that for each rise of 0.1 per cent in unemployment around the levels we are considering output falls by five times as much. So the margin of unused productive capacity associated with unemployment rate of say 1.8 per cent is therefore rather larger than it appears at first sight.†

* R. G. Lipsey, *Economica* 1960; L. Dicks-Mireaux, *Oxford Economic Papers*, October 1961; A. W. Phillips, *Economica*, 1962.

† I have deliberately not stated how large a margin of unused capacity is implied in the various unemployment percentages in order to dodge the problem of where the capacity ceiling lies. The argument can be stated in terms of unemployment percentages without having to take a view on this tricky question.

Incidentally the 'capacity' in question is not necessarily physical capacity – which may be out of line with the country's labour force – but the maximum production which could be achieved in normal peacetime conditions if overall demand were increased sufficiently across the board.

Some of the Treasury's policy thinkers would accept this loss of production as a once and for all sacrifice. But having established this margin, they would henceforth allow output to rise just as fast as the underlying growth of capacity.* From this point onwards the doctrine becomes in theory not one of deflation, but of growth; and provided this margin were preserved, there would be no need for policies which cut back production. One analogy might be that of a man standing in a rising lift with a few inches head-room. He is rising as fast as the lift, but, if the Treasury has its way, never bumps his head against the ceiling.

Considered by itself, the doctrine under discussion has quite radical implications. For it suggests that once a sufficient margin of unused capacity has been established, production should grow at the maximum rate physically possible. The sterling problem would presumably then – with some help from an incomes policy – take care of itself. But if it didn't the doctrine could well imply that devaluation, or import controls, or some other expedient, would have to take care of the balance of payments.

This implication would not be an easy one for the Treasury to swallow, and the outsider cannot help wondering how seriously the whole set of ideas would be taken if having established an unemployment percentage of about

* This is the underlying reasoning behind the expression 'sustainable expansion' of which Chancellors so frequently speak. The Treasury practically stated the doctrine in question in condensed form in para. 28 of the *Economic Survey* of 1962. Speaking of the situation as it appeared at the beginning of that year the *Survey* writer suggests that provided the pressure of home demand were kept in check and an incomes policy widely applied, the country would be able to take advantage of the favourable opportunities which the year then seemed to offer. He went on: 'If this is done production could expand without damaging increase in the pressure of demand upon resources and without a renewed risk to the balance of payments. This is the only sound basis for sustaining economic growth.' In the 1961 *Survey* there was a sentence saying: 'The Government do not believe that running the economy with greater pressure of demand than at present would in fact increase the sustainable rate of growth.' (para. 24).

1.8 per cent, there still seemed a long-term conflict between growth and the pound sterling. This question cannot be conclusively answered because in the past the Treasury has managed to justify to itself non-expansionist policies by asserting that it was still engaged in establishing the right margin of unused capacity.*

But even taken at its face value there are serious objections to this sort of 'surplus capacity' doctrine. It is one thing to try and prevent unemployment from falling below 1.8 per cent in a boom. But once having overshot the mark (as is extremely likely for the reasons discussed in the account of the Macmillan cycle) it is quite another thing to hold production down for months or years at a time until the required unemployment percentage is re-established. Frequent squeezes of this kind have, in all probability, undermined the growth of capacity itself in the period since 1955.

Nor is this the only objection. For even if the 1.8 per cent unemployment percentage could be permanently established with a minimum of deviation in either direction,

---

* The Treasury variant of the doctrine in question differs from the Paish version in at least two important interrelated ways:

1. Professor Paish envisages an unemployment percentage of just over two, which is appreciably higher than many people in the Treasury regard as desirable.
2. Unlike Paish the Treasury does not believe that the control of demand is sufficient to stop the inflationary spiral, but insists that there must be an incomes policy as well. This last point is of course obvious from Chancellors' statements. Paish's view about the relation between demand for labour and the pace of wage inflation would be regarded as rather too optimistic by many in Great George Street.

It is of course all too likely that if the maintenance of any chosen unemployment rate, whether 1.8 per cent or two per cent, failed to do the trick, the more conservative economists and officials would simply say that the structure of the economy had changed and that a higher percentage was now necessary. But if this escape route is chosen, the doctrine loses all its intellectual interest and becomes simply an excuse for deflation.

we are still left with a joker in the pack. To operate a policy of this kind a view must be taken of the probable growth of productive capacity in the future. Otherwise policy makers will not know how far they can expand demand without reducing unemployment below the critical level. Unfortunately attempts to estimate future growth are fraught with difficulty and leave room for great differences of opinion.

The Treasury house doctrine has in fact been associated with a view of capacity based largely on long-term historical trends. The great danger of this approach is that if demand is regulated year after year on the assumption that capacity can only grow by three per cent or three and a half per cent per annum, the prediction may well prove self justifying through its dampening effects on incentives to invest and modernize. In that case we would not get the automatic rise in unemployment which is the main check provided by the doctrine against an over-restrictive policy. One of the objects of the planning exercise inaugurated by NEDC is to break out of this vicious circle by using an estimate of capacity growth based on industry's own view of the possible future.

But although estimates of the growth of capacity prepared on a 'NEDC basis' would be an improvement, we should still be left with a further difficulty. This is that no one can be certain of the effects of a given reservoir of unused labour and productive capacity on the incentive to invest and to modernize. Is it not possible that businessmen may prefer to eat up their existing margin of slack before they will think seriously about labour-saving devices? May not labour shortages themselves be one of the most powerful incentives to modernization? If this were so a tight control of demand might slow down the long-term growth of capacity well below what it might otherwise be. Many European countries which are theoretically less committed to full employment than Britain have found that expansion has brought extremely low unemployment percentages; and it has not been possible to eliminate the labour shortages without bringing their booms to a halt.

A final, and really important, objection to the 'surplus capacity' type of theory is that it makes no distinction between different ways in which the margin of slack might be created. The closure of uneconomic railways, mines, shops, or farms might have the same effect on the unemployment percentage as demand restriction by the Chancellor. But whereas the first way of releasing surplus labour is a positive stimulus to growth (and if it were properly organized would consist mainly of people in the course of changing jobs) the second holds everyone back.

What are we left with at the end of it all? *Other things being equal* an unemployment percentage of say 1.8 (provided it is not too heavily concentrated in a few depressed areas) may be preferable to an 'overfull' employment level of one and a half or less (especially if successful regional policies can prevent unemployment being concentrated in certain areas). If the higher percentage could be brought about by the elimination of feather-bedding practices in industry, trade, and agriculture this would be excellent. If it could be brought about by moderating the pace of a boom, there may still be an arguable case for it, provided that the growth of production is carefully watched to see that – taking one year with another – it keeps in pace with a NEDC type of growth target. But if the achievement of this higher unemployment percentage involves long periods of stagnant or slowly rising production, the game is not, in my view, worth the candle.

Part III
CONCLUSIONS

CHAPTER 10

The End of a Myth

IN the last few chapters, the twists and turns of British financial policy have been traced back over a number of years. At the end of it all, can any general conclusion be drawn as to who was mainly responsible for the course of Britain's financial policies in the 1950s and early 1960s? If the reader would like a one-word answer, before going on to the qualifications and complexities, it is: officials. For it is they who provided the framework of thought within which the Government acted.

Even though one Party remained in office during this period there were frequent attempts to give economic policy a new look. Chancellor succeeded Chancellor, but the underlying policy assumptions, and sometimes the very phrases remained largely unaffected.

The traditional relationship between ministers and Civil Servants has broken down because of the sheer complexity of the issues. It is precisely because the British Civil Service is not a ruling bureaucracy that economic policy has been so uninspired. The Whitehall administrators are meant to be among the checks and balances of the British constitution. Their function is supposed to be to warn ministers of snags and dangers, to point out what Bagehot called the persistent facts that seem to live in the office – and also to work out policy details. The worst rebuke a minister can give a Civil Servant is to say: 'Why wasn't I warned?' People trained in this school are always bound to advise the Chancellor to play for safety. For this system to work successfully the guiding lines of policy must come from ministers themselves.

In the last decade the Treasury knights have had to step into the vacuum, and have had to make essentially political decisions for which they neither had the background nor the training. The function of 'knowing what the minister thinks better than he does himself', has been blown up from a whimsical extravagance into a main part of the duty of senior Treasury officials.

The weakness on the ministerial side was aggravated by a growing staleness in the Civil Service itself after the last wartime temporaries left and the Service returned to normal. The habit of asking distinguished lawyers or other outsiders to pronounce on essentially political issues, such as wages or restrictive practices, showed how badly the normal machinery of government was working.

When a new minister enters a Department he is alone among the people who have advised the outgoing one. Although the problem has been most frequently discussed in connexion with a change of Party after an election, it is perhaps most serious when there is a change of ministers among the Party in power. Is it surprising that constant changes of Chancellor in Conservative Governments made so little difference when the new man was invariably briefed by the same Permanent Secretary, the same Economic Adviser, and the same Civil Service experts as the old? Indeed he would spend a large part of his time in the House of Commons defending their activities on the basis of briefs they had written. He was far too dependent on their expertise to exercise any independent control over them.

Indeed, for most practical purposes the Civil Service is responsible for its own promotion and movements of personnel. Departmental ministers are consulted, mainly as a courtesy, about the filling of vacant posts. If a minister wished to oppose the official choice he would have to appeal to the Prime Minister against the decision of the Permanent Head of the Civil Service – not a battle upon which an ambitious politician would lightly embark. The Prime Minister can and does play a part in deciding who should be Permanent Secretary to a few key Departments; and a strong Chancellor could stand out against the appointment of a new Permanent Secretary whom he disliked. But in the key positions just below this level (and in the case of existing Permanent Secretaries) he pretty well has to accept who he gets. For a long time no political party has dared to criticize the Civil Service system for fear of being accused of tampering with a cherished non-political machine for party political ends. 'The Civil Service has therefore,' as the Fabians remark, 'tended to be left to play the role of prosecuting counsel, defending counsel and judge of its own case.'

Many senior Civil Servants, it must be said, would regard the above account of their influence as grossly exaggerated. They are conscious not only of innumerable occasions (some are given in earlier chapters) when their advice has been rejected, but of the futility of even proffering advice which is opposed to a minister's own political standpoint.

No one would deny that politicians are able to push through peripheral measures that please their own supporters, but which are irrelevant to the main economic issues of the day. A good example is the abolition of Schedule 'A'. On the main issues politicians have interfered enough to prevent the Treasury policies from being carried out logically and consistently, but have not been able to produce a substitute policy of their own.

The 'but' clause is the heart of the matter. Politicians may prevaricate, they may accelerate (but how rarely!), they may tone down, or add verbal glosses. In so doing they produce perverse results such as the four-year cycle, which gives everyone the worst of all worlds. But the one thing ministers, especially Chancellors, are rarely able to do effectively is to question the analysis on which the advice given to them is based. And having accepted the analysis they are ninety per cent of the way towards accepting the policies implied by the advice, in one form or another, sooner or later. A casual conversation with an outside economist, or the exchange of private memoranda, is no substitute for the stream of official papers (which is far, far

305

Advisers

larger than anyone outside Whitehall would imagine), and the few attempts to operate on the basis of outside advice have come sadly to grief.

Many recent Chancellors have acted as buffers, passing on criticisms of official policy which they themselves only half understood and which the Treasury advisers found only too easy to answer. But although the politicians could not pick flaws in the answers, many of them left the Exchequer with an inarticulate feeling that something was not quite right.

The whole idea of impartial advisers analysing 'means' and politicians choosing 'ends' has long been due for debunking. For it to be valid the following conditions, at least, would have to be fulfilled. Men of competence (and there would have to be an agreed yardstick for determining competence) would have to agree on the main alternative courses of action open to a Chancellor or an Economics minister. They would also have to agree on the probable consequences of the different alternatives and on the degree of probability to attach to each. These consequences would have to be such that they could be set out in simple terms so that the average minister could understand them, and make as a result the same choice as he would have made had he been himself an expert with time to follow closely and critically all the stages of the investigation. And the minister would have to be good at making choices where there are no certainties but only different kinds and degrees of risk. If these conditions were fulfilled, the present system would still be in working order, and one could concentrate on improving the quality of the existing machine. But merely to state these conditions is to show their artificiality.

It may be possible to provide an analysis of the factors determining spending on hire purchase which stands or falls by simple statistical tests on which all experts can agree (and judging by the controversies on hire purchase even this example may be admitting too much). But neither

economics, nor any other study, is in a state to provide
such an analysis of the probable consequences of devaluing
sterling, operating the economy with a slightly higher margin of unemployment, or even of more humdrum suggestions such as the fixing by NEDC of maximum rates of
return on capital in exchange for a bargain with the unions
on wages.

Behind the conflicting analyses of different economists
and officials are different (and changing) pictures of the
world in which factual generalizations, pieces of logical
reasoning, preferences for certain types of language, 'value
judgements', and personal judgements of what is important,
are inextricably mixed. Considerable technical knowledge
is required to ascertain what the real political choices
are.*

On the key question of policy towards sterling, which has
overshadowed all other economic issues, the Treasury is
itself dependent on the Bank of England's technical expertise, or – as the latter prefers to think of it – its knowledge
of markets and men. On many vital questions concerning
the pound, the Treasury has stood in the same relation to
the Bank as ministers normally do to Departmental
officials.

Whereas the Treasury maintains the polite fiction of
having no views other than the Chancellor's, this is not true
of the Bank even in theory. In the last resort it has to obey
his will; but, despite nationalization, it is an independent
self-perpetuating entity with a distinctive viewpoint of its
own. On issues like devaluation or exchange control it does
not pretend to be impartial. It is professionally against them
both.

* The logical distinction between 'is' and 'ought' statements (like
the related one between statements of fact and value judgements) is of
course crucial. There is *in the last analysis*, as Hume long ago pointed out,
no bridge between them. But the extreme trickiness of the distinction
between factual statements and value judgements is brought out well by
one of its foremost advocates, Professor R. G. Lipsey, in the first and last
chapters of his *Positive Economics*, 1963.

The Bank of England has much fewer inhibitions than the Treasury knights about making its views public. The Governor's speeches occasionally criticize Government policy with little attempt at concealment, and the Bank's views are also echoed in certain parts of the financial Press. This would be all to the good, were it not for the fact that Chancellors feel it improper to answer back, fearing perhaps that an attack on the Bank would damage sterling: it probably would.

The objectionable feature of the Bank's position – compared with that of other high-powered pressure groups such as the Ministry of Agriculture – is the odour of sanctity which surrounds its views. They are supposed in popular mythology to be those of disinterested experts and not lightly to be disregarded. The fashionable Bank line during the period this book was being written was that sterling could no longer be devalued unilaterally even if Britain wanted to do so. The world was no longer like that.

The argument is impaled on an internal contradiction. For if sterling cannot be devalued in any case, why bother to protect it? Why not go full steam ahead on domestic expansion? Yet this line was lapped up uncritically by most people on London's economic talking circuit, including people who once held other ideas.

The appointment of a Chancellor who has some personal knowledge of economic controversies by no means solves the problem. Some of the arguable points depend on detailed calculations (such as 'Have we gone far enough?'), which the Chancellor, with his many other duties, could not hope to perform himself. Others involve practical experience, vast numbers of facts and figures and knowledge of the records, or of the attitudes of other Governments. In addition there are all sorts of possible directives (such as 'take a tough line with the I.M.F.') on which he must be very dependent on the practical interpretations put by his officials upon his instructions.

THE END OF A MYTH

Professor Neustadt gives two rules of conduct for an American President.* 'On the one hand he never can assume that anyone or any system will supply the bits and pieces he needs most; on the other hand he must assume that much of what he needs will not be volunteered by his official advisers.' This applies in their lesser spheres to British Chancellors too. Neustadt comes even closer when he writes: 'One gains by joining in the argument. Presidents are always told to leave details to others. It is dubious advice. . . . To be effective a President needs to be both his own director of intelligence and his own executive assistant.'

No one took these words more to heart than Robert McNamara, the U.S. Secretary of Defence – not even the late President Kennedy. One of McNamara's first acts was to abolish the old-fashioned Pentagon briefings. 'McNamara wants it in writing first, so he can question it, and wants it in writing after (his advisers) go, so other people can come in and argue with it.'

McNamaras, however, do not grow on every tree; and even McNamara never imagined he could go it alone; one of the keys to his success was his very careful selection of the top twenty or thirty civilian policy makers (which in the U.S. are not necessarily Civil Service appointments).

The best solution in British conditions would probably be to create a new class of adviser distinct from the main Civil Service. Their job would be both political and technical. They would be selected in accordance with the personal preferences of ministers and move freely in or out from the academic world, industry, the professions, and elsewhere. They would tend to change with governments, but this would not be a rigid rule. An incoming minister from a new Party might well want to keep a certain adviser, while another from the same Party might not feel able to work

---

* *Presidential Power*, p. 154.

with him at all. The system would be above all a flexible one, and could take account of the fact that many of the real divisions of opinion and of personal compatibility cut across Party lines.

The main point about these new advisers is that they would not be what Mr Andrew Shonfield has called in a broadcast discussion 'a separate kind of man', set apart from the rest of the community. These new men need not be introduced in one overnight revolution; non-Civil Servants have occasionally been introduced in the past into ministers' private offices; and this precedent should be developed and extended until these offices have become more like continental-style *cabinets*.

It would be wrong to suppose that this new class of adviser would be concerned with policy and the existing Civil Service with execution. In the Treasury above all, nearly all the Administrative Civil Servants are concerned with advice to Chancellors, which is constantly necessary as changes occur in the exchange market, in economic indicators or in government spending plans.

The new advisers would be a sort of politically appointed brains trust. They would examine the whole framework of assumptions on which day-to-day policy is based and also inject specific new ideas on particular topics. One of the Chancellor's troubles has been that (like most other ministers) he and his Civil Servants have been so absorbed in a sea of immediate problems that he has not enough time to think through what he is trying to do. There is always a decision about Bank Rate, an embarrassing wage claim, a difficult Cabinet Committee, quite apart from a busy annual round of events culminating in the April Budget and the September I.M.F. meeting.

Non-political Treasury economists would continue as at present to work out national income forecasts and assess their implications for the Budget. The brains trust would, one hopes, have something to contribute on the settling of objectives; what unemployment percentage to aim at, what to do if there is a conflict between growth and the balance of payments, the social objectives of tax policy, and hosts of other topics. On none of these would the non-political appointees be debarred from speaking. On the contrary, the arrival of the brains trust would probably stimulate them into a much greater outspokenness. The idea would be to break down barriers, not create them. (This suggestion seems to strike even at the most broad-minded of traditional Civil Servants on a sensitive spot. Lord Bridges, for example, who is very willing to consider many other suggested reforms, will have nothing to do with ministerial *cabinets*, remarking that, 'It is significant that one wants to use the French pronunciation here. It is an idea foreign to us, with political overtones.'*)

The present post of Economic Adviser might well be split into two. There could on the one hand be a Director General of Economics inside the Treasury, which would develop out of the present post and remain 'non-political'. The main job of this Director General would be to do what he can to ensure that the Treasury's behaviour made economic sense. He would try and persuade the Expenditure Group to think a little more in terms of real resources, when these diverged from money calculations; he would examine what the Finance divisions were doing in the light of current monetary doctrines; he would supervise short-term economic forecasts; he would be in charge of all the Treasury's own economists and of economic education for Treasury recruits. All this would add up to a high-level and time-consuming job; indeed it should be higher in rank than it is at present.

Under such a system there would also be an overtly political Economic Adviser, to advise on the big questions involving choice between conflicting objectives. But again there would be no hard-and-fast demarcations. I would expect each to invade the other's territory. The main

* 'Whitehall and Beyond', the *Listener*, 25 June 1964.

difference is that one would be a political appointment and the other a Civil Service one.*

The suggested reform ought to do away with the whole feeling of inarticulate suspicion which separated Chancellors from their advisers in the years discussed. Ministers would feel less worried that something alien to their basic convictions was being 'put across' them; and – much more important – the advisers themselves would feel far less inhibited in putting over their views by the need to seem neutral and purely technical. One of the things that has made a Chancellor's task so difficult and increases his isolation in the Cabinet is that the political principles on which he has been brought up seem to have no relevance to many of his most important decisions, and the deeper one goes the truer this is. An avowedly Conservative Economic Adviser could put the case for say a capital gains tax much more eloquently and forcefully to a Conservative Chancellor than a man who was supposed to be above the political fray. Similarly an avowedly Socialist Adviser could, if he wished, argue with no holds barred in favour of a reduction in profits tax to a Labour minister with whom he had a close personal relationship.

The main argument against the proposed scheme is that it might discourage some of the best people from joining the permanent Civil Service. This could be overcome to some extent by recruiting the new class of advisers not only from the universities, industry, and the professions, but also from among established Civil Servants with the right interests and aptitudes. A Civil Servant in the *cabinet* of one minister, might, it is true, find himself in an embarrassing position after an election. But such difficulties are not insuperable. There are innumerable high posts, both

* A situation apparently resembling the one described may be brought about if responsibility for economic policy is split between the Treasury and a new ministry. But my formula still seems worth recording, as responsibility for overall economic policy will probably come to reside again under one roof.

in the Treasury and elsewhere, where his political and economic views would not matter over much, to which he could be transferred. It is a bad and not a good feature of the present system that high officials should be able to opt out to the extent that they do from the political consequences of their advice.

The creation of a special class of policy advisers might even have administrative advantages to compensate for its lack of tidiness. A Permanent Secretary at the moment has three separate and large burdens: he has to run his Department, be responsible as Accounting Officer for its expenditure, and be the minister's senior policy adviser. Sir James Dunnett, the Permanent Secretary to the Ministry of Labour, has expressed doubts 'whether the qualities required for all these roles are likely to be found in one man or woman'.* A reform that left Permanent Secretaries free to devote most of their time to running their Departments is not to be sneezed at.

Career Civil Servants could do their job far more effectively if they could rid themselves of the legalistic doctrine that every word they say, even in confidential inter-departmental committees, commits their minister. The fiction of ministerial accountability for every action of the most junior official should be replaced by a more realistic arrangement in which the Permanent Secretary is put clearly in charge of running the Department.

If the new politically appointed policy advisers were well chosen the excessive veto against new proposals on practical grounds might with luck go. But these suggested brains trusts are not meant as a substitute for the changes in the Civil Service itself, aimed at breaking down the barrier between it and the outside world, which Chapman and other writers have urged.

The case for breaking down some of the barriers between the Administrative Civil Service and the outside world has been argued often enough. But there is not much chance of

* *Public Administration*, 1961.

progress so long as Civil Servants are recruited almost exclusively in their early twenties, and do not emerge from Whitehall again until retirement. Some of them who reach the top of the Service retire early and go into industry, but there is no movement at all in the other direction.

Whitehall itself would maintain that it is almost impossible to persuade a promising executive of say thirty-five to forty to spend a few years in a Government Department. This may be, however, because such moves are regarded purely in terms of interchange; if a new entrant from industry had the same chance of rising to the top of the Civil Service and becoming Permanent Secretary as those who had come in straight from university, it might be very much easier to find new people. There is something in Professor Brian Chapman's suggestion that all posts above Assistant Secretary should be advertised.*

As a *quid pro quo*, to make such changes acceptable, there should be faster promotion within the Civil Service at all levels. There has been a retrogression here since before the war when young men could often do important and responsible work in their thirties and even twenties.

The announcement in the summer of 1964 that Civil Servants will now normally be able to leave before the age of fifty without loss of accrued pension rights should help secure a faster turn-over. The Civil Service Commission also announced at the same time that it would be prepared to recruit up to three Assistant Secretaries a year between the ages of forty and forty-five, as well as six Principals. These reforms may either be stepping stones to a more open Civil Service, or defensive modifications to keep the reformers at bay. Why after all should the number of Assistant Secretaries recruited from outside be three – or any other fixed figure? And why should entry be limited to the ages of forty to forty-five irrespective of personal qualities? The *Economist* commented at the time, 'A sort of

* *British Government Observed.*

polite, trade-union like restriction is entirely inappropriate at this level of management.'

There is something to be said for a much faster turnover of personnel among the top echelons of Whitehall. The Civil Service Commission would then have to recruit more people who would on average stay a shorter period. Staleness seems a quality endemic to Whitehall (and it is partly fear of acquiring it that makes many knights leave in mid-career).

One suggestion now going the rounds in Whitehall is to have more interchange of staff between the nationalized industries and the Civil Service. This is a good idea, provided it does not strengthen the partition between the State sector and private industry. More interchange between central and local government is another much canvassed, but worthwhile idea. A much more far-reaching proposal, however, would be to unify the Home and Foreign Civil Service. The typical Treasury or Board of Trade knight might spend ten years of his career in different parts of the world, and the Foreign Office man concerned with 'Britain's vital interests', would do a stint at the Ministry of Power or Labour. Such a unification would widen the horizon of both branches and might have an interesting effect on the residual class consciousness that still separates the two sides. The very ferocity with which the proposal would be resisted shows how near the bone it reaches.

The broader pattern of experience I am suggesting should not be forced on people irrespective of temperament and inclinations. There would be no need to make a misery of the life of a brilliant expert on local government finance who cannot stand going abroad, or of a diplomatic genius who loathes social and economic affairs. But most men do not have one-sided abilities and deficiencies on this scale, and are readily adaptable to a fairly wide range of environments if only given the opportunity.*

* This suggestion need not encourage amateurism. See Chapter 1, p. 32.

Mention of the word 'expert' brings one to another almost opposite criticism of the Civil Service – its lack of expertise. It is certainly true that the training of Civil Servants who have to handle economic topics (to take the example covered in this book) has until recently been woefully inadequate. The greatest need is to provide people with a theoretical framework on which they can hang their practical observations but which they will not adopt uncritically. It is very rarely satisfactory to leave the acquisition of subjects such as economics to voluntary spare-time reading.

On the other hand the subject studied at university is often unimportant in determining a person's later performance and attainments. Even today there is still a case for enjoying one's time at university and not treating it as a grim preparation for a future career. I have also been impressed by how much more quickly people can learn things outside school or university, when occupational pressures are substituted for the pedantries of teachers and examiners. If all these points are correct they point irresistibly to something like a Civil Service Staff College. The new Centre of Administrative Studies may one day provide a nucleus for such a College. At the moment it is for Assistant Principals only; but it would be a good idea if eventually officials in their forties and fifties about to take up important appointments went along for fairly extensive refresher courses.

This suggestion has now been aired by a House of Commons Select Committee which remarks, 'The value that the Assistant Principals may obtain from the Centre for Administrative Studies would to some extent be nullified if thereafter their trading is confined to a possible two weeks' course as an Assistant Secretary.'

One might have thought that it was no longer necessary to make out the hackneyed and obvious case for sending the typical Civil Servant for a few years during his career to work in industry or other outside employment. Yet as recently as March 1964, a senior Treasury official told a

THE END OF A MYTH

Select Committee that in the short career of a Civil Servant 'there are limits to what, I might say, are the sort of fancy things you can do'.*

Having said this, a little cold water needs to be poured on the cry for more professionalism. Of course more ideas and more expertise would be beneficial, whether they come from academic economists, investment analysts, or anywhere else. But these are not necessarily the same thing as professionalism. The organized professions with their rigid demarcations, examinations, and entrenched conservatism, have not always, to put it mildly, been forces for enlightenment. In a field close to the Treasury, accountants are professionals, yet they have provided the hard core of opposition to most tax reforms and their traditional conventions have been a retarding influence in British business. One should think many, many times before erecting a rigid demarcation between professional economists, sociologists, and other social scientists, and the rest of humanity.

There is a special point about the drift of present-day economics, to take the 'profession' most relevant to this book, best made in the words of a lecturer in the subject, M. D. Steuer. 'Questions of economic policy as a whole receive much less attention from economists than in the past. . . . Since the mid-40s this branch of the subject which used to be regarded as an integral part of the economist's job has been sadly neglected.'†

The trouble with the present vogue for research and statistical investigation is that it can too easily be exploited by those in Whitehall who want to avoid making difficult policy choices. It can in this form become just a modern version of the time-honoured expedient of setting up a committee. One would be less sceptical of current fashions

* Fifth Report from the Estimmates Comittee, Treasury Control of Establishment; Session 1963–4, No. 228, Paragraph 40 and Minutes of Evidence Q.1014.

† M. D. Steuer in *Industrial Relations*, edited by B. C. Roberts, Chapter 8, pp. 228–9.

if there were more detailed and systematic research in the Treasury and elsewhere on the probable consequences of alternative policies to the present ones. Such studies are not 'mere opinion' but can be just as 'scientific' and a good deal more fruitful than the study of existing trends to which so much effort is devoted.

Some of the most important economic controversies could, moreover, not be solved by unearthing more statistics. The biggest internal obstacle to full employment in the U.S. is not lack of statistical research but the public attachment to the principle of a balanced budget. This is not a genuine value judgement but a compound of false analogies, linguistic muddle, and dim historical recollections. The U.S. economist who wants to overthrow this attitude requires not more figures (he already has more than enough) but a rare combination of logical analysis and evangelical zeal.*

The position becomes even more absurd when the results of such research are not even revealed to the public. Advice given to ministers is regarded in Britain as on a par with the secrets of the confessional. A Chancellor was recently able to announce a decision to give £250m. in tax relief as a 'personal judgement' with no accompanying explanation.

* Nothing in this chapter is meant to justify an *a priori* approach to the social sciences. My sympathies are with the Popper view (reproduced in Professor Lipsey's book) that the question to ask about a theory is whether it has been subjected to a test where it has a real chance of being refuted. My doubts about the concept of research in vogue in Whitehall, apart from the one given in the test, are the following:

(a) The therapeutic function of economics, pointing out inconsistencies, or bringing to the surface the logical implications of certain political beliefs is in the present state of the subject often more important than its scientific one. Lipsey gives many interesting examples of this function.

(b) The progress of economics towards scientific status (on the really interesting questions) has been very slow. Why this has been so is a very large subject which could occupy a team of philosophers and economists for a very long time. In the meantime the Treasury has to decide what to do, and it may be more important (given that resources are scarce) to make a best guess about a really big problem in the international financial field than make a more scientific assessment of a minor puzzle.

The blame does not attach to Mr Maudling, who as we saw adroitly avoided an embarrassing situation, but to the conventions which allowed him to get away with it.

There is no great difficulty about ascertaining Treasury or Bank of England views on a great many subjects. But there is the greatest difficulty about reporting them as such. There is an excessive temptation under the present system for financial and economic writers to express official views in the guise of personal comments of their own – an unhealthy state of affairs with implications going far beyond economics.

The publication of economic forecasts suffered a blow as a result of the sneers the Labour Government experienced from the Opposition when its own went wrong. In the Budget Speeches and *Economic Surveys* of 1960, 61, and 62 there was something of a revival, and the introduction of a few rough figures enabled economists to see what sort of outlook the Treasury envisaged. Indeed Mr Selwyn Lloyd sometimes insisted on publishing more than his advisers thought wise. Mr Maudling, seeing Lloyd's fate, went into reverse; and actually abolished the *Economic Survey*. As Mr Andrew Shonfield has put it 'the one serious piece of economic reporting by the government which reached professional standards has now been turned into a meagre and hurried ministerial commentary attached to the tax changes announced on Budget day'.*

The publication of the White Paper on the Government's long-term spending plans at the end of 1963 caused much heart-searching among officials anxious to 'protect' ministers against public commitments. It is not certain whether the exercise will be repeated frequently. Yet the pattern and size of Government spending is one of the biggest issues of domestic politics, and if this is covered under a smokescreen, political discussion becomes shadow-boxing, while the real decisions are taken behind closed doors.

One of the latest international reports on the U.K.

* Article in *Suicide of a Nation*, edited by Arthur Koestler.

economy, the O.E.C.D. Survey for 1964, minces no words in condemning recent British practice.

Informed discussion of economic policy has become even more necessary now that demand management is geared to maintaining conditions favourable to achieving a medium-term growth target. But such discussion is handicapped by the absence of a systematic attempt to quantify the impact of policy decisions on the economy. Since the abandoning of the publication of quantitative annual forecasts in the Economic Surveys, no such data are provided regarding the consequences of the Budget.

Such censure could hardly have got past the Review Committee, if at least some British officials had not been happy for it to see the light of day.

Civil Servants often argue that the whole basis of their relationship to ministers depends on their advice remaining confidential. The argument begs the question of whether the present relationship is a healthy one. Whether a particular report is public or private is sometimes almost an accident. The Buchanan Report on motor transport, and even more the Trend Report on Government Science, could easily have been private Departmental documents. The quality of advice might well be improved if officials had more often to defend it in public against expert criticism.

It is sometimes argued that certain economic predictions, for example ones that indicate a worsening of the balance of payments, would affect foreign confidence adversely. But the Americans, who are just as worried about the dollar as Britain is about sterling, are constantly publishing every variety of official, unofficial, and semi-official balance of payments forecast. If Britain is heading for a payments deficit, there will be no dearth of gloomy private forecasts for foreign bankers to read. By keeping silent Treasury officials may keep British ministers and M.P.s in the dark. They will fool few people who matter in New York, Paris, Frankfurt, or Zürich.

Another objection is that a realistic prediction might differ from the Government's professed aims; wage increases may be above the guiding light. A little political imagination might be able to turn even this type of forecast to advantage. It could be used, for instance, to highlight the dangers or to show how little room for manoeuvre is left. But in the last resort, there is no reason why a democracy should acquiesce in conventions designed to save the Government any embarrassment in all circumstances.

Too much recent discussion has concentrated on prediction. It is at least as important to know the destination a Chancellor or Economics Minister is trying to reach and his reasons for choosing it in preference to other alternatives. In other words one would like to know, not merely what output might be in twelve months' time, but what the Government's target is, why it has been chosen, and how it fits into the Government's economic strategy. Where a Chancellor is following a Treasury doctrine it would be better for everyone concerned if one of the officials responsible for it were allowed to explain and defend it at suitably chosen gatherings.

Professor Ely Devons once wondered whether there was not 'a deeper, although unacknowledged, reason for reluctance to admit the public to a full view of events: a mistrust of the general public; a fear that they will not understand or will be unwilling to face the truth; a feeling that the public must be cajoled, wheedled, seduced, and exhorted, rather than convinced by logical argument and debate; a dread that if the whole complexity of the situation is revealed it will be misinterpreted and misjudged. These plus the temptation to keep information secret, because exclusive knowledge means power, seem to me to be the main motive forces behind the passion for cliques, confidentiality, and secrecy.'* This still seems a convincing view. In Sweden every official document is open to public inspection, unless it is declared a matter of national security; and there is no evidence that Swedish officials have had

* 'Government on the Inner Circle', by Ely Devons, the *Listener*, 27 March 1958.

to pander to obscurantist popular prejudices as a result.

The traditional system has in any case half broken down; all sorts of recent incidents, including the public inquest on Mr Selwyn Lloyd's ill-fated 1962 Budget and the fracas following Mr Cairncross's defence of the two and a half per cent guiding light before NIC, show that we are passing through a period of transition. With the proliferation of international and national economic organizations, officials are having to appear in public more and more, and can no longer hide behind ministerial apron-strings. The old relationship between ministers and officials is disintegrating, but new principles of public accountability have still to be invented. Hence many of our present embarrassments.

Both of the reforms discussed in this chapter – a new corps of politically appointed ministerial advisers and more public explanation of Whitehall thinking – would be easier to introduce if accompanied by changes in the political system. The most natural bodies to cross-examine the government's policy advisers would be the specialized House of Commons Committees so often advocated. Better pay and working conditions for M.P.s might help to get enough high quality members who could sit on such committees. It is to be hoped that the Lawrence Committee on members' and ministers' salaries will have something to say on these wider issues.

But in the last analysis, no weakness in either the Civil Service or the House of Commons can excuse the government from its own responsibilities. Although Civil Servants laid down the basic framework of economic policy over the last decade, it was largely the Government's fault that this was allowed to happen. The growing complexity of economic policy is something that Prime Ministers should have borne in mind when appointing Chancellors. By the time Mr Macmillan acted on this realization and appointed Mr Maudling in 1962, it was too late to give economic management a new look. (See pages 163–6 for a general discussion of Conservative Chancellors.)

The staleness of the Civil Service itself, in the 1950s and early 1960s, reflected the casual approach of ministers, who felt disinclined to go too deeply into intellectual controversies. Economic management was in a worse plight than other subjects because it was further from ministers' interests than others. The endless discussions on issues, such as the price of school milk or prescription charges, were far removed from the central economic issues. The most powerful ministers were mainly interested in foreign affairs and defence. The big questions that moved them were those of power and how Britain could retain it, rather than the state of industry and trade. It is therefore hardly surprising that rapid growth was not achieved.

But it is far from certain that British Governments excelled themselves even in the overseas field, or indeed that they would not have given themselves more room for manoeuvre on the world political scene had they been better at cultivating their own garden.

CHAPTER 11

Choosing Priorities

'WHY is it that when one meets these Treasury people individually they seem so enlightened and sensible, but when they all get back in their office, they produce such painful results?' This is a question that is often asked, but the answer to it is by no means simple.

One must start off by admitting that even as a collective body the British Treasury has had some very great virtues. In its attitude towards government spending and towards the Budget it has for some years – despite its backslidings and mistaken forecasts – been ahead of most other Finance Ministries in the world. Not only is it prepared to use surpluses and deficits to regulate the economy. But it has even abandoned the theory that taxes are levied to pay for the government's own spending. In principle it decides the level of taxation solely by the speed with which it thinks production can safely rise.

Yet for all the sophistication of their ideas, many Treasury officials have been inclined to panic during foreign exchange crises. In this respect they failed to display the qualities of detachment and perspective which are supposed to be the strong point of the British Civil Service. This is partly explained by the Bank of England's dominating expertise in this area.

There are, of course, highly regarded experts on international finance inside the Treasury, but these tend to share the Bank's 'sterling first' attitude in essentials. One senses that most other Treasury officials do not feel at home in the foreign exchange and gold markets, or in the world of tough, opinionated foreign Central Bankers. Not feeling at home, they are temperamentally inclined to play safe and concentrate on other subjects.

But to say that the Treasury is very good except on the question of sterling is like saying that a performance of Hamlet was first class with the exception of the Prince. Moreover, the complexity of the foreign exchange market cannot explain away the error of principle in allowing import controls to be abandoned even as a reserve weapon when there was no sign that exports were rising sufficiently fast to pay our way in the world, and we had no other weapons to hand. Mr Maudling's change of front here has already been welcomed in the last chapter. This came after many years had been wasted in doctrinaire opposition to the whole idea, during which Sir Roy Harrod's protestations on this point were brusquely brushed aside.

In an article in the January 1964 issue of *Encounter*, Harrod points out that one of Keynes's most persistent themes was that we must not allow full employment policy to be impeded by balance of payments considerations. Lord Keynes would have liked both Free Trade and full employment, but he never deviated from the doctrine that full employment came first. Harrod has convincingly argued that 'the failure to achieve the full growth potential of the economy, thereby losing year by year a growing amount of wealth that could be produced' is a crying evil involving similar wastes to pre-war unemployment. 'There is a great wide world of suffering humanity whose lot could be improved if only the U.S. and Britain raised their production to their true potential.'

The provisional answer to Harrod's question about whether the Treasury has really been converted to Keynes is in techniques, yes (more so than Harrod acknowledges), but in basic belief and approach, no. To be absolutely sure of the answer to this question one would need to see how the Treasury would react to high unemployment at a time when sterling was really weak. But the un-Keynesian belief of some leading Treasury men that there is little the Government could do to secure full employment in the face of adverse world forces, is not encouraging.

The failure to give economic growth a higher priority over most of the last decade can probably be traced to three fundamental causes (leaving aside the Bank): (a) general attitudes in the upper reaches of British society; (b) the Treasury's traditional role as the watchdog over government spending; (c) the absence of any alternative centre of power to put forward other priorities.

At bottom the decision to put the pound first stems back to a deep-seated 'outward-looking' tradition on Britain's part. This tradition is not enamoured of supranational institutions, and it does not particularly look towards the Continent of Europe. It does see Britain as an island with far-flung interests in North America, in the Far East, and in the countries which used to be part of the Empire.

One has only to take a walk in the City and look at the titles of some of the banks – Bank of London and South America; Hong Kong and Shanghai; Ottoman; Barclays Dominion; Colonial and Overseas, (D.C.O.) or to attend a few political or City lunches to absorb this spirit.

To have risked the cohesion of the Commonwealth by devaluing its sterling balances, to have risked destroying the international monetary system, and alienating the Americans into the bargain for a few doubtful points on the production index was unthinkable according to this tradition. It was in this spirit that the Labour Government of 1950–1 plunged into a rearmament drive at a time when Britain's main European competitors were engaged in rebuilding their export drive. This same tradition probably explains the insouciance with which Britain merrily abandoned import controls and disdained export aids, without asking what reserve weapons she had left to control her balance of payments other than domestic deflation.

One does not have to accept such 'outward-looking' arguments on their own terms. It can be argued that the best form of international economic good behaviour would be for all advanced countries to give high priority to domestic expansion; and that this in the long run will do more to keep world trade expanding (and thus keep up primary product earnings on which the poorer countries of the Commonwealth are so dependent) than an unconditional liberalization of trade between developed countries under a regime of immutable exchange rates.

It is, moreover, a pity that the word 'internationalism' which most people associate with world peace, spreads its favourable aura to cover the present network of understandings between Central Bankers. One could envisage a new type of cooperation aimed at expansion rather than currency stability, based on links with bodies such as the U.S. Council of Economic Advice, the French and Indian Planners, and the U.N. Regional Commissions. (Would that one could add the Common Market Commission to the list!) But this other internationalism is still, alas, just an intellectual alternative. Emphasis on domestic growth has seemed psychologically to many influential people in Britain, an inward-looking policy.

Another national characteristic which has powerfully contributed to British economic policy is the puritan tradition which attributes all our troubles to self-indulgence. It is rampant among the general public in a widespread belief that good times cannot last and that there 'isn't any money' to pay for public spending programmes. In times of trouble the automatic response among many top officials and politicians is to don the hair shirt rather than to see what one can get away with.

This showed itself in the way in which, during the 1961 run on sterling, some members of the Cabinet could not feel happy until they had converted it into a moral crisis.

It also shows itself in a general, and sometimes personal asceticism in the Treasury, and in school prefect ideas of national discipline inside the Bank of England. Puritanism is perhaps an Anglo-Saxon rather than a purely British instinct. It consists not in abstinence from worldly goods but in guilt feelings about them. It is strong even in an overtly materialistic country like the United States, where many people seemed disappointed that, after asking for sacrifice, President Kennedy in the end campaigned for tax cuts.

There is also the psychological point that 'the pound' is easier to worship as an abstract symbol, however little it is understood, than a technocratic concept like growth or expansion, which needs a great deal of explanation and is even then not a good slogan with which to lead troops into battle.

Quite apart from all these psychological intangibles, there has been an inherent ambiguity about the Treasury's own position. On the one hand it was supposed to act as the guardian of the public purse. On the other hand it was the ministry responsible for promoting growth.

It succeeded in combining these two responsibilities better than anyone had a right to expect. But the contradiction between the two roles remained. As one would expect, the Treasury was at its best on those issues where economic efficiency could be promoted by 'cutting out surplus fat' – one of its favourite metaphors. The Treasury was keen on closing down high-cost pits and on backing Dr Beeching. But it could hardly be expected to see the economic case for subsidizing urban public transport, for putting up New Towns to secure a better distribution of population, or for institutions to provide overseas market research for small businessmen on easy terms – to take three random examples.

In fact, there was no ministry whose job it was to spend money in a way that would promote growth. The Ministry of Housing saw housing as a social service intimately tied up with local authorities; it did not think of putting up houses for workers moving from one part of the country to another. The Ministry of Labour was interested in adult re-training, but was not inclined to push ahead with it too aggressively for fear of spoiling relations with the unions. Most so-called spending ministries looked after special interest groups or points of view. They did not pretend to be the custodians of anything as abstract as 'growth'. The popular idea that the Ministry of Labour is 'Labour' while the Board of Trade is on the other side of the political and industrial fence is not as childish as one might suppose. The Treasury's role was that of referee rather than that of initiator.

Moreover, even in dealing with the balance of payments and home financial policy, the Treasury was influenced by its tradition as a housekeeping ministry. Before the war it worried about balancing government income and outlay, and avoiding a Budget deficit. Today it worries about balancing expenditure and resources for the nation as a whole and avoiding an overstrain. The instinctive reaction of the traditional type of Treasury Administrator to a run on the reserves is that it must in some way be due to excessive spending at home.

The 'cutting out surplus fat' metaphor tends to be applied right outside the sphere of government spending where it was first coined. The merits of more competition for industry are easily seen in Great George Street. The case for import controls or export incentives, or of tax devices on the late President Kennedy's model to reduce an outflow of capital, is less easily appreciated. These look too much like 'soft options'. (What, incidentally, is wrong with a 'soft option'?)

The great gap in Britain during much of the post-war period was an institution that would promote the claims of growth as against those of sterling, or as against those of a quiet life for existing producers.

The real significance of the setting up of NEDC was that it was a potential pressure group for growth. The same ought to apply to any new ministry that takes over its function. The existence of either body or both should make it one degree more embarrassing for any Chancellor, Conservative or Labour, to hold back output in the interests of the balance of payments. This, rather than detailed planning of individual industries, is its ultimate justification.

People often ask 'What powers has NEDC got to see that different industries fulfil its forecasts?' and 'What powers does it have to see that there is a market for the amount of steel laid down in its plan?' It has, of course, no such powers; and heaven forbid that it should. The key to wisdom is that a planning body can be useful without them.

Broadly speaking, a planning organization in a free society can fulfil many small functions and one big one.

There is a large number of individual things it can do to improve efficiency. It can spotlight the need for regional policies, for training and redundancy schemes, tax reform, and many similar needs, and put forward ideas for policy. (I emphasize *policy* since exhortation to industry, not backed up by financial incentives or deterrents, ought not to come high on its list.)

It could also, as the French planners have tried to do, encourage industrial mergers when – but only when – these would promote efficiency or exports. More important, it could devise means by which the buying power of the State could be legitimately used to favour technological progress – a topical example being industrial building. Eventually, too, the 'little NEDCs' for particular industries might be a means of exercising gentle pressure on the long inefficient tail that exists in so many industries.

In each of these fields the planning body may only have a small contribution to make. It can exert a most useful chivvying and diplomatic function. Proposals which would, in isolation, arouse the ire of either side of industry, can be much more acceptable when presented as a necessary part of a programme which will bring greater prosperity to everyone. Here is where incomes policy fits in.

But all these individual functions should be seen in

relation to the one big thing. This can be simply stated. The four per cent growth target, if it means anything at all, is a Government commitment to do everything in its power to see that the *demand* for goods and services rises by an average four per cent a year. No individual manufacturer or industry can have his sales guaranteed ... he will have to fight for his share. The commitment would refer only to the total size of the national market. (The Chancellor's acceptance of the four per cent growth target in the 1963 Budget Speech was something much vaguer than what is here suggested.)

The role of the 'targets' for individual industries would be illustrative only. They are an attempt to show in practical terms what a four per cent growth rate *might* mean for, say, glass, washing machines, or cement. They are a *prediction* about how total demand will be divided up among different goods and services. In a free economy such predictions are very liable to go wrong; and individual businessmen must be completely free to disregard them if they wish. The key figure on which the government can and should operate is the overall growth of demand.

A commitment to a four per cent growth on the Government's part would mean that if, for any reason, output suffered a check and only rose by two per cent in one particular year, it might rise, say five per cent, in each of the two following years. The exact pattern need not worry industry very much, *provided that it is known that the ground lost in any one year will eventually be made up.*

Against such a background, temporary setbacks would have less effect on business psychology and investment decisions than they have had in the past. Similarly, temporary spurts of activity would also be much less likely to trap businessmen into planning on the basis of an over-rapid rate of sales expansion, although nothing can prevent human error or the excesses of optimism from which so much progress springs. The best way to reduce unwanted cycles in business investment is to keep consumer spending rising at a steady rate.*

At the time of the 1964 election NEDC still had a very long way to go before it attained the status described. One of its difficulties was that it was held at arm's length by Whitehall. It was absent from many of the main Whitehall committees; and Government Departments gave it less information about their plans than private industry has. Its estimates of Government spending in its 1961–6 Survey were mainly derived from inspired guesswork.

The Chancellor, moreover, did not consult the NEDC Office about his Budget judgement, and the Office was excluded from the Treasury's work on the short-term control of the economy. This is the most vital point of all. The long run is a way of describing a series of short runs, and the fate of the long-run growth objective will depend partly on what the Treasury does year by year.

Should then the NEDC office be inside a Government Department, as a large body of opinion both in the Labour Party and Whitehall would like?

This might turn out a high price to pay for access to the

---

* It is sometimes suggested that if industrialists voluntarily undertake to base their investment decisions on the assumption that demand will grow by x per cent a year, this will be itself sufficient to ensure that it will do so. This belief seems to lie behind a great deal of French writing on planning.

There is no need to decide in advance to what extent it is justified. A Government commitment to maintain the growth of demand can be regarded as an insurance policy just in case it doesn't come about as automatic consequence of the collective act of will.

Mrs Joan Robinson's studies of 'golden' and 'near-golden' ages are relevant to the conditions in which self-sustaining growth is possible. If I may dare to draw a moral from them, it is that a general belief by industry that demand will grow by the desired percentage each year would give a powerful impetus in the right direction. But the process of growth is liable to so many disharmonies, accidents and shocks that it cannot be relied upon in itself without supporting Government stabilization policies. (See *Essays on the Theory of Growth*, Macmillan 1962 and *The Accumulation of Capital*, Macmillan 1956.)

innermost circles of Government. The confidence with which both sides of industry treat NEDC at present is in large part due to the feeling that it is their own organization and not just a creature of the Government. Many Whitehall officials would, for obvious reasons, like to keep the Council but dispense with the office; but the members of the Council would soon lose heart if they did not have their own staff, or if the staff were reduced to a rump.

The great advantage of the NEDC office, which cannot be sufficiently stressed, is that it is not a Government Department. It is not circumscribed by the ritual described at the beginning of this book. Civil Servants are inhibited in their dealings with the outside world, and even with each other by the thought that every word they say commits a minister. NEDC officials are able to act unhampered by this scholastic concept of responsibility; and although their ideas are frequently turned down or toned down by the NEDC Council, at least they are free to put them forward.

The NEDC Office would have been more effective even in the form it existed in 1963-4 if ministers had wanted to use it more, and had not seen it so exclusively in terms of incomes policy. Nor is there any reason why a member of the NEDC office should not sit on the Budget Committee on a confidential basis. (One could think of precedents.)

Some moderate-minded men would argue that those of NEDC's functions which relate to the removal of obstacles to growth should still be performed in an independent Office, but they see no reason why the Office should work out an economic model and set of long-term predictions rival to the Government's own. This, it is said, is a waste of manpower and a source of confusion. If Whitehall needs competition in the study of general economic trends they can be best provided by outside academic bodies like the National Institute. (A distinction is sometimes made in terms of 'Orange Book' and 'Green Book' policies – named after the colour of the covers of different NEDC publications!)

The main objection to this line of thought is that a process of model building is not as innocent as it looks. As we have seen a political disagreement about priorities between NEDC and the Treasury recently took the form of a statistical argument about the rate of productivity increase on which we should count in 1961–6; such political disagreements could happen again irrespective of the colour of the Government in power.

Admittedly the result of the election is crucial here. If a new Economics Ministry is now set up with a set of priorities different from the Treasury, this would amount to a change of circumstances and NEDC might be advised to let this new Ministry work out the finer elaborations of alternative growth targets. This is what a branch of the French Finance Ministry has been doing for the Planning Commission for years. And yet any NEDC Director General would be well advised to keep a very close watch on these seemingly technical subjects. The fate of the Treasury's Economic Section – formerly a band of licensed rebels which have long since become absorbed into the Treasury machine – should serve as an awful warning.

Much in the preceding pages would point in the same direction as the Production or Economics Ministry favoured by the Labour and Liberal Parties. But the snag in most of these plans is that they assume that there is something called 'finance' quite apart from economics and production. In act, of course, the instruments by which production is influenced in this country are the Budget, monetary policy, exchange rate policy, and one or two very general controls. Despite all the talk of 'physical intervention', this is likely to remain the case. If the Treasury remains responsible for the balance of payments, for taxation, for the Bank Rate, and for the use of devices like the Regulator, it is likely to remain the effective Economic Ministry, whatever nominal changes are made.

Nor is the idea that the Economics Ministry should determine strategy and the Treasury tactics very convincing. An example often quoted is that if production needs a stimulus, the Economics Ministry will say 'Give away £250m.' and the Treasury will suggest how to do it. But £250m. can mean a lot or a little, depending on the kind of reliefs given and the time when they take effect. It would be a poor Treasury official who could not trim away a recommendation he considered dangerously expansionary. It is also doubtful wisdom to multiply the number of deadlocked inter-departmental committees. Wherever there is such disagreement there is a bias in favour of inaction.

The organization of economic policy represents an impossible dilemma. It has at least two aspects – probably many more. There is the overall management of demand and the balance of payments, international financial negotiations, incomes policy, long-term output targets and the like. Then there is a host of specific industrial decisions ranging all the way from redundancy compensation, to encouragement of management education and the future of the aircraft industry. Both kinds of decision have a large general impact on the economy and only an intellectual bigot would argue that only one or the other is important. (Even this suggested classification leaves a vast number of highly important loose ends such as overseas trade and tariff policy which in my view ought to be put together with the overall macroeconomic decisions.) The solution to which the Heath–Maudling division of labour in the years before the 1964 election was pointing, was a partition, with one man responsible for the physical and industrial side and the other for the overall financial one. This is not really satisfactory as economic policy is indivisible; the two kinds of decisions interact at every level. Nevertheless no one man can handle in detail the vast range of issues involved and any Department that tried would become hopelessly distended.

There are no final solutions. My own suggestion would be to start off with the existing Treasury as a base and hive off some of its functions. The control of Government spending would go to a separate Expenditure Bureau.*

The control of the Civil Service could then go to an enlarged Civil Service Commission. In this way the Treasury would be rid of some of the main psychological impediments to its acting as a proper Economics Ministry. There would be left a small group of people who would have their hands on the main fiscal and monetary taps, and be responsible also for the balance of payments. Whether they were then still called the Treasury or not would be a detail. But once they had got rid of their watch-dog functions they would be specifically responsible for urging on spending projects conducive to growth which they could do with a clear conscience. It would also be possible for them to enlarge their functions, take a more detailed interest in industry, and bring in some outsiders, without becoming overblown.

They might then have a wide brief to think about economic policy as a whole. They might for instance ask questions such as 'Do we still favour the maximum liberalization of trade if we cannot secure a sufficient increase in international liquidity (i.e. means of payment) to support it?' Or 'How can we provide a stimulus to industrial efficiency comparable in character to the I.C.I.–Courtauld take-over fight?' Or 'Can we use selective tariff cuts to back up an incomes policy?' Some of the functions of my revamped Treasury would be similar to those suggested for the Labour Party's proposed Production or Economics Minister. But it would have the specific operational tasks of managing home demand, and looking after sterling. The emphasis should be more on 'conditions favourable to growth' rather than detailed intervention in specific industries.

* I have in mind something like the U.S. Bureau of the Budget, but have avoided the title in order not to give people the impression that it will be responsible for taxation. Some of the functions of the Treasury's Pay and Management group would fall more naturally into the lap of the Expenditure Bureau and others would fall to the Civil Service Commission.

The fundamental defect of the British Cabinet system from the point of view of coherent strategy in economics or in any other field is one that does not concern the structure of ministries at all. It arises from the fact that Britain has what American political writers call a plural executive. No minister has the power to give orders to any other ministers – not even the Prime Minister. This accounts for the great profusion of committees in place of individual leadership, and the inability of Chancellors to get their way on many important occasions over bodies like the Ministries of Labour or Pensions. To advocate a more formal move towards a Presidential system, which would avoid the defects of Congressional vetoes, would take us into very deep waters a long way from the central themes of this book.

The Prime Minister has, however, been handicapped from exerting effectively the very great influence he already possesses by the lack of adequate staff – he has had at his disposal most of the post-war years a few Private Secretaries and two officials of senior rank in the Cabinet Office. During the war, by contrast, Winston Churchill had a Central Statistical Section, under the supervision of Lord Cherwell, which was essentially personal to him with a loyalty to no one else.

It can be argued that ministers should be left to get on with the job. But, as Sir Donald MacDougall, who has served in Churchill's Statistical Section, has argued, someone must decide what the job is, especially if there is a clash between ministers or a fundamental change of policy is required. Many such problems are economic or statistical. 'Is it right,' asked MacDougall in a post-war symposium, 'that when ministers meet to discuss such matters, the Prime Minister alone should be largely unsupported by expert advice?'*

It would, however, be quite wrong to end the book on an institutional note. People are already far too tempted to introduce institutional gimmicks as a way of avoiding policy

* *Lesson of the British War Economy*, edited by D. N. Chester, p. 68.

issues. 'When in doubt, appoint a minister' is an old adage still observed, and there are more sophisticated variants of this idea.

If we are to maintain a faster economic growth than in the past, we require not a reshuffle of desks and ministries, but a clear-cut economic decision. It needs to be accepted that the maximum expansion of real wealth (of which leisure is a part) is the main aim not of human life, nor necessarily of national policy as a whole, but certainly of *economic policy*.*

As a corollary of this decision, the restriction of home demand must cease to be the main weapon for protecting sterling or controlling the balance of payments. (The brake may still be necessary if there really is a domestic over-strain, but this is by no means the same thing.)

If there is trouble on the sterling front, adjustments should be made in other spheres of policy. There are numerous alternative weapons. Exchange rates can, despite the Bank of England, be moved; there can be import controls or levies, export incentives, long-term overseas borrowing, higher Bank Rate offset by tax reductions; or, perhaps even a partially successful incomes policy. These weapons can be used singly or in combination. The important thing is to agree that one or more of them should be used, rather than restrict domestic output.

The war cry of the financial conservatives has always been 'You can't plan exports'. This is factually misleading, unless the world is moving into a deep recession brought on by the people who say these things. The devices listed in the previous paragraph can increase exports, reduce imports, or help to balance payments in other non-deflationary ways. One has only to look at overseas experience. There has been a long and indecisive discussion on how much French planning has contributed to growth in France. The only conclusion to have emerged with any clarity is that planning contributed something (it is difficult to say how

* The necessary qualifications are made in Chapter 5. They do not affect the argument of these concluding paragraphs.

much) but readiness to devalue contributed a great deal more.

There is no reason why a Chancellor or Economics Minister should show his hand in advance on these expedients, especially as he may not need to resort to any of them. His real task is the subtler one of giving the impression that he means business – that the next sterling crisis will not be tackled in a deflationary way, and that demand will go on rising by at least four per cent a year. It will have to carry on doing so for quite a while before the present cynical mood towards the target is dissipated.

If this new order of priorities is accepted, we shall somehow get the right institutions. But it is all too beguiling an error to suppose that some institutional trick can be an adequate substitute for the right policy decisions.

Bibliography

This is not intended to be a comprehensive list. The works mentioned below are simply ones that I have personally found helpful in the course of preparing this book. I have also added two introductions to economic theory which some readers may find useful for reference.

The sub-headings into which the list is divided cannot, in the nature of things, be watertight compartments; some of the works listed under 'History' could, for instance, equally well have come under 'Economic Policy' and vice versa.

WORKS ON THE TREASURY

Lord Bridges: *The Treasury*, Allen & Unwin, 1964

Sir Herbert Brittain: *The British Budgetary Mechanism*, Macmillan, 1959

S. H. Beer: *Treasury Control*, Oxford University Press, 1956

Control of Public Expenditure. (The 'Plowden Report'), H.M.S.O. Cmd 1432, 1961

Viscount Amory: 'Preparing the Budget', article in *Parliamentary Affairs*, autumn 1961

Public Administration. Spring 1963. This number contains relevant articles by D. N. Chester, R. W. B. Clarke, and W. W. Morton.

The Reform of the Exchequer Accounts, H.M.S.O. Cmd 2014, 1963

J. R. and U. K. Hicks: 'The Reform of the Budget Accounts', *Bulletin of the Oxford Institute of Economics & Statistics*, May 1963

Alan T. Peacock: 'Problems of Government Budgetary Reform', *Lloyds Bank Review*, January 1962

A. J. D. Winnifrith: 'The Treasury', Article in *Country Life*, 14 November 1957 (on William Kent's Treasury building)

MACHINERY OF GOVERNMENT

Sir Ivor Jennings: *Cabinet Government*, 3rd edn Cambridge University Press, 1959

John P. Mackintosh: *The British Cabinet*, Stevens, 1962

Walter Bagehot: *The English Constitution*, Introduction by R. H. S. Crossman, The Fontana Library, 1963

Brian Chapman: *The Profession of Government*, Allen & Unwin, 1959

Brian Chapman: *British Government Observed*, Allen & Unwin, 1963

Bernard Crick: *The Reform of Parliament*, Weidenfeld & Nicolson, 1964

J. W. Grove: *Government and Industry in Britain*, Longmans, 1962

J. Donald Kingsley: *Representative Bureaucracy*, Yellow Springs, Ohio, 1944

Bank of International Settlements: *Eight European Central Banks*, Allen & Unwin, 1963

A. Koestler (ed.): *Suicide of a Nation*, Hutchinson, 1963

Herbert Morrison (now Lord Morrison of Lambeth): *Government: a survey from the inside*, Oxford University Press, 1954

Richard E. Neustadt: *Presidential Power*, John Wiley, 1960

A. Sampson: *Anatomy of Britain*, Hodder and Stoughton, 1962

John Sheahan: *Promotion and Control of Industry in Postwar France*, Harvard University Press, 1963

M. D. Steuer: 'Economic Policy and Union Activity', Chapter 8 of *Industrial Relations*, edited by B. C. Roberts, Methuen, 1962

E. Strauss: *The Ruling Servants*, Allen & Unwin, 1961

The Administrators: *Reform of the Civil Service*, by a Fabian Group; Fabian Tract 355, June 1964

Sir Edward Bridges (now Lord Bridges): *Portrait of a Profession*, Cambridge University Press, 1953

Hugh Thomas (ed.): *The Establishment* (Article on the Civil Service by Thomas Balogh), Anthony Blond, 1959

Royal Commission on the Civil Service: Cmd 96,113, 1955

Committee of Inquiry into the Organization of Civil Science (The 'Trend' Report) Cmd 7171, H.M.S.O., 1964

The Formation of Economic and Social Policy (symposium dealing with several countries). The section on Great Britain is by B. St J. Trend (now Sir Burke Trend). *International Bulletin of Social Sciences*, Vol. VIII, No. 2, UNESCO, 1956

Treasury Control of Establishments: Fifth Report from the Estimates, 1963–4, H.M.S.O.

Thomas Balogh: *Planning for Progress: A Strategy for Labour*, Fabian Committee Pamphlet, 1963

Business Economists Group: *Planning:* Report of Oxford Conference; introduced by Sir Robert Shone; obtainable from 21 Godliman Street, E.C.4

Change or Decay: Conservative Political Centre, 1963

Ely Devons: Government on the Inner Circle, the *Listener*, 27 March 1958

Ely Devons; Economic Management in Whitehall, *ibid*, 2 July 1964

Robert Neild: New Functions: New Men?, the *Listener*, 27 August 1964

J. C. R. Dow, 'Problems of Economic Planning', *Westminster Bank Review*, December 1959

Federation of British Industries: *The Next Five Years*, Report on the Brighton Conference of November, 1960

Sir Robert Hall: 'Reflections on the Practical Application of Economics', *Economic Journal*, December 1959

Ian Little: 'The Economist in Whitehall', *Lloyds Bank Review*, April 1957

J. Selwyn Lloyd: 'NEDDY and Parliament', *Crossbow*, October–December 1963

P.E.P.: *Economic Planning in France* (Report of a London Conference) 14 August 1961

P.E.P.: *French Planning: Some Lessons for Britain*, September 1963

E. H. Phelps Brown: *The National Economic Development Organization, Public Administration*, autumn 1963

Paul Samuelson: *Problems of the American Economy*, University of London, Athlone Press, 1962

HISTORY AND MEMOIRS

Nora Beloff: *The General Says No*, Penguin Books, 1963

Lord Birkenhead: *The Prof in Two Worlds: Lord Cherwell*, Collins, 1961.

D. N. Chester (ed.): *Lessons of the British War Economy*, Cambridge University Press, 1951

The Memoirs of Lord Chandos: The Bodley Head, 1962

Lord Dalton: *High Tide and After*, Frederick Muller, 1962

J. C. R. Dow: *The Management of the British Economy, 1945–60*, Cambridge University Press, 1964

Ludwig Erhard: *Prosperity Through Competition*, 3rd English edn, Thames and Hudson, 1962

Sir Roy Harrod: *The Life of Keynes*, Macmillan, 1951

Earl of Kilmuir: *Political Adventure*, Weidenfeld & Nicolson, 1964

Norman Macrae: *Sunshades in October*, Allen & Unwin, 1963

Joan Mitchell: *Crisis in Britain 1951*, Secker & Warburg, 1963

Graham L. Rees: *Britain and the Post-war European Payments Systems*, University of Wales Press, 1963

A. A. Rogow and Peter Shore: *The Labour Government and British Industry*, Basil Blackwell, 1955

Andrew Shonfield: *British Economic Policy Since the War*, 2nd edn, Penguin Books, 1959

Sir John Wheeler-Bennett: *John Anderson, Viscount Waverley*, Macmillan, 1962

Memoirs of the Rt Hon. the Earl of Woolton, Cassell, 1959

G. D. N. Worswick (ed.): *The British Economy, 1945–50*, Oxford University Press, 1952

G. D. N. Worswick and P. H. Ady (eds): *The British Economy in the 1950s*, Oxford University Press, 1962

Economic Surveys: 1947–62, H.M.S.O.

Economic Trends: Economic Report for 1962, H.M.S.O., March 1963

Economic Trends: Economic Report for 1963, H.M.S.O., March 1964

O.E.C.D.: *Surveys of United Kingdom, 1962* and *1964*, obtainable from H.M.S.O.

M. June Flanders: 'The Effects of Devaluation on Exports', *Bulletin of the Oxford Institute of Economics and Statistics*, August 1963

Sir Robert Hall: 'Britain's Economic Problems', two articles in the *Economist*, 16 September 1961 and 23 September 1961

Sir Horace Hamilton: *Sir Warren Fisher and the Public Service*, Institute of Public Administration, 1951

ECONOMIC DIAGNOSIS AND POLICY

A. K. Cairncross: *Factors in Economic Development*, Allen & Unwin, 1962

A. R. Conan: *The Rationale of the Sterling Area*, Macmillan, 1961

T. W. Hutchison: *'Positive' Economics and Policy Objectives*, Allen & Unwin, 1964

Angus Maddison: *Economic Growth in the West*, Allen & Unwin, 1964

Not Unanimous: Institute of Economic Affairs, 1960

F. W. Paish: *Studies in an Inflationary Economy*, Macmillan, 1962

P.E.P.: *Growth in the British Economy*, Allen & Unwin, 1960

Lord Robbins: *Politics and Economics*, Macmillan, 1963

M. Shanks: *The Stagnant Society*, Penguin Books, 1961

M. F. G. Scott: *Study of the Behaviour of U.K. Imports*, C.U.P., 1963

Richard M. Titmuss: *Income Distribution and Social Change*, Allen & Unwin, 1962

S. J. Wells, *British Export Performance*, Cambridge University Press, 1964

Bank of England: Quarterly Bulletins, esp. March 1964

Committee on the Workings of the Monetary Systems, (Radcliffe Report) Cmd 827, H.M.S.O., 1959

Committee on the Workings of the Monetary System: Principal Memoranda of Written Evidence, Vol. I – Bank of England, H.M. Treasury, etc. H.M.S.O., 1960 (63–161–1)

Committee on the Workings of the Monetary System: Minutes of Oral Evidence, H.M.S.O., 1960 (63–150)

Report of the Royal Commission on Taxation, H.M.S.O. Cmd 9474, 1955

N.E.D.C.: Growth of the U.K. Economy, H.M.S.O., 1963

N.E.D.C.: Growth of the U.K. Economy, Progress Report, H.M.S.O., 1964

N.E.D.C.: Conditions Favourable to Economic Growth, H.M.S.O., 1963

N.E.D.C.: Export Trends, H.M.S.O., 1963

N.I.E.S.R.: Economic Reviews

Council on Prices, Productivity and Incomes, First and Second Reports, H.M.S O., 1958

Public Expenditure in 1963–64 and 1967–68, Cmd 2235, H.M.S.O., 1963

The Financial Objectives of the Nationalized Industries, Cmd 1337, 1961

O.E.E.C. The Problem of Rising Prices, obtainable from H.M.S.O., 1961

O.E.C.D. Policy for Prices, Profits and Non-Wage Incomes, 1964

'The Manchester School', Vol. 27. No. 1. *The Bank Rate Tribunal Evidence: A Symposium*, 1959

Report of the Committee on Turnover Taxation, H.M.S.O., 1964, Cmd 2300

Statement by the 'Group of 10', H.M.S.O., 1964

Lord Aldington: 'The Select Committee on the Nationalized Industries', *Public Administration*, spring 1962

F. T. Blackaby: 'The Recent Performance of the British Economy', *The Advancement of Science*, March 1963

BIBLIOGRAPHY

Sir Robert Hall: 'Incomes Policy – State of Play', the *Three Banks Review*, March 1964

Business Economists Group: *Incomes Policy*, Report of 1963 Oxford Conference, obtainable from 21 Godliman Street, E.C.4

S. Brittan: 'Too Many Regulators?', *the Banker*, September 1962 'No Stopping Stop-Go?', the *Banker*, March 1963

L. Dicks-Mireaux: 'The Interrelationship of Cost and Price Changes, 1946–59', *Oxford Economic Papers*, October 1961

J. C. R. Dow: 'Fiscal and Monetary Policy as Instruments of Economic Control', *Westminster Bank Review*, May, August, and November 1962

W. A. H. Godley and J. R. Shepherd: Long-Term Growth and Short-Term Policy, *National Institute Review*, August 1964

Sir Roy Harrod: 'Are We Really All Keynesians Now?', *Encounter*, January 1964

K. G. J. Knowles and D. Robinson: 'Wage Rounds and Wage Policy', *Bulletin of the Oxford University Institute of Economics and Statistics*, May 1962

Lord Robbins: 'Notes on Public Finance', *Lloyds Bank Review*, October 1955

R. G. Lipsey: 'The Relation between Unemployment and the Rate of Change of Money Wage Rates in the United Kingdom, 1861–1957', *Economica*, February 1960

Robin Marris: 'The position of economics and economists in the government machine: a comparative critique of the United Kingdom and the Netherlands', *The Economic Journal*, December 1954

A. J. Merrett and Allen Sykes: 'Financial Control of State Industry', the *Banker*, March and April 1962

P. W. Paish: 'The Economic Position of the United Kingdom *Westminster Bank Review*, August 1962

A. W. Phillips: 'Employment, Inflation, and Growth', *Economica*, February 1962

A. W. Phillips: 'The Relation between unemployment and Rate of Change of Money Wage Rates in the United Kingdom, 1861–1957', *Economica*, November 1958

Austin Robinson: 'Re-Thinking Foreign Trade Policy', the *Three Banks Review*, December 1963

P. Vandome: 'Econometric Forecasting for the United Kingdom', *Bulletin of the Oxford Institute of Economics and Statistics*, November 1963

TEXTBOOKS ON ECONOMICS

Richard G. Lipsey: *An Introduction to Positive Economics*, Weidenfeld & Nicolson, 1963

Paul A. Samuelson: *Economics: an Introductory Analysis*, 6th edn, McGraw-Hill, 1964

Index

Hall, Sir Robert, Economic Adviser (1947–61), 37, 66–9, 132, 155
compared with Cairncross, 67, 69
disciple of Keynes, 68
and price controls, 70 *n.*, 170
opposes Operation Robot, 173
Thorneycroft and, 187
on 1958 pre-Budget tax concessions, 201, 202 *n.*
favours a 'guiding light' for incomes, 206
on the effect of 1960–1 boom on productivity, 207 and *n.*, 226–7
attitude to Common Market, 214
on Maudling's 1962–3 re-expansion, 257

Hamilton, Sir Horace, 'Sir Warren Fisher', 49 and *n.*

Hare, John, later Lord Blakenham, as Minister of Labour, 220, 237, 347–8

Harrod, Sir Roy, on failure to achieve growth potential, 325
Life of Keynes, 49 and *n.*

Heath, Edward, 37, 41
and the Board of Trade, 12, 75, 265–7
becomes Secretary of State for Industry, 172, 265
and Maudling, 266–7, 272
his R.P.M. Bill, 268
and NEDC, 269

Helsby, Sir Laurence,
Joint Permanent Secretary to the Treasury, 32, 55, 56 and *n.*
at the Ministry of Labour, 237
reports directly to the Prime Minister, 56 and *n.*

Henderson, Arthur, 39

Hire-purchase, Government policy towards, 129, 130, 131, 132, 178, 183, 201, 206, 217, 244

Hogg, Quintin, formerly Lord Hailsham, 220, 245

Home and Overseas Planning Staff, 172

Home Office, 57 *n.*

Hopkin, Bryan, 71, 72, 73

Hopkins, Sir Richard, Permanent Secretary to the Treasury (1942–5), 49

House of Commons,
its Standing Order 78, 79–80
its Public Accounts Committee (P.A.C.), 80
the Select Committee on Estimates, 80–1, 84
its Select Committee on the Nationalized Industries, 96–7
case for specialist committees, 322

Import Controls, 1951, 252–3, 275, 287

Incomes,
a 'guiding light' for, 132, 187–8
a policy for, 171, 172, 187–8, 206, 239, 240, 263, 269–70, 281

opposes certain tax reforms,
225, 258-9
International Confederation of
Free Trade Unions, 240
'International liquidity', 276-9
International Monetary Fund
(I.M.F.), 62, 89, 130, 132,
176, 192, 233
the 'gold tranche', 123
Britain's drawing right on,
275
and Maudling's plan, 276-9
Italy, her economic recovery,
137, 138, 139
secures a competitive start in
export markets, 281

Jacobsson, Dr Per, 89, 233, 234
Japan, 1949 U.K. devaluation
and, 160
Jennings, Sir Ivor, *Cabinet Gov-
ernment*, 79 and *n.*
Jobs, treated as a scarce com-
modity, 151
Johnston, Sir Alexander, 119
and the Budget Committee,
101
Jones, Aubrey, Minister of
Supply (1957-9), 84

Kennedy, President J. F., 131,
214, 255, 328, 329
and O.E.C.D., 241
Kent, William (1684-1748),
his 'Treasury', 44
Keynes, John Maynard, 1st
Baron, 26 *n.* 91, 93, 258 *n.*

his influence on Hopkins, 49
on Hall, 68
and the function of the
Budget, 51
Butskellism based on his
doctrines, 162
degree of influence on Treasury policy, 325-6
Korean War, 138, 139, 156,
158-60, 162
Kuwait, 130, 189, 387

Labour Governments of 1945-
51,
move away from a planned
economy, 51, 155-7
rearmament programme, 129,
138, 158-60, 326
policy, 1945-51, 154-61
and Butskellism, 156, 162
'Long-Term Programme'
(1948), 157
attitude to the nationalized
industries, 294
economic forecast, 319
Labour Party,
proposes a new Economics or
Production Ministry, 12,
75, 172, 334
and the space-missile field,
85
and the Budget, 107-8
possibility of rival Ministers,
267
and Heath's R.P.M. Bill, 268
Law, Sir Toby (later Lord
Aldington), on the Com-
mittee on Nationalized
Industries, 97

becomes chief economic ministry (1947), 50

its Permanent Secretaryship split into two (1956), 52

and the Economic Steering Committee, 53

its lesser ministers, 54–5

its organization (1964), 55

its main groups, 55–9

its say in salaries and wages of public sector, 57 *n.*

and promotion within the Civil Service, 58

transfers within, 59

links with the Bank of England, 60

compared with the Bank, 62

and the foreign exchange market, 65

presents a unified front, 70

and N.I.F., 71–2

and long-term forecasting, 73–7

and NEDC, 73, 74, 221, 222, 240–2, 260, 269

weaknesses of its economic organization, 74–7

concerned with controlling Government expenditure, 75, 78, 89–91

distribution of Administrative officials within its groups, 78–9

basis of its authority, 79–80

auditing of Accounts, 80

delegates some powers, 83, 85

and the Concorde, 85

and long-term planning of Government expenditure, 86–91

its national growth target (1961), 89

basically a coordinating and regulating Department, 90

how far converted to 'real resources' approach, 91–3

its definition of public spending, 93–5

and the nationalized industries, 95–9

and Budget preparations, 101 *ff.*

concession to NEDC's 4 per cent growth target, 106

and the Budget speech, 110, 111

and Budget Accounts, 113, 115, 124

attitude to tax reform, 118 *ff.*

relations with Revenue Departments, 118–20

presents a bad image of Britain's economic position, 122–5

and Exchequer Accounts, 124

meaning of 'Treasury policy', 12, 154

and Dalton, 155

advises a wage pause, (1948), 157

and Labour's rearmament programme, 158–9

advice during Butler's Chancellorship, 169

supports Operation Robot, 173, 176

attitude to a flexible exchange rate, 175

*Some other new Pelican books
are described on the
following pages*

FACT AND FICTION IN PSYCHOLOGY

H. J. Eysenck

Here is the long awaited final volume of Professor Eysenck's Pelican trilogy: *Uses and Abuses of Psychology, Sense and Nonsense in Psychology* – and now *Fact and Fiction in Psychology*.

The author's style is as incisive and his wit as keen as ever, while the range of subjects that he deals with is, as always, provocatively wide. Of special interest in this volume is his application of behavioural therapy to the theory and practice of neurotic behaviour and especially to the severe clinical problem of the alcoholic. Also Professor Eysenck's most recent views on the criminal personality are set out with challenging authority.

Further chapters on the psychology of road traffic offenders and a hard look at the more exclusive claims of depth psychology complete a fascinating volume.

BRITISH HISTORY IN THE
NINETEENTH CENTURY AND AFTER
1782–1919
G. M. Trevelyan

Between 1780 and 1920 Britain underwent the most rapid change of character any country had ever experienced until then. Despite the most stable political structure in Europe the nation changed with startling speed. The first industrial state was created; the world shrank under the impact of steam power and the electric telegraph; man's scientific, social, and political attitudes were revolutionized; an Empire grew at the same time as a parliamentary aristocracy transformed itself into a parliamentary democracy. And Britain, almost alone, was without violent revolution.

G. M. Trevelyan's famous study of the period is focused on the political stage, on which the central themes of the century were played out by such actors as Pitt and Gladstone, Wellington and Queen Victoria, Disraeli and Parnell. The author employs his gift for divining the logic of events to show how developments in science, industry, economics, and social theory made themselves felt on the conduct of the nation's affairs.

THE UNATTACHED

Mary Morse

Resentment, apathy, mistrust – the dead-end job, the Beat sound, and a rejection of the values of adult society. These are the kind of words with which journalists have tried to catch and understand the unattached – the teenagers who don't belong to anyone or anything. What kind of people are they? What are their attitudes, needs, aims, or resentments? How can they be approached or understood?

In 1960 the National Association of Youth Clubs set up a pioneer experiment to discover the answers to these questions and possible solutions to the problem of the unattached. Three young social workers were sent, each to a different town, under concealed identities to find and to scrape an acquaintance with these particular teenagers. Over three years, the three, one of whom was a young woman, eventually became the trusted friends and confidants of the bored, the apathetic, the rebellious, and the defiant. This account of the workers' experiences offers an utterly authentic insight into the world of the unattached. But the book is more than this: it is also a fascinating description of the difficulties, loneliness, fears, and setbacks of three social workers, working out on a limb in isolation and under assumed identities. It is a fascinating account of a remarkable experiment.

A HISTORY OF MONEY

E. Victor Morgan

Adam Smith regarded 'a propensity to truck, barter and exchange one thing for another' as one of the basic ingredients of human nature. Certainly in the growth from the earliest exchanges of rice and honey to the complexities of modern international monetary systems, the invention and development of money ranks with the great dynamics of world civilization – the domestication of animals, the culture of land, and the harnessing of power.

Dealing with money only in its broadest sense, Professor Morgan surveys the ideas, concepts, and institutions associated with it and ranges the whole diversity of this fascinating subject, from money and other means of holding wealth to banking, the money market, the origins of accounting and the system of 'double entry'. The meaning of 'capital' leads to an impressive analysis of the relationship between government and money, ranging from government finances in Athens to the International Monetary Fund.

Two final chapters survey monetary theory and policy, making clear the relationship between money and fluctuations in business, employment, and prices. Professor Morgan ends a description of the modern British monetary system with a discussion of the highly contemporary problems of full employment and inflation, and shows how governments have tried to control money as part of the effort to secure stable economic growth.

For a complete list of books available please write to Penguin Books whose address can be found on the back of the title page